DISCLAIMER

I am a fully-qualified experienced hypno/psychotherapist. I am not a medically trained Doctor or Psychiatrist. I have taken every care to ensure that the information presented in this book is both ethical and responsible, and the information and techniques within this book have been safely used with my clients during my career.

However, if you have been diagnosed with, or believe you may be suffering from any form of psychiatric condition, you should seek professional help, and you should not use this book without the consent and blessing of your qualified formal medical healthcare provider. To all readers, please ensure that you read, understand, and agree to the following disclaimer before proceeding:-

This book is provided on an "as is" basis. I cannot assess nor guarantee that this book is suitable for your needs, or for use by you. You use this book at your own discretion. The information offered in this book is offered as complementary therapeutic information. Information and content offered throughout this book are not offered as medical treatment, or diagnosis of a medical condition, and no such suggestion may be implied by you or me. If you are suffering from any medical condition or believe that you may need medical or psychiatric treatment, you are advised to see your Doctor or formal healthcare provider. By your use of this book, no medical, advisory, therapeutic, or professional relationship is implied or established between you and myself. Any information provided in this book is for information purposes only and does not replace or amend your Doctor's advice. Any action you may take arising from your use of this book, or any of the exercises contained within, including the use of relaxation recording/s, is undertaken entirely at your own risk and discretion. If any of the exercises contained within this book make you feel uncomfortable or distressed in any way, you agree to discontinue using them immediately. Use of this book does not guarantee a cure of any mental, emotional, or medical condition, and no such suggestion may be implied. This book and the information contained within it have not been audited by any official bodies, either, professional, regulatory, or governmental.

HOW THIS BOOK CAN HELP YOU

"Anxiety Relief" is a complete and professional guide to recovery for people suffering with stress, anxiety, or depression. I have been a professional therapist, successfully helping people to recover from anxiety, depression, panic, phobias, and OCD for more than thirteen years. My vocation isn't merely academic though. I also know the territory intimately myself. Before becoming a therapist, I suffered with severe anxiety and depression myself for the best part of a decade. I know first-hand the complete despair of trying to recover, and repeatedly failing, so I know how important it is that you receive the help you need, and fast. This book is here to help!

Anxiety and depression can make each moment a torment to be endured, rather than a life to be lived. My personal recovery took much longer than it needed to because I didn't have the right understanding in place, in the right order. I want to make sure that you don't suffer the same fate.

This book will help you to understand:-

The scientific, evolutionary basis of stress, anxiety, and depression.

* That you have an *emotional* brain and an *intellectual* brain. Why the "emotional" brain creates states of anxiety, depression, stress, and panic, and how we can work *with* this understanding to recover.
* Why anxiety and depression often persist, despite well-meaning attempts to heal, and what can be done about it.
* How and why anxiety and depression can reduce our control levels and make us temporarily less intelligent. Why this matters, and how you can regain control.

How to create the correct mind-set for deep and lasting recovery.

* Understanding the important difference between "curing" and "healing".

* How to avoid energy-zapping, time-wasting, fruitless wrong-turns!
* The importance and respective roles of love, skill, and resources as recovery tools.
* Understanding therapy, medication, and self-help.

The accumulation of stress and tension in your nervous system, and how to "empty your bucket" effectively.

* Neuro plasticity - Neural pathways, habits of negativity, and how to rewire your brain.
* Why your bucket is "overloaded", and how to stop adding to it.
* The role of sleep in reducing emotional arousal levels.

Why "fear of fear" is at the root of most anxiety disorders and exactly how you can overcome it.

* Why going to war with anxiety or depression will make things worse.
* How to stop beating yourself up for being anxious or depressed.
* Why consistency is "safe" and conditionality is "unsafe".
* How to soothe your anxious or depressed self with empathy and acceptance, and break the "fear of fear" stalemate.
* Why are eight little words so important?

Staying S.M.A.R.T - Why how you think and behave matters. Learning practical skills for eliminating negative thinking and avoidance.

* How the language in your internal dialogue can alarm you, and how you can master the simple skills necessary to speak to yourself using language which soothes.
* Some of the basic principles and strategies used in Cognitive Behavioural Therapy (CBT).

The importance of creating practical solutions to unhappy circumstances, and how to deal with your resistance to change!

* The principles underpinning Solution Focussed Brief Therapy, and how to use them without the need for a therapist.
* How to accurately identify your "needs" using "the miracle question", and create the change necessary to have them met with minimum resistance.
* Practical strategies for worrying less, and gaining clearer perspectives on problems.
* How to avoid disappointment and failure by accurately assessing the level of "control" you have in any given situation.

How to deal with obstacles to progress.

* Recognising what may be holding you back from healing.
* Resolving the struggle between unconscious "needs" versus conscious "wants".
* How to recognise unhealthy relationships and why it's important to change your position within them.
* Why the word "no" is important, and how and why to be more assertive when necessary.

How to use tried and tested emotional de-arousal tools which really work.

* How to use many practical stress reduction tools effectively, and enjoy them! A free twenty eight minute deeply soothing relaxation recording (by me) is provided via a download and streaming link. (Worth the book price alone!)
* How and why what you believe affects the way that you feel, and how beliefs can be amended at the core level.
* Understanding the principles of hypnotherapy and how you can use self-hypnosis to reduce your anxieties.
* Exploring forgiveness as a gift to yourself, and learning how to "let go" gently and respectfully.
* How to recognise and re-negotiate restrictive negative "contracts" you may have made unwittingly with yourself.
* Why sweeping your emotions under the carpet will fail, and how to integrate difficult feelings successfully.

* Understanding the power of stories; where they come from, what they mean, how they affect you, and making sure that you surround yourself with helpful narratives.

A deeper look at depression, and what's necessary to move out of the pit.

* Exercise, nutrition, brain chemistry, and drugs. How to support your brain and body during your recovery.
* How to deal with the main obstacles of depression such as apathy, lethargy, lack of pleasure, and de-motivation.
* A check list for recovery.

Anxiety and Depression as an opportunity.

* How suffering with anxiety and depression can bring you strength and richness of character when you've recovered.
* My personal journey of recovery. The pitfalls I faced, and how I overcame them.

Emotional Rescue

* How and why you can't "think" or "talk" your way out of an anxious state. What to do instead!
* Plenty of encouragement, reassurance, and answers to questions along the way.
* How to have realistic expectations about your recovery journey, and how not to freak out if you have a "blip".
* This section is a complete reference section which you can refer to on difficult days.

There is much else here as well. I offer it to you with the sincere wish, as a fellow human being, that it will help you to stop your suffering, and find your way back to joy as quickly as possible.

PREFACE

There is really nothing more miserable in this World than feeling chronically anxious and depressed. It's a lonely place. You could be in the most beautiful landscape on the planet, surrounded by your best friends, with a seven figure bank account, and still feel utterly bereft. Not only can very few of the people around you truly empathise with, or understand the inner torment you're experiencing, but you may find yourself utterly puzzled by it too. It's very easy to feel victimized, frustrated, frightened, angry, alone, useless, and desperate. Despair will tell you that there's no end in sight, and you will probably believe that with every fibre of your being. I really do understand how incredibly wearing and miserable it is to suffer like that because I've been there too. I had a decade of it. If you're suffering with anxiety, depression, or both, you have my sincere empathy. It's pretty awful. This book is here to help.

My opening lines above break every rule in the hypnotherapy handbook. There are no positive suggestions in sight...yet! But, I wanted you to know that your distress is properly witnessed. Suppose you'd opened this book to find the first lines read: "Anxiety is just a feeling. It won't hurt you. Take a lavender bath, think positively, and try not to let it get you down." Nice advice maybe, but rather useless when you're in a crisis I'm afraid.

The reality is that there is an emergency. You're in quicksand. The harder you try to pull yourself up, the further down you sink. This is how anxiety and depression operate. The more desperate we become for escape, the more enmeshed we find ourselves. You've tried to "Just be more positive". Believe me, I know you have tried! It's simply impossible when you're waist deep in soul-sucking mud. Extricating yourself from anxiety and depression is more complex than that. Positive focus will come later, when we're around the fire, showered, in dry clothes, with a glass of brandy, relieved and reminiscing about the lucky escape we just had. This book will honour that fact, and we'll get to the positivity once we're out of this pit and back at the lodge!

I wrote this book with a very clear vision. Over the years I have learned that there is an order in which instructions for recovery need to be implemented. It's something like building a house. Firstly, we must clear up the site. Then, we work on creating strong foundations, and only then can we complete the build itself. Get this right, and you will have an unshakeable inner certainty that the structure will remain solid. This is not a quick fix manual. It's a guide to fixing your life properly, from the foundations up.

Whilst it's simply not possible that a book can fully replace the therapeutic magic of two souls in a consulting room, I want this book to be as close to a personal therapy as possible. I always began my clients' therapy with the assumption that they could be helped, even if they'd tried unsuccessfully with other therapists before. I don't mind admitting that there have been a small number of people I couldn't fully reach over the years for one reason or another, though I'm sure I helped everyone in some way. The vast majority of people though were inspired by my unshakeable belief in them, and have gone on to make full recoveries, and lead great lives. As a therapist it's not supposed to be personal, but for me, it was always personal. I have been unfailingly tenacious in my conviction that my clients could recover. If I had to dig deep to go the extra mile, I always did. I just wasn't willing to do things any other way. This book is written with that spirit and commitment firmly at its heart.

Nothing in this book should be overly onerous. You won't be asked to fill out forms for weeks on end, or spend hours and hours on therapeutic exercises that you don't really believe in. This book is designed to seep into your being as you read it, expanding your understanding, and offering many lightbulb moments which will create shifts in your perception and feelings. You will simply need to make time when you can, to practice the important exercises suggested, and remain committed to your own recovery. There are optional extras to engage with if you wish to. With application, the processes and understanding set out in these pages can be used to facilitate deep self-healing. There is enough here to provide you with the tools you need to clear the rubble, install strong foundations, and build a new home to live in that you can love.

This also isn't a book reserved solely for the very unwell. Most people could use a helping hand with managing the demands of modern life.

When you understand how your brain and mind work clearly, you will be able to make improvements in all of those areas that have been bugging you for years. You'll probably have a much better understanding of why you are the way you are, and why others are the way they are too. That's always going to help! There's something here for everybody.

Beyond anxiety, depression, and high-stress living, there is an amazing, loving, beautiful, exciting World to be reunited with. Have hope. Relief from anxiety IS possible! You can learn to manage stress much more skilfully. You can know joy again. I sincerely wish with all of my being that this book will help to make that happen for you. I'm cheering you on from the sidelines. You'll hear me whooping!

John Crawford – Bristol – April 2016.

INTRODUCTION

There are no words to describe the horror I felt at the moment that something inside me just snapped. It was an odd sensation. I literally heard the snap. It sounded like the tearing crack of a whip, and accompanying this sickly sound was the undeniable sense that an earthquake-like fissure had opened within my being, shearing me into two pieces diagonally. The nerve endings in my hands suddenly started firing uncontrollably, and I felt every muscle in my body contract and lock violently. I felt sick to my stomach as deep shock poured through my being in thick waves, like some sickly sticky bitumen, coating every cell with blackness and terror. In a single moment, all joy was gone. A crushing sense of finality poured through every cell of my being as I realised that I wouldn't bounce back from this one. This wasn't just a panic attack. I had literally broken myself. I knew it was bad, very bad.

Looking back it was hardly surprising. It was foolish of me to think that I could put myself under that sort of pressure, for that long, and walk away unscathed. I should have seen it coming. The signs had been there all along, but I was a man in the grip of a mania, and I wasn't slowing down for anything, or anyone. It would take a nuclear sized explosion to take the wind out of my sails. And so it was. I'd weathered storms before, hurricanes even. Fear was an old friend. We'd travelled together many times, but this was something else; an apocalyptic explosion of anxiety. Sheer mortal terror is as close as words can come. As I shook the stars from my head, I was left gasping for air, alone, freezing, in shock, and clinging to a piece of driftwood in a dark raging ocean that seemed a million miles from land. I knew it would be a long time before I ever reached shore. I genuinely didn't know whether I could even make it. Only my biological desire to survive made me start paddling. Were it not for that, I wouldn't even have tried.

I have had the great displeasure of personally experiencing the very worst of what anxiety and depression has to offer. I know what it is to feel each moment as a torture, and that all is truly lost. I have literally paced the halls in despair for days, and I have known what it is to be so anxious that I would not move an inch because every movement sent another sickening wave of terror through my body. I know how it feels to desperately need to sob my heart out, and be unable to mobilise even a single droplet from my eyes. I really did sadly lose nearly a decade of my youthful years to anxiety and depression, and I can never get them back. Perhaps though, with a different perspective, I can recognise that they were not wasted because as I paddled my way back to land I learned about the ocean, and I mapped the territory. In sharing that map with you, I can honour those lost years by pointing you towards home, and hopefully, sparing you the long, arduous, and often misguided journey I took. If I had known then what I know now, I'm sure I would have saved myself a whole lot of wasted time and heartache.

My personal apocalyptic moment happened in 1993. I was just twenty two years old. The poetic vignette above was only the beginning of a long and difficult journey of recovery. I read many self-help books during that time, and I'm sure that every one of them helped in some way, but it didn't feel like it at the time. There was never a single book that delivered all that I was looking for. As my mind has matured I can look back and see that some of those books contained vital pieces of information that somehow I managed to completely overlook, despite their being right under my nose. I searched frantically for Epiphany and simply didn't recognise that I was looking at the pieces of the puzzle that would fit together to make the overall finished picture. After inspecting the puzzle pieces and deciding they weren't "It", I tossed them asunder and went on searching fruitlessly. With the wisdom of hindsight, twenty three years on, and with thirteen years spent working as a hypnotherapist specialising in the treatment of anxiety-related disorders, the anxiety-busting jigsaw picture is now incredibly clear to me. This book is all about passing that knowledge and understanding on to you.

The vision behind this book is to present you with the book I needed. I want to present you with a deep understanding of the causes of stress, anxiety, and depression, and then to guide you through the process of undermining their stranglehold on your life, once and for all. It is not a quick fix manual, though you will find approaches within these pages which can yield fast and effective results. It is a very accessible human guide, based on good science, which will allow you to tackle anxiety and depression from the deepest level possible, with results that match. It is practical and realistic. It is not a book of hype, or of wild promises. It is a sincere offering of useable in-depth understanding about how to eliminate anxiety, depression, and stress from the roots up.

Technique-led therapy (do this and you'll get better) can frustrate people because the application of pure technique often doesn't help people in understanding themselves, and their relationship to the difficulty. To my mind, such understanding remains central to all healing. I will offer these connections as we proceed, building a complete picture of how all the elements fit together to produce a user-friendly model of how to take your life back. I hope that this is what will make this book at least partly unique. I'd like this book to help you to connect with levels of yourself which really count. Though there is technique here, it will take a back seat to the important levels of understanding which are essential to overcoming anxiety and depression fully.

Not everything in this book is original. If it were, I would have re-invented the wheel. I hope I have honoured the knowledge-bearers who have been my teachers over the years, both in person, and via the written word. There is much input here from others, but this book is not a simple regurgitation of ideas. What I have aimed to do here is to tie all of the disparate threads together, and present them in a circular and coherent package. Much has been elaborated upon, and many new ideas introduced.

For those readers who are well-versed in the terminology and theory of anxiety I ask for your patience in moving through those parts of the book which are known to you already. Your patience will, I hope, be rewarded with some gems that will help you in ways that nobody else has yet offered. Equally, you may have arrived to this book with it being the first thing you've ever read about anxiety. I want to make sure that this book is totally accessible to you. It's my intention to provide you with information that is free from "psychobabble", meaning that I've kept the fancy therapeutic language to a bare minimum. I'm much less interested in impressing the clinicians than I am in giving you the information you need in a language that you understand. Most importantly, I aim to give you full explanation of the reasoning behind each section of the book.

So, while you may be raring to get on with the "how do I fix this?" question, there's groundwork to do first. It might appear academic initially but eliminating anxiety and depression requires a rounded picture of cause and effect, so what follows will have great value later. Let's get started with some explanation about what anxiety and depression actually are, and why they exist!

Chapter One – What Is Anxiety? What Is Depression? Why Do They Exist?

What Is Anxiety?

Anxiety is nature's way of alerting you to the possibility that you are in danger. All animals have the capacity to experience anxiety when they feel threatened. There is evidence that even plants react to the presence of threat! Anxiety's job is to demand your attention and prepare your body so that it is immediately ready to take evasive action. In an appropriate situation anxiety could save your life.

Nature has designed anxiety to be powerful enough that it cannot be ignored. It is meant to be uncomfortable.

Anxiety itself is not a bad thing. It only becomes a problem when anxiety is triggered inappropriately. Sadly, this can happen very easily.

Why?

Well, briefly, your brain actually contains two brains. At the base of the brain is the "limbic system" which is your "animal" brain. The limbic system deals with instinctive and emotional responses, while your cortex, particularly your frontal lobe, processes higher thinking such as logic, reason, planning, and control. The human brain has doubled in size throughout the course of human evolution and the frontal lobe sits at the pinnacle of that evolution. The mental processes of logic, reason, planning, and control, are higher functions of intelligence. By comparison, the limbic system is ancient. This doesn't make it stupid. The limbic system is incredibly fast on its feet in its own way. It's just that the basic function is to keep us alive. It is not by definition a "thinking" brain. It is a "feeling" brain. It functions instinctively. Therefore:-

The frontal lobe is primarily an intellectual brain while the limbic system is primarily an emotional/instinctive brain.

16

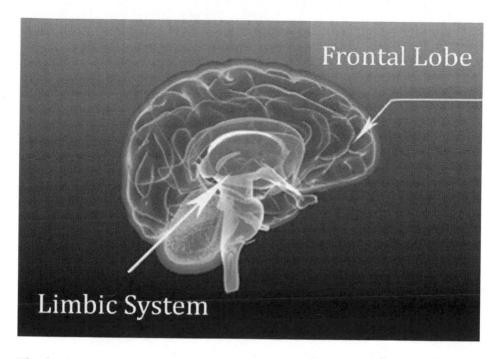

The limbic system is concerned with survival. These survival functions are often referred to as the four f's. That is fear, feeding, fighting, and ahem...procreation. The limbic system works by the process of association, or what is known in psychology as a "conditioned response".

Conditioned response is easy to understand. Famously, a Russian scientist called Ivan Pavlov published research which is now well known as "Pavlov's Dogs". He showed that when dogs were called to feed by the sound of a bell they learned to associate the sound of the bell with the presence of food. Dogs salivate in anticipation of feeding, and Pavlov realised that after a period of conditioning, the dogs would salivate in the presence of the bell alone, in the expectation of food being present. Without prior "conditioning", the sound of a bell alone would not make a dog salivate, but once the bell becomes associated with food, then the bell itself is enough to produce the physical response (salivation), even when no food is present. If we look at the fact that the limbic system deals with feeding as one of its areas of control, we can easily see that the response belongs to the limbic system, and that the response itself is not "intellectual", but "instinctive", that is, automatic. When considering fear then, we see the same process in action. Once the limbic system has

17

learned that a certain situation contains an actual or potential "threat", then we come to fear the entire situation, even if the threat is not actually present. We have been conditioned to expect that the threat will be present, much like Pavlov's dogs expected food when the bell was sounded.

In the diagram below we can see this process in action. What we are seeing here is the limbic system scanning the current situation (?) against its held repository of knowledge (Experience Library). Whatever is held in the library will influence how the limbic system responds. If the scan match is recognised as non-threatening, then the limbic system gives a green light which says "This situation is safe. Proceed." We feel no anxiety and go on to engage with a sense of ease. If however, the template of experience suggests a threat, then the limbic system will raise the alarm with an emotional response designed to help us act appropriately, according to the perceived threat level. Something perceived as mildly dangerous creates a minimal response, and something perceived as life threatening creates a powerful response, such as panic or rage.

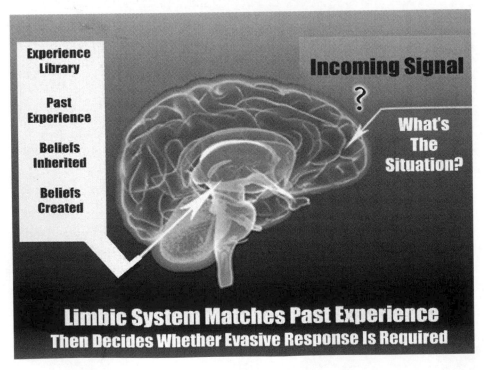

You will note that we show the library contents as being comprised of past experience, beliefs created, and beliefs inherited. For the sake of clarity, let's expand on what this means in practice:-

Past Experience – This is quite self-explanatory really. If, for example, you are bitten by a dog and wounded badly, then that experience is recorded here. It is likely that you will at the very least have a healthy respect for the possibility that some dogs, sometimes, have the potential to damage you in the future. If you were particularly traumatised by the experience at the time, this could set up a phobic template, meaning that you might have extreme emotional responses such as panic in the presence or anticipation of, dogs.

Beliefs Created – Less obvious, but extremely important. Sometimes we ourselves decide for some reason, perhaps known only to ourselves, and sometimes not known consciously, that something is much more dangerous than the evidence suggests. This is a complicated area because there are potentially many reasons that this could happen. Uncovering why we have concluded that something is more dangerous than it actually is involves reviewing personal history. There is likely to be a string of assumptions, often faulty, that have been made along the way. Many, if not all of these assumptions will be subconscious, that is, just outside of our conscious understanding. In any case, for now, just note that we ourselves can draw alarming conclusions about things that really don't need to be feared so intensely. Faulty logic is often to blame, particularly the kind of faulty logic we are at risk of in our younger years. These beliefs can easily be carried into adulthood without being recognised as faulty.

Beliefs Inherited – Parents, teachers, peers, lovers, culture, media, politicians, preachers, books, internet, movies, storytellers: Life! Anything that has any input into our thinking about ourselves, other people, or the World at large, has the potential to create an emotional imprint here that can affect us for the rest of our lives. Despite liking to think of ourselves as free thinkers, the truth is we are all massively influenced and shaped by our environment. The greater our awe of the source of the message, the deeper the imprint will be. This too, is a hugely important area when it comes to anxiety-busting because not every belief we inherit is either true or helpful. Anxiety itself often runs in families. The official explanation for this is that it must be something to do with genetics, and there's clearly some truth in this, but it's also easy to see that anxious mums and dads often make anxious children. Studies have shown that identical twins (with identical genetic information) who are raised in different environments don't automatically develop mental or emotional health difficulties equally. The environment clearly has a part to play. If we are asking whether the onset of anxiety related problems relate to nature or nurture, it's almost certainly a bit of both. Some beliefs may be encoded in the genetic information passed down through generations, such as fear of spiders or snakes. Culture also plays an enormous role in creating both wellbeing and anxiety. An anxious culture makes anxious people.

THE EVOLUTIONARY PERSPECTIVE

Consider that early Human beings date back over two million years. According to historical data it is generally accepted that advanced civilisation began to flourish around ten to twelve thousand B.C. The relative safety and security we enjoy today is recent. The World you see around you today of city office buildings, houses, buses, cars, and supermarkets, has been here for less than the blink of an eye in evolutionary terms. Human beings have literally spent more than 99% of their existence on this planet living as hunter-gatherers. For that entire period the limbic system has been honed to take care of survival. For our ancestors, dealing with truly life-threatening situations was an everyday occurrence. Historically that might be predatory animals, warring tribes, famine, drought, plague, pestilence, or ice age. You name it. As a species we've endured it. Undoubtedly, anxiety has been a constant throughout human evolution. Our anxieties today are just about different things. Anxiety is relative however. Yesterday it was lions and tigers, and today it's the mortgage. In any case, the anxiety remains real enough. Pain is relative. It doesn't change things for us personally to say "Hey, what do I have to worry about? Our ancestors were fighting off tigers once a week!" We can honour their struggle and give thanks that they got us this far against huge odds, but what's really important here is to understand that it's hardly surprising that we're a bit jumpy! Our limbic systems don't necessarily understand that when we become stressed it's because of the mortgage and not that we're about to become lunch for the local lion pride. Anxiety is fine when you really are face to face with a tiger, but when that response is triggered because you're standing in the queue at your local supermarket (or insert trigger here) then we have a problem.

Here's somebody who had a bad time last time they flew:-

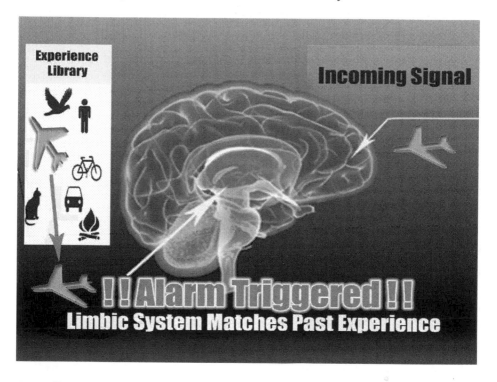

Actually, anxiety isn't the only response that the limbic system throws up. Depression and anger are also key responses. When considering the role of the limbic system, it's helpful to recognise that from the limbic system perspective, it's all emotional arousal. That's why these states often co-exist. They are in fact all part and parcel of the same thing. That's an overload of limbic system based emotional arousal.

Anger is the "stand and fight" response, clearly necessary for dealing with warring tribes or dangerous animals, but again, inappropriate when expressed as road rage or shouting at a customer. Depression is the "withdraw from life" response. This would have been useful for our ancestors in times of no food to conserve energy. It's not so useful when we're trying to lead productive lives in the 21st Century. These responses were literal lifesavers for our ancestors. They would serve us too, in a crisis, just as well. The problem is that most of us are not dealing with genuinely life-threatening situations. Our emotional mind, being a primitive mind, doesn't know that though. We can then experience feeling like we are in a life or death crisis over something quite harmless. Of course threats can be emotional as well as physical. A threat can be defined as anything which might cause us pain or damage. The limbic system response is commonly referred to as "fight or flight", meaning anger (fight) or anxiety (flight). Sometimes "freeze" is also included, meaning paralysis caused by fear, which could be a useful survival mechanism because being very still would reduce the likelihood of being noticed by a predator, or even taking just one more step towards the danger. Freeze is a far less common response.

In summary then, the emotional brain, the limbic system, is responsible for our emotional responses including anxiety, depression, anger, and obsessional problems. The emotional brain is primitive in nature and cannot assess situations with the same logic that the frontal lobe uses. It relies entirely on past experience and current beliefs, that is, what we are "buying into" right now, consciously and unconsciously, to assess the relative danger of any situation.

Why then doesn't the frontal lobe, the intellectual brain, help out a bit more? Well, actually it can help a great deal, and in non-anxious individuals it does help out, all the time. As we'll see later, CBT (Cognitive Behavioural Therapy) capitalises on the fact that the frontal lobe logic can be a very useful ally in tackling anxiety. It is true however that the frontal lobe has a much greater anti-anxiety effect when used as a preventative medicine. When an anxiety crisis is already underway, logical thought is of limited usefulness in the moment. Here's why:-

There is a threat perception threshold where the frontal lobe's input is, to a degree, disregarded. What this means in practice is that we experience "knowing" that the way we feel is irrational, but still seemingly, can do nothing to stop those feelings from overwhelming us. This is because emotional arousal trumps intellectual assessment when we're in an emergency. From a survival perspective, we're more likely to come out alive if we respond instinctively, as opposed to intellectually because instinctive response is deemed more powerful and immediate. We know that our eyelid closes to protect our eye in milliseconds, long before we've become consciously aware of the tennis ball hurtling towards us at eighty miles per hour. That's instinct, and it's faster by far than thinking. When facing a significant threat, running or fighting is deemed preferable to thinking, in survival terms. So when a significant threat is sensed, the limbic system will, to a degree, disregard a considered perspective in favour of a more direct and immediate instinctive-emotional response.

We know that in an emergency we can go into a trance-like state and perform seemingly super-human acts. Common are the stories of women lifting cars to release their trapped children. Though these tales may be modern folklore based only partly on truth, we know that extraordinary changes to the body and perception really do occur when we are in an emergency. Most people are familiar with the sensation of seeing everything in slow motion when something "big" happens, and many people can relate to the sense of having access to strength beyond their normal limits when in an emergency situation. Experiments have shown that the brain actually speeds up its perception of reality in such moments, and it is this that gives one the sense that time is slowing down. It's not that time actually slows down, but rather that we receive and process more frames per second of information. One interesting experiment involves a person free falling from a great height into a soft inflatable landing pad while an electronic board is held in sight displaying a secret number programmed into its digital face. The number is flickering on/off at a frequency which is invisible to normal perception. As the experimenter falls from the great height (what we might term a "big" event) he is able to read the secret number and report it at the bottom. His perceptual speed, that is, the rate of frames per second that his eye and brain is receiving and processing, speeds up to a rate able to receive the otherwise invisible information on the number board. So, instinct works much more quickly than intellect and is favoured by nature as a strategy for dealing with perceived threat. This explains the reason that logical thought is often overwhelmed by emotional arousal in an anxious moment.

Physical Effects Of Emotional Arousal (Anxiety)

The effects of instinct aren't limited merely to perception. There are physical changes too. When it comes to increased physical strength there is science at work. When the limbic system perceives a threat, it quickly moves into alarm mode, and a number of physical processes begin. Within a few milliseconds of sensing a significant threat, an electrical impulse is sent through the nervous system. This is the metallic electrical jolt of alarm that you feel when a panicky feeling begins. Less than half a second later, powerful chemical hormones are released into the bloodstream. Amongst these are the hormones Adrenaline, often now known as Epinephrine, and Cortisol. You are of course free to study the effects of these hormones independently but for the sake of explanation I will keep things deliberately simple. Suffice to say that when the body readies itself for evasive action or battle it aims to be in a state of peak physical performance because that will increase our chance of survival. If we are evading an enemy, then obviously the faster we can move, the greater chance there is of a successful escape. If we are engaging in a battle, the stronger we are physically, the more chance we have of overpowering our enemy and surviving the encounter. So when the fight or flight mechanism is activated, the body releases these powerful performance-enhancing chemicals into the bloodstream and a number of physical processes quickly occur:-

Physical Symptom	*The Reason The Symptom Occurs*
Shortness of breath. Shallow fast breathing.	The body demands more oxygen to supply the limbs with additional energy.
Dry mouth.	Saliva is redirected to the blood stream to help blood pump faster.

High blood pressure. Racing heart rate.	The heart pumps blood harder and faster to supply the limbs with additional oxygen and energy.
Dizziness/Dissociation. Feeling "spaced out".	Blood supply to the head is reduced as oxygen is diverted to the limbs. Powerful chemicals have a pharmacological action on the brain designed to keep us at maximum alert levels.
Poor digestion.	Blood and energy is redirected from the stomach to major muscles.
Urination. Defecation. Vomiting.	A body even one pound lighter can move faster.
Sweating. Clammy hands and skin.	A wet body is more slippery and therefore more difficult to catch. The body attempts to stay cool so as to preserve peak performance temperature.
Visual distortion.	The pupils widen to receive more information.
Time distortion.	The brain speeds up to receive more frames per second.

Aching muscles. Shaking.	The large muscle groups such as the back, shoulders, legs and arms become tense and energy laden.
Butterflies/tension in stomach.	The solar plexus area contains complex nerve bundles that alert us to the presence of danger by tightening.

Of course, here we are talking about extreme or emergency situations, and not all anxiety symptoms are as intense as those shown in the table above. If we can understand how anxiety affects the body in an acute phase though, we can then begin to understand why we experience these physical symptoms, perhaps to a lesser degree, chronically, when our stress levels rise generally. Being constantly or regularly primed for evasive action is simply exhausting. In practice we usually experience some of these physical symptoms in a mild form when we feel anxious generally. The difference is in the degree.

So, when a threat is perceived, the limbic system is forced to respond or take over. This taking over of our brain is referred to as "hijacking the intellectual brain". What's really going on is that the signals from the limbic system become so intense that they overwhelm the intellect. It's not that we can't choose to think intellectually, but that the data that comes from the limbic system simply feels truer, and more powerful, than our usual sense of logic. Our focus shifts powerfully away from rational thought to a much narrower and more acute awareness of our senses and feelings. So, when we experience negative stress we go through a shift of relative control from the intellectual brain to the emotional brain. Thus, we can easily become overwhelmed with irrational emotional content because the limbic system is a primitive mind with a limited ability to think things through logically. In practice, the result of this is that we become more emotionally and instinctively driven, meaning that we are at greater risk of buying into irrational, and frightening conclusions. The greater our anxiety, the greater the relative control of the limbic system, and the greater our subsequent loss of logical perspective. In other words, as anxiety increases, intellectual control decreases. This creates an unpleasant cycle. Anxiety creates irrational and alarming thoughts and feelings, which then create further anxiety.

WHAT IS PANIC?

We all understand what panic is, but in truth, there is panic, and then there is PANIC!! Everybody knows the first. Not everybody knows the latter. Let's put it this way. Our accident and emergency units see people every day who are convinced that they are about to die, but who are, in fact, having an episode of panic, otherwise known as a panic attack. If we return to our list of physical symptoms of anxiety, we can see that this is hardly surprising. We see high blood pressure, racing heart, palpitations, sweating, vomiting, extreme fear, nausea, and dissociation. It sounds like a heart attack! It feels like a heart attack! Anyone who has ever experienced a full-blown panic attack will tell you that they wouldn't wish it on their worst enemy. It is among the most unpleasant experiences in existence.

Panic is an extreme form of anxiety. So let's understand how it arises. There are really three ways in which panic can occur. The first of these is the pressure cooker effect. Some people are really good at holding everything in; sometimes because they have to be, and sometimes because they're as yet unaware of the repercussions this may have later. What you have here is the person who will at some point become so overloaded that they will simply not be able to contain the stress any longer. This could go a number of ways. It might end in rage. It might end in tears. Sometimes though, it will produce panic. I call it an elephant-sized bag of anxiety trying to escape through a mouse-hole sized opening. This person has simply not recognised the amount of pressure which has been building up in the background. Then, the pressure cooker just cracks, and panic is the experience of all that pressure suddenly releasing from the container. The second way in which panic can occur is when a person comes face to face with their worst fear/s. We touched on this earlier with the example of dog fears. If the detection of threat is judged by the limbic system to be enough of an extreme danger, then it can jump straight to full-blown red alert in seconds. An extreme phobia is a good example of this. This can seem very irrational, but I have met people who have told me that they would rather jump from a window than be in a room with a person who is vomiting. For them, it's very real indeed.

The third way in which panic can occur is the most common. Here we have fear of fear, or put another way, anxiety which rises exponentially. Since anxiety is a very uncomfortable feeling, the inexperienced person can find it quite a shock to the system when they first experience it. What you end up with is an anxious feeling which alarms the person greatly. So now there is anxiety about anxiety. It has doubled. Next there's a recognition that things appear to be getting out of control. This sends a further signal of alarm, which again, doubles the fear. Now the anxiety is huge, and so on. All of this can occur in a matter of seconds. Soon we're becoming alarmed by our racing heart rate, which is thumping as though we've just run a hundred metre sprint. It's difficult to breathe because the solar plexus is tight. The negative thoughts are swirling around, "What if I were to drop dead right now? What if my heart gives out?" On it goes. It is particularly terrifying if it's the first time you've experienced it. Feelings can quickly escalate to a complete conviction that death is imminent, hence all of the A&E admissions.

Usually, panic attacks don't last a long time. They burn themselves out. It's a process. Unfortunately though, very anxious people can have repeated episodes, and it is possible for someone to feel panicky generally. This is a direct result of a complete overload of stress. You need to be absolutely clear that these are not occurring for no reason at all. Take it as a given that if you suffer regularly with panic, your anxiety levels generally are way too high.

I do have some good news for you then. Here it is.

When you successfully reduce your overall level of stress and anxiety, your panic attacks will reduce, and eventually cease.

If panic attacks are part of your problem, then the understanding in this book will give you the tools you need to overcome them. Don't ask the question "How can I stop my panic attacks?" Ask instead "How do I reduce my anxiety levels?" This will lead you to solution.

WHAT IS DEPRESSION?

The main criteria most usually used to diagnose depression are as follows:-

* Depressed (Low or disturbed) mood

* Sleep disturbance

* Decreased energy

* Increased or decreased psychomotor activity (fidgety or apathetic)

* Decreased concentration

* Suicidal ideation

* Appetite or weight change

* Guilt or feelings of worthlessness

* Loss of interest or pleasure in everyday life

Of course, everybody feels some of these feelings some of the time. This doesn't necessarily indicate depression. This indicates that you're human and you have ups and downs. When we experience difficulties or loss in life it is quite normal to experience a period where we feel the same feelings which characterise depression. These feelings usually pass normally with the healing passage of time. Clinical depression though is characterised by a persistent and deeply pervasive experience of the above difficulties with little or no rational reason to be feeling those feelings. It is true that depression tends to run in families. It is also true that genetic research has failed to identify a single defective gene which might be responsible for creating depression, and researchers believe it is unlikely that one will be found. Some studies have shown that identical twins (sharing the same genes) will more often than not both suffer with depression, which lends weight to the argument that there is a genetic pre-disposition towards the disorder. Interestingly though, those twins who were separated at birth and grew up in different environments show less incidence of twin development of depression, arguing that there must be other factors involved, namely of course, the effect of environment on mental and emotional development. It is clear that depression runs in families at least in part because families have "atmospheres". This is an unscientific way of saying that different families do things their own way, and behavioural traits are passed down from generation to generation. Thinking styles are also passed down. If the general atmosphere of a family is negative and oppressive, it is easy to see how this general gloominess is passed on to family members. Michael Yapko makes this case beautifully in his important book "Hand me down blues". When we think about it clearly, it's not difficult to make sense of. Did your family possess or provide you with the coping skills you require to make a success of life? If you were not taught how to see the World positively in your formative years then is it any wonder that the World feels negative, hostile, or threatening today? If you were not taught the skills you need to interact healthily with people, how to get your needs met in a functional way, how to have self-esteem, then is it any wonder that the competitive world we live in feels overwhelming? In any case, let's conclude that what we do know for sure is that people who grow up in unsupportive or hostile environments are more likely to suffer from mental and emotional disorders later in life. If our environment is uninviting (and this includes our mental and emotional environment), then depression can thrive. Conversely, a positively-focussed life filled with satisfying activity and success leaves little room for depression.

So, what does cause depression? This can be summarised with two words: Hopelessness and helplessness. Or put another way, having no control. That's the core of it. Of course there are other peripheral considerations such as poor nutrition, lack of exercise, age atrophy, medications, addictions, illness and loss etc. It can be a complicated picture for sure, since good health requires many factors to be balanced, but essentially we experience depression when it feels like we can't be helped, and that there is no hope for the future. At that point something dies inside us (metaphorically speaking) and we stop trying.

Let's also have a quick look at depression and its evolutionary purpose. Depression is a physiological response to certain conditions; namely hopelessness. Our ancestors were hunter-gatherers. They gathered their food on a daily basis. They relied heavily on natural crops and game for survival. Without agriculture, and the subsequent storing of surplus food, drought and famine would have been a common occurrence. Nature generally favours survival, and we find ourselves therefore equipped to deal with such emergencies. So, if the rains had failed to fall on a particular year, and consequently food had become scarce, then the best way to ensure survival is to conserve energy, since when starvation threatens, every single calorie saved equals a better chance of long-term survival. In a famine, with no immediate chance of food, the situation becomes temporarily "hopeless". So, what would be the best way to make sure that a human being conserves energy? Feelings of exhaustion, lack of interest, lack of hope, and low motivation will fit that request nicely. Then we are much more likely to turn inwards, become intensely reflective, and cease physical activity. The brain learned that to survive, it was necessary to inhibit energy use in times of crisis. So, we can see then that the physiology of depression is very real indeed. The unpleasant feelings of lethargy and disinterest that depressed people experience are in fact powerful shifts in internal chemistry. The brain and body go into an "opt out" mode of existence, which quite literally grounds a person. It sends us into an inward looking trance-like state of external disinterest and exhaustion. This is what depression is. A physiological response designed to save lives when conditions become temporarily hopeless. It can be a relief to sufferers of depression to learn that these feelings are a response, and are not indicative of their core being. You are not your depression. You are not a "depressive". It is very important to remember this fact. You are a human being suffering an inappropriate physiological response to stress and negative environment.

That is very interesting, but we're not in a famine!

No famine I agree, but are you starving? I'm not meaning to be clever or dismissive here. This is a serious point. The feelings of hopelessness we might experience in our complex lives today are every bit as fraught with angst and seriousness as those our ancestors will have experienced in the absence of food. The depression response too is every bit as powerful. It didn't just disappear because we started living in houses and shopping at the supermarket. So follow the logic and you can see that this powerful response pattern can be activated just as powerfully by today's modern "emergencies" as it has always been by floods, famines or warring tribes.

So, what are today's modern "emergencies"? Well, we have the obvious of course, being immediate emergencies; divorce, bereavement, losing a job etc. These emergencies can trigger depression, but again they don't necessarily. If we possess good coping skills and a strong constitution, we can ride these things out without going into depression. But, there are longer term emergencies too. It's long been recognised in solution focussed psychology that as individuals, as human beings, we have needs. This is a fact. Though our needs are somewhat subjective, there are certain needs which we all have to some degree; the need for physical safety and security for example. Most (though not all) people have a need for positive human interaction. Other needs include having a purpose in life, being financially secure, employment, peer recognition, friends, interests, to love and be loved. For each individual there will be certain areas which stand out more than others as being critically important to that individual's sense of okay-ness with the world. If that need is very important and is not being met, and it appears to that individual that there is no way that need will be met any time soon, then this constitutes a crisis or emergency as far as the mind is concerned. To put it simply then, if our needs are not being met, then emotionally speaking we are starving. To the mind, the feeling of hopelessness is exactly the same as that feeling our ancestors experienced. So the antidote to this starvation then is to go to find food. Finding food here means having our needs met. We'll be looking at depression again later in the book but that's the essence of what we need to cover for now.

Understanding The Emotional Brain (The Limbic System)

We now know that the limbic system is responsible for creating survival-based responses to threat which include anxiety, depression and anger. In order to understand that we are not being victimised by the limbic system it pays to understand exactly how this response system works, and why it does what it does. This is vitally important information. If you take the time to fully understand what follows you will be in a much stronger position to end unnecessary anxiety forever.

The emotional mind, the limbic system, is not an intellect, and therefore cannot assess intellectually whether something is truly dangerous or not. It must rely therefore on information gathered from past experience, inherited beliefs, and rational assessments made by the frontal lobe as discussed earlier. Once a rational assessment of any subject carried out by the intellect (frontal lobe) is assumed to be true it is metaphorically stamped with the stamp of approval by the limbic system and filed away in the limbic system's experience library as "fact".

From this point forward the limbic system will treat this information as though it is indisputably true.

The problem here is that not all information stored in the experience library is necessarily complete or entirely true. There are two poignant expressions in CBT that allude with tongue firmly in cheek to this fact:-

I've made up my mind, don't bother me with facts. Or, Feelings are facts and to hell with the truth.

Therefore:-

The emotional mind does not know intellectually whether something is true or not.

If the library says it's true, then as far as the limbic system is concerned, it's true! Straight away we begin to see why there is often a conflict between knowing that something is irrational intellectually, and yet feeling it to be an indisputable fact emotionally. We have a faulty template in the library, and the emotional mind has no option but to

33

treat that information as fact. This means that if there is a template in the library that tells the limbic system that the situation under consideration is potentially dangerous, even if we know rationally that it isn't, the limbic system must respond with anxiety. We should not underestimate the degree to which this principle can operate under worst case conditions. OCD is an anxiety-related mental illness which can cause people to take the toaster to work with them in an effort to reinforce the recognition that it wasn't left dangerously plugged in at home. They can sometimes report that they then still feel worried that they have left a fire hazard despite the absolutely incontrovertible evidence to the contrary. Alarming as this sounds, such extremity isn't always a bad thing. When anxiety becomes that irrational the OCD trick makes a farce of itself, revealing its illusory nature to the sufferer. Anxiety is also largely illusory. It's just less obvious that this is so.

The emotional mind doesn't create these responses to give you a hard time. It doesn't hate you. It isn't victimising you. It literally does the only thing it is programmed to do. It can only work with the information that is available to it at any given time. This is a vitally important point to understand because ultimately it is our own personal responsibility to ensure that the limbic system has accurate data to work with. Exactly how you go about doing that is what this book is all about.

The next equally important point we need to understand about the limbic system is that it doesn't respond only to current situations. It also responds very powerfully when anticipating danger. What this means in practice is that we can easily become anxious about the future. If you think about it clearly, all anxiety is future based. You literally cannot be anxious about an event that has passed because fear is the mechanism by which your mind and body alerts you to the presence of imminent danger. That danger cannot be imminent if it has already passed. You can become anxious that the past may repeat itself, but do recognise that this is still anxiety about the future, not the past. We can, however become angry about the past, and depressed about the past. It is for this reason that people suffering with emotional arousal difficulties, and that includes anxiety, should remain careful to keep rumination about past events to an absolute minimum. Ruminating on negative past experience in the mind will not help with anxiety. It will simply create more emotional arousal right now, which will contribute greatly to both depression and anxiety.

The problem with anticipating future threat is that it makes us feel anxious in the present because imagining the situation, with its associated pain and threat, is, from a limbic system perspective, the next most real thing to living it. It has been said that he who worries dies a thousand deaths. Reflect on that for a moment. In fact, the limbic system sees very little difference between what's real and what's imagined because it's not an intellect. That means that it responds to all situations, actual or imagined, in a very similar way. If you experience problem anxiety, you'll know straight away that this is true. Just thinking about an object of concern very quickly makes you feel anxious doesn't it? The limbic system responds almost equally to actual threat and anticipated threat. It has been wisely said that worrying is praying for what you don't want.

Now taken in isolation this needn't be a problem under normal circumstances. If I am generally calm then I can cope with the odd bit of anticipatory anxiety. If I am already overloaded emotionally, then the effect of this is greatly magnified because once the limbic system is aroused generally it becomes hyper-sensitive to the presence of further danger. If we track this back to our ancestral roots we can see this process in action:-

An ancestor is walking back to the camp through the forest and he becomes aware of a rustling in the trees ahead. He knows that there is a family of lions that live nearby and he is always on guard when collecting wood for the camp fires. In a tenth of a second he freezes. He is alerted to the presence of danger and feels the familiar jolt of alertness that attends such moments. His heart beats quickly and he puts the wood quietly down on the ground, crouching, still. His hearing becomes hyper-sensitive as he listens carefully and a bead of sweat forms on his forehead. He enters a trance like state and the world seems to stop. Only his hearing, his sight and his sense of smell are in focus now. He looks hard into the undergrowth, his eyes, sensitive to the slightest movement. The distinction between every leaf and twig is now in sharp focus...and then he sees it. It's just a squirrel. He takes a deep breath and continues on his journey back to the camp but he remains on high alert...now sensitised to the slightest sound and movement...

In his alert state, our ancestor becomes highly sensitised to the presence of all stimuli, and begins to see potential danger in every inch of the forest. In this state, the slightest sound, smell, or movement would create further alarm. This state is called hyper-vigilance and it is part and parcel of the anxiety state. Again, here, we are using an acute situation to illustrate the mechanism by which hyper-vigilance occurs, but this also can occur chronically. As we become more anxious generally, we can easily become generally hyper-vigilant. In practice, this means that we begin to perceive potential danger at every turn. Since the danger is perceived as being "hidden", the feeling is something resembling "At any moment, out of nowhere, something terrible could happen." Do you recognise this feeling? To make things worse then, now that the limbic system is convinced that there is hidden danger in the environment, it sets about trying to define that threat. It starts looking for the source of our discomfort, the perceived threat. It says "It could be this. It could be that. What if this happens? What if that happens?" In the presence of such alarm, the limbic system sees everything we bring to mind in such moments as a perceived threat, and very quickly the imagination starts working overtime. Negative scenarios begin to act themselves out in our imagination, and it is here that we really start to work ourselves into a terrible pickle. The more anxious we are, the more we start to imagine terrible things happening, being unable to cope, and each one of those negative imaginative scenarios will be responded to as real possibilities by the limbic system. It has only one option under the circumstances, and that is to do what it is programmed to do, which is...supply anxiety. Thus, we have a very unpleasant vicious circle. More anxiety creates more negative imaginings, and more negative imaginings create more anxiety. This is in fact the basis of obsessional difficulties. Hyper-vigilance can cause us to overestimate threat where there isn't any, and since threat detection creates anxiety, we can end up feeling fear with little cause.

If this limbic system explanation leaves us feeling a bit deflated, let's not forget that the limbic system is capable of creating some very pleasant enjoyable response patterns too. It is an emotional brain, and if anticipation can be negative, it can also be positive. This feeling we know as "excitement". When we are well, we can wake up every day excited to start the day. Your limbic system can be a great friend, but it does need some positive material to work with if it is to provide you with positive emotions. The good news is we have a helper here; the frontal lobe. The bad news is, as we mentioned, the frontal lobe's input is weakened by anxiety.

UNDERSTANDING THE INTELLECTUAL BRAIN (THE FRONTAL LOBE)

The human brain is the most highly organised matter in the known universe, and the human frontal lobe stands at the pinnacle of that evolution. The frontal lobe is a much more advanced piece of hardware than the limbic system. Our ancestors of two million years ago didn't have this equipment as we find it today. In fact, the human brain has doubled in size during that two million year period. The frontal lobe performs a number of very important functions. Most notable of these are:

* An ability to synthesize future expectation in a "virtual" simulation of an event. In other words, to be able to imagine how something which has not yet happened, will actually turn out.

* Using that information, the frontal lobe can then develop a "plan" of the best course of action to achieve the desired outcome using:

Logic, Reason, Planning, and Control.

In short, the frontal lobe deals with higher thinking. It operates primarily intellectually, as opposed to emotionally.

In 1868, a physician, J M Harlow, was working with a patient named Phineas Gage. Phineas had suffered severe damage to his frontal lobe due to a freak accident with some dynamite while working on the railroads. Though Gage made a good recovery in most respects it was noted that his ability to make executive decisions had been seriously impaired. Harlow concluded that the frontal lobes serve as a kind of "executive" brain: making decisions, forming goals, planning, organising, devising strategies for attaining goals, and changing strategies when initial plans fail. These observations have been repeatedly confirmed as study and research has continued throughout the decades. Welsh and Pennington (1988) defined the executive function as "the ability to maintain an appropriate problem-solving set for the attainment of a future goal". In other words, having a plan and seeing it through to completion.

Luria in 1973, and Damasio in 1994, also note importantly, that the frontal lobes have greater interconnectivity to the sub-cortical regions of the brain (the brain underneath the cortex, which we have looked at and called the "emotional brain") than any of the other lobes of the cortex. The frontal lobes have extensive and reciprocal connections to the thalamus, basal ganglia, limbic system, and also posterior portions of the cortex.

Okay, that is wordy I know so stay with me and we'll plain English it. What this is saying is that the frontal lobes (the "executive" brain) have greater access to the "emotional brain" than any of the other lobes. The frontal lobes, and the emotional brain (thalamus, basal ganglia, and limbic system), are reciprocal, meaning that they can, and do, feedback information to one another. Cognitive Behavioural Therapy capitalises on this understanding by using intellectual assessment to adjust emotional responses.

Nature dictates that an instinctive response is preferable to an intellectual response when we are under attack. So when the emotional brain is called to act in the presence of a perceived threat it actively blocks access to the higher brain functions associated with the executive brain. When the emotional mind is in control therefore, we lose access to the part of the brain that controls our ability to create solutions. Put simply, we become less rational. In addition to this we also lose a certain amount of access to our sense of control.

Pennington and Ozonoff (1996), note that central to the executive function is: "...maximal constraint satisfaction in action selection, which requires the integration of constraints from a variety of other domains, such as perception, memory, affect, and motivation. Hence, much complex behaviour requires executive function, especially much human social behaviour."

"Maximal constraint satisfaction" is another way of saying "control". They go on to note that "control" requires the correct use of perception (how we view things), memory, and proper motivation, and that these factors all affect how we behave.

LIMBIC SYSTEM VERSUS FRONTAL LOBE?

When we are in a non-aroused emotional state then, the frontal lobe exerts continued control over the limbic system impulses. This is why you don't beat your boss to a pulp when he or she disrespects your efforts. We learn to control our limbic system impulses early on in life. By the time we are five years old we've generally learned that throwing toy bricks at people because we're not getting our own way doesn't usually provide a very good return on investment of energy. If our parents/educators are doing their job properly, the message we receive from the environment is that constructive behaviour is rewarded, and destructive behaviour is ignored or punished. Later, we learn that eating everything in sight makes us fat. Later still, we learn that indulging in drugs, alcohol, smoking, casual sex, late nights, poor nutrition and so on, all extract a cost. We learn naturally to control our emotional responses, and the urge to over-consume. There are two processes at work here.

Process one: We are training the limbic system via a feedback loop of reward and punishment to understand what creates "pleasure", and what creates "pain".

Process two: We are also using the frontal lobe to make decisions based on logic, which will ultimately be passed to the limbic system for automatic processing.

So in process one there are simple connections which make easy learning for the limbic system such as:-

Fingers in fire = immediate pain. Therefore, avoid putting fingers in fire.

This type of learning is quickly established and will pretty much always be taken care of by the limbic system without the need for any great intellectual consideration.

Then, in process two, there are more complex-abstract connections such as:-

Eating candy bar now = future pain because it's uncomfortable to be overweight.

Learning to control how much chocolate we eat is much more complex than learning not to touch fire because cause and effect is not immediately emotionally obvious. We actually need the input of our frontal lobe to exert control over the limbic system impulse. This comes under the heading of "planning", which you'll remember is a frontal-lobe function. By choosing to forego the immediate pleasure of eating the chocolate bar, I am planning ahead to make sure I can fit into my clothes next month. It's not difficult to see then that we are involving some fairly complex processing here because the limbic system works purely by association, while the frontal lobe has a much greater capacity to plan ahead using logic and reason. We can therefore easily end up with conflict when the two brains fail to reach an agreement. Using the chocolate bar example above, what's happening is that the limbic system truly believes that eating the chocolate bar right now is a good thing because it's tasty, sweet, and provides immediate gratification. That's about as far as the limbic system goes in processing. If it looks good, and tastes good, felt good last time I ate it, and Mum always gave me candy for being good (I have learned to "associate" candy with reward), then it must be good! The limbic system has learned that chocolate is good, and provides an urge to indulge. It is the frontal lobe that provides the additional information that all may not be as it seems. Our higher rational brain is capable of connecting our weight gain to the over consumption of chocolate, and must exert "control" over the indulgent limbic system impulse in order to avoid future pain. What this means in practice is that we "know" we should stop eating candy (frontal lobe) and yet we "feel" that we must have it immediately (limbic system). Thus, we have conflict. When you understand this process you can see that the same thing is happening in many situations we encounter in life.

I feel	I know
Like staying home from work today and eating ice cream all day in the sunshine.	I need to keep my job so that I can pay my bills and save for my retirement.
Like throwing myself on the floor and beating my fists because my friend beat me on Xbox	That I am expected as an adult to be a good loser and gracefully accept defeat!
Like leaving my screaming children on a faraway island so I can have five minutes peace.	That would be quite wrong. I would feel terribly guilty abandoning them like that!
Like going out and getting totally trashed on Mojitos.	I'll regret it tomorrow!
Like eating these clotted cream scones.	I'll regret it at the weigh in next week.

These are humorous examples of course, and these types of conflicts we manage mostly to deal with quite easily, but there is a serious point here. We can see that we do in fact constantly use what we know intellectually to temper what we feel emotionally. Thus, we see here, the frontal lobe exerting continued control over the limbic system, often fairly effortlessly. As a general rule then, most of our actions are controlled by the frontal lobe. Generally, we operate from a place of intellectual understanding rather than emotional urge. The question is then, why do we sometimes lose this sense of intellectual control?

The answer is simple. We lose intellectual control when we become emotionally overloaded. Think of a set of scales. "Control" is relatively weighted between "emotional" and "intellectual". When we are generally calm the intellect retains control, but as stress builds, the relative weight of the emotional brain increases, and the scale tips in favour of instinct and emotion. Now, what would have seemed easy to control intellectually when we were calm starts to feel a lot more emotionally driven. Using our table above, what this means in practice is that I am likely to start favouring, and acting upon, "I feel", over "I know". We all know this to be true in practice, right? When we are stressed out we make poor decisions and to hell with the consequences, whether it be stuffing our faces, or kicking the furniture! On occasion, arguably, this can be a release of stress, but beating pillows is known to be ineffective as an anger management tool! Though I might not leave my kids on an island, I might partly fulfil that agenda by dumping them on my mother for a day. Had I not been stressed, I might not have considered that an option, but right now I just don't care. A moment of stress can cause us to act emotionally. When we relax, control returns. The real problems begin when our stress levels are so high generally that we begin to function almost exclusively from the limbic system. Then, I might start dumping my kids on my mother every day. I might start drinking more regularly too. Then our level of intellectual control continues to reduce as more of our life feels "out of control". The net effect of having your life out of control is misery. Your weight increases. You feel hungover. You don't exercise. You upset your loved ones. You lose your job. You are irritable and short tempered. Your self-esteem suffers, and so on it goes. Each of these miseries actually compounds the problem because you then become more stressed, and this simply increases your loss of control, when control is the very thing you need to get things back on track. Make no mistake about it - losing intellectual control makes us feel more anxious. It's not a solution, and we need to dig deep to ensure that doesn't happen.

SUMMARY

* Anxiety, anger, and depression are evolutionary responses to threat.

* Anxiety is designed to create discomfort because it is not meant to be ignored.

* The limbic system is responsible for generating anxiety, depression, anger, and obsessional thought/feeling patterns. It is primarily emotional, and works by conditioned response, not by intellect and reason. It cannot accurately assess whether something is "true" or not, and can react inappropriately by triggering anxious responses to "imagined" or "anticipated" threats.

* The limbic system learns about life through past experiences, other peoples' input, media, environment, and via our own personal conclusions arrived at by rational, or irrational, thought. Since such information can be incorrect, the limbic system library can be corrupted with inaccurate information causing inappropriate triggering of negative emotional responses.

* Once an idea is established in the limbic system library, it is acted upon as "fact" from that point on regardless of how "true" the idea is intellectually.

* Anxiety is triggered when something in the environment (both physical and/or mental) matches with something in the experience library that the limbic system recognises as a potential threat.

* When anxiety is triggered it unleashes powerful physiological processes which are designed to ready us for survival situations. This is known as fight or flight. These responses are very uncomfortable when triggered inappropriately, and can in themselves cause further anxiety.

* The brain favours an instinctive response over an intellectual response when a threat is detected because instinct works more quickly than intellect, increasing the chance of survival in a life-threatening situation.

* The frontal lobe is our "higher thinking" executive brain, and it deals with Logic, Reason, Planning and Control. The frontal lobe generally holds limbic system impulses in check but is less able to do so in the presence of high emotional overload.

* When anxiety is triggered, higher thinking is temporarily over-ridden by the limbic system's emotional response, making it more difficult for us to perceive a situation accurately and rationally.

* Generally high stress levels cause the limbic system to take a greater degree of relative control generally, meaning that we become more emotionally driven overall. We lose some measure of intellectual control in our lives leading to decisions, thoughts, and actions that may ultimately increase anxiety.

Okay. So we've established then that the usually brilliant frontal lobe becomes overwhelmed by negative emotion when we're overloaded with stress. That's bad news. But, we've also explained exactly how and why that happens. So, now that we understand the mechanics of it, we're better placed to do something about it.

Think of it this way. Ordinarily, our frontal lobe keeps everything ticking over automatically and we more or less take it for granted that all is well. As stress levels rise and anxious signals increase, the frontal lobe is swamped by emotion, and will function less brilliantly than it would if things were calm. So the usually automatic function of making clear rational judgements ceases to be quite so automatic. This doesn't mean however that the frontal lobe has no say whatsoever, only that it's relative power is temporarily diminished. Our frontal lobe can in fact still be put to good use. The difference is that the function is no longer fully automatic. When we're anxious, depressed, angry, or obsessive, we need to take conscious control of our frontal lobe, and start instructing it in how to present something positive that the limbic system can work with. This isn't necessarily easy, but at least you know now what needs to happen if we are to eliminate anxiety and depression. The next question is "What can I do about it?" Let's have a look at the immediate options. I want to begin with some information about the correct mental preparations necessary to make a success of it.

Chapter Two – Understanding How You Will Fix Yourself

Curing Or Healing?

Many people walk into the consulting room with a specific problem (symptom) that they want fixed, or cured. The word "symptom" is an interesting one. It alludes to the fact that we have a visible sign of a deeper problem. Most people recognise that the symptom is not necessarily the illness. It is in fact the visible tip of a greater iceberg. The subconscious mind often uses symptoms to alert us to deeper distress which requires our attention.

The difference between curing and healing is that curing is the removal of a symptom while healing is the re-balancing of that which has caused the symptom. If you skim off the top of an iceberg, what's underneath will simply float up to the surface and create a new tip!

Headaches for instance, are often caused by dehydration. You can take ibuprofen to cure a headache but the headache will recur when the drug wears off if the dehydration issue is not addressed. If we re-hydrate we are much less likely to experience another headache. Can we take anti-depressant drugs and have them fix us without addressing the underlying causes? This is an important question because your beliefs in this area will directly affect your ability to fully and permanently recover, for better or worse. Let's explore the question and clarify.

Medication

Whether to use medication or not ultimately has to be a personal decision, albeit one guided by the advice of your medical practitioner. There are undoubtedly pros and cons. Experiences and outcomes are mixed. Some people say that medication has ruined their lives. Others say it has saved their life. It is commonly understood that a person may have to try numerous medications before they find one that works for them, but some find relief with their first course of treatment. Some trial and error may be involved, but for those willing to ride this process out, more often than not, the correct drug that helps, is usually eventually identified. It's worth understanding that although these medications are normally referred to as antidepressants they can often help with anxiety disorders too. Beginning a course of treatment with SSRI antidepressants (the most commonly prescribed) can be a bumpy ride, for some people, for a few weeks, as the body adjusts due to side effects. Initially, some of these medications can increase anxiety but this will often settle fully within four to eight weeks or less, depending on the type of medication prescribed, and the person taking them. After the initial adjustment period, the medication may actually decrease anxiety levels significantly. It is also common, then, for many of the side effects to reduce considerably. The really bumpy part doesn't usually last longer than two to four weeks. There can be a risk of increased suicidal tendency for some people, particularly younger people. Treatment usually continues for six months to a year but this can be flexible depending on your needs, and the supervision of your Doctor. Withdrawing from antidepressant medication must be carefully staggered over a period of time under medical supervision. Some people find withdrawal problematic in terms of symptoms, but antidepressant medications are not considered "addictive" in the usual sense.

There are a number of possible medications. I will leave it for you to research these if you wish but they fall broadly into the following categories.

* *Selective Serotonin Reuptake Inhibitors (SSRI/SNRI) – Anti-Depressant Medication – SSRI's* are considered modern treatment, and they are the most commonly prescribed anti- depressant medication. They work by decreasing the rate of reabsorption of neurotransmitters within the brain, thus increasing the availability of useable serotonin/norepinephrine. There is some evidence that SSRIs may also regenerate brain material atrophied by stress (this is still being researched).

* *Tricyclic – Anti Depressant Medication* – Older style anti-depressants, sometimes with gentle relaxant properties, but also potentially more side effects. Low doses are often used for chronic pain reduction.

* **Anti-psychotics** – Used more rarely for people with extreme difficulties such as clinical paranoia or delusions.

* **Beta Blockers** – Used to treat the physical symptoms of anxiety such as shaking, racing heart rate, and sweating.

* **Tranquilizers/Benzodiazepines** – Very short term prescriptions. Usually offered to get one "through" a difficult event or period of time. Potentially addictive, but generally safe if used as prescribed. Should never be mixed with alcohol (potentially fatal combination).

One caution when doing any research here though. The internet can be full of horror stories. There are risks associated with the use of medications, but that does not mean that the risk is not worth taking, or indeed that you will personally encounter any of the problems you may read about. I recommend that you also look for antidepressant success stories so that you can come to a balanced conclusion, as well as informing yourself accurately by using professional medical information. One thing that most people agree on though is that if the causes of your anxiety or depression are not addressed, then there is an increased probability that medication alone will not be sufficient to create a long term solution.

THERAPY

During the last decade we hear of more doctors recommending therapy to patients, sometimes alongside medication, as a solution. This is heartening. Unfortunately, therapy costs money. While a visit to the doctor for ten minutes to receive a prescription for anti-depressants is acceptable, the ten to twenty hours of one to one care one might receive in a brief therapy programme remains an unaffordable expense for the NHS when it comes to wide-scale provision. A radio programme I was listening to recently made the point that if therapy were widely available on the NHS, the call for it would be enormous, since so many people suffer with emotional disorders of one form or another. It really would be a drain too far for an already stretched NHS. In some areas of the UK, mental/emotional health services are available, but they are generally reserved only for the most serious of cases. State funded provision of mental and emotional health services are improving in some areas, but the services that are available are limited and they can be insufficient. At the time of writing, this looks set to get worse. Typically, following a long wait, one might be offered four to ten sessions of Cognitive Behavioural Therapy or Counselling. While such intervention will be helpful for some, it leaves others only half-helped. Worse still, in some cases, half a therapy can lead a patient to erroneously feel that they are un-helpable. If the therapy is offered as complete, but actually isn't, the assumption that can be easily drawn is that "therapy doesn't work on me". In fact, it's often the case that not enough attention has been extended to create full solution.

The NHS's own advisory council, The National Institute for Health and Clinical Excellence, recommends that antidepressants should not be used as first-line therapy for mild to moderate depression. Instead, they say that patients should be offered guided self-help and psychological therapies in the first instance. There is a problem with this though; time, and finance. Marjorie Wallace, chief executive of the mental health charity SANE, tells us, "GPs are now encouraged to diagnose depression, yet without the availability of qualified counsellors and therapists, they have little choice but to hand out a prescription - or send the patient away empty-handed, leaving them with less hope of treatment and recovery."

Medication has its place. There will be many people who are helped solely through the use of medication. The lift in mood and perception that anti-depressants can supply for some people can be enough to create a window of opportunity for recovery. Anti-depressants can act somewhat like stabilisers on a bike that help a person to regain their balance and start peddling again. Once they are up and running, the stabilisers can be removed and the person will find that they have enough momentum and positive focus in their life to move forward without a recurrence of chronic anxiety or depression. This is most likely when a normally positive person has encountered a short period of anxiety-provoking stress which then naturally passes. It can also be appropriate for people who have restored order in their lives but still find that their body/brain chemistry has not automatically recovered. A little chemical support here can do wonders. This is not however the case for many others. For many, their anxiety and depression is the result of ongoing longer term patterns of unaddressed negativity. In such cases, the anti-depressant acts only to remove the symptom, and not the cause. Though the medication may lift mood for a time, if the underlying lifestyle and perceptive style, the cause of the anxiety or depression is not adjusted, the disturbance is more likely to recur with or without medication, often leading to greater hopelessness.

AVOIDING FALSE STARTS

When you break your leg, you don't expect it to miraculously heal overnight. You recognise that there has been some wounding and that wounds require time, attention, and convalescence to heal well. Healing is organic. We need to understand therefore that recovery from emotional or mental illness is also an organic process, and likewise requires time, attention, and convalescence. A ten minute visit to the doctor is often simply insufficient to deal with the scale of the difficulty, and two or three sessions of counselling, hypnotherapy, acupuncture, CBT, or any other therapy might be equally ineffective. Choosing the wrong kind of therapy is equally precarious. It is a great mistake to assume that this means we cannot be helped. Sadly, many people suffering with anxiety or depression do just this. They visit the doctor, maybe get some medication, try two sessions of possibly inappropriate therapy and find it doesn't "work" before spiralling immediately into helpless-hopeless mode, believing they've fulfilled their duty to themselves without result. So the logic goes, "I've done everything I'm supposed to do. I've even been to therapy! Nothing works. Nobody can help me!" Such a conclusion clearly encourages a sense of hopelessness, and hopelessness is public enemy number one when it comes to anxiety and depression busting. The reality is that when we do this, we are in fact vastly underestimating the scale of the undertaking before us, and failing to recognise the true nature of our position. I've been working on myself for most of my adult life and I'm still learning new things about how to reduce my emotional disturbance. It doesn't take a lifetime to stop being anxious, but let's be clear that there is always something that can be improved. If you find you are telling yourself that you've done everything you can to improve your emotional health, you are probably not being completely honest with yourself. It may be true that you've done everything you currently know how to do, or even all that you're willing to do, but that's not that same thing as all that can be done. Let's begin then with the recognition that no matter how bad things seem, there is room for improvement even if it's not obvious at this point.

Emotional illness has taken hold because the conditions for illness to thrive have been allowed to flourish. When your garden has become overrun with weeds, you don't expect beautiful roses to bloom throughout because you weeded a small area in the corner of your acre. If we want our garden to be a pleasant place to be, we need to weed out the weeds, cultivate the soil, and plant seeds which will grow into beautiful blooms through time. Our emotional being is much more akin to a garden than it is an electrical appliance.

We can be neither half-hearted nor frantic.

People "grow", like gardens grow. We need therefore to cultivate a realistic expectation of what is required if wellness is to return. You can attain relief from anxiety, but it's organic, not mechanical. Recovery takes time, patience, and attention, but if we hold a realistic expectation from the outset, then we can begin to relax about going forwards without unhelpful urgency.

Do I Need A Therapist?

Not necessarily. Some problems will resolve themselves. It's natural for instance to feel very low following a difficult time such as a divorce, a bereavement, or big life change. If everything else is okay in your life, it's likely that you'll feel much more like your old self in the passing of time. There's always room however, to help that process along by improving your understanding and applying some helpful measures. The chances are though, that if you're reading this book, you've probably found yourself in a difficult place.

So, where do we start? Who do we turn to? Well the quick answer is that we need to engage with some form of therapeutic agenda. How you choose to do that is up to you. There are many avenues available to you. There are books, and this is one of them. There are online Cognitive

Behavioural Therapy (CBT) services. If you're persistent, you may be able to procure some free therapy from your GP. There are charities like Sane, Mind, and The Samaritans, who can offer you support. The most direct route however, is to consult an experienced private therapist. What we need is someone who understands the causes of, and solutions to, emotional and mental distress. This is not to say that we can't recover with the help of friends, family, books, internet, common sense, and other support. Many people do just that, but not everyone does. Your friends and family, well-meaning as they may be, may simply not have the skill set needed to help you recover, and are often too close to encourage impartiality in either direction. When recovery does not take place organically, then we are wise to seek specialist help. I'm painfully aware that this will sound biased coming from an ex-therapist, especially one specialising in anxiety, but if you consider it logically for a moment, it's easy to see that this is sensible thinking. What do therapists do all day? Therapists spend their days helping people to resolve emotional and mental distress. Who else is better placed then to help you with your difficulty? Therapists learn what really works, and what doesn't, in practice. The tools that don't cut it in practice are abandoned because they are an embarrassment, and those that really help are refined. There is no substitute for experience, and when you consult with an experienced therapist you are hiring their understanding and experience. It's not that therapists are better than anyone else as people. Neither can they guarantee outcomes. They're still human, flawed, and have blind spots just like everyone else, but most of them will fight for you like mad. Good therapists won't come across as all high and mighty; quite the opposite in fact. Good therapists will recognise that the human condition is by definition flawed and imperfect. Good therapists will teach strategies for managing the complexities of life more comfortably. They'll help you to understand the roots of your difficulties, and assist you in healing. They can help simply because they are experienced in solving the problem that you have. They know where to look, and they come equipped with a box of tools to go about getting the job done. Trying to work it all out on your own is like looking under the bonnet of your broken down car, having an empty toolbox, and expecting to be able to get the thing purring like a kitten! With ingenuity and an infinite amount of time you might actually succeed, but it's not the easiest way to

51

get things done. Don't fall into the trap of thinking that consulting a therapist is an admission of weakness. That's twisted thinking.

The one drawback is that therapy costs money, and usually isn't cheap. I can promise you though that most therapists are not profiteering from your need. The work is intense, so most therapists can't energetically see more than fifteen to twenty clients per week as a maximum. Many see fewer people than that. Consulting room hire fees are expensive and there are many hidden costs. These include professional memberships, monthly supervision, insurance, materials, no holiday pay (during which time they usually still pay for room rental), mandatory annual professional development courses, advertising, accountancy fees, travel costs, tax, and so on. They may charge much more than you earn per hour, but after everyone else has a slice of the pie, their net profit is probably less than fifty percent of the fee. Multiply that by fifteen or twenty maximum and that's their net earnings. They make an average wage at best. They also do a lot of work behind the scenes that nobody pays them for. This is information worth considering if you are feeling reticent due to fees. In the end, your complete therapy might cost you the same as a decent washing machine. I know personally that the money I spent on therapy was the best money I ever spent. If you really are struggling financially, it's always worth asking whether a therapist is willing to offer you a concessionary rate. Many will do so, even if they don't advertise it, and if you spread it out to having one session every three weeks or so, that can be really affordable. Longer term treatment spread over a longer period is, in my opinion, a better option than trying to cram your healing in by having more sessions faster. You're a garden, not a vacuum cleaner. You'll learn skills that you can then take away and work with, and it will take time to master each area of learning. Recognise then, that you're simply calling on a person with greater experience in this particular area. Recognise that if you are very lost, it may take some time to get to where you're going. Be okay with this. Wherever you are, you'll feel better once you have some support, a map, and are back on a road that goes somewhere! Therapy is worth considering.

To Flit, Or Not To Flit?

Flitting is defined as moving in an erratic and fluttering manner. Animals in shock tend to flit. So too do anxious, frustrated, desperate people.

Any therapist who's been in practice for any length of time will have encountered persons who flit between therapists and therapies, frantically searching for a solution to their woes. These are some of the most difficult types of clients to help because their whole premise for being in the consulting room can be skewed from the outset. It is likely that this person has not yet fully assumed responsibility for their problem, but is still looking for someone to magically cure their ills.

So when approaching your solutions, my advice is to choose an approach, and then stick with it for long enough to master it. Your approach can of course be drawn from any number of sources, but the point here is not about where you get your information from, but what you do with it once you have it. If you are impatient, and prematurely abandon what you know because everything wasn't fixed in the first five minutes, then it's likely that you'll end up flitting from one thing to another, and mastering nothing. In the end, this is a false economy. Learning to bust anxiety is a skill which takes time and application to master. The quicker you can get on board with this understanding, the better equipped you'll be for creating a permanent solution.

Spread yourself too thinly and you lose potency.

By all means, if something really isn't working, then do something different, but do be mindful to give every approach enough of a chance to prove itself before discarding it and flitting on to the next thing. As one of my teachers reminds us, though perhaps not meant to be taken too literally, there are at least seven ways to solve any problem. It's not about finding *the* way. It's about finding *a* way, and then sticking with it long enough to master it.

So, that's some practical thoughts about how to prepare for the journey ahead. Before we get to the tools and how to use them though, there is just one more area of great importance to consider. We're about to get deep for a moment, so put your philosophical hat on and you can take it off when we get to the other side.

UNDERSTANDING YOUR HUMANITY

It sounds deep doesn't it? It's important though. Beyond our personal uniqueness, we all share some basic similarities.

Our human-ness is rather wonderful. Sidestepping any religious implications, I think we could rightly call it a bit of a miracle. What's miraculous about our human-ness is its enduring nature. It's like a cork in water. You can hold it down for a while, but as soon as you release it, it pops back up to the surface. Our human-ness has a dark side and a light side. We are potentially capable of great acts of love, and also atrocious cruelty. This is a hard fact to swallow for those of us who like to think that we are "nice" or "good" people, but as we will come to discuss later, having a dark side to one's nature isn't the same thing as being a bad person. Though it is true that disowning our darker side can lead to painful repression, and by extension, inappropriate expression, there is a way to integrate that dark side of ourselves so that it is not feared or damaging. It's ultimately about what we choose to cultivate. Having a dark side to our nature doesn't mean that we choose to be nasty people. We can still choose to stand in the light.

What I want to draw your attention to initially though is that in the light part of our humanity we find some wonderful qualities naturally existing. What I mean when I say that these qualities exist naturally, is that we don't have to manufacture them. They are inherent to our being. They are there with us from the moment that we take our first breath, and whether we are aware of their presence within us or not, they stay with us, I will argue, to our dying day. The light side of our shared humanity includes, but is not limited to, the following:

* A desire to be happy.

* A desire to help other people to be happy.

* A desire to love and be loved.

* Empathy – (An awareness of other peoples' pain and a desire to help others when they are suffering).

* Passion.

* Sensuality.

* Excitement.

* Aesthetic Awareness. (A natural appreciation of beauty).

* Constructiveness.

* Creativity.

* Interest.

* Curiosity.

* Hope.

* Optimism.

* Intelligence.

* Innocence.

* Capacity for joy.

* A sense of adventure and exploration.

These are all the qualities of being we feel when we experience states of positive emotional health. If you're anxious or depressed, you will probably be finding it difficult to relate to some, or all of the above in any substantial way. You may feel that you knew these qualities once but that things have now changed irrevocably. You may feel that some of these qualities you have never known or felt. It's easy to conclude that all is lost when we're worn down with anxiety or depression, but I want to present you with a different, much more hopeful model.

It has been my experience both personally and professionally that these human qualities are never truly "lost". A much more accurate understanding is that these qualities can become temporarily obscured from our awareness. The human heart (emotionally speaking) is like a precious jewel. All of the above qualities the human heart exudes in effortless abundance when it is open and unwounded. The problem is, while the heart is unfathomably radiant by nature, it is also very vulnerable and prone to wounding. Few of us live with truly unwounded open hearts. It seems to be part of the deal with living a human life, that at some point in our lives, we each will have our heart broken in some way. In fact, most of us have our hearts broken many times over, sometimes in huge and devastating ways, and sometimes in small subtle ways.

Metaphorically, what happens when a heart is emotionally wounded is that initially it hardens a little. This is quite normal. A protective shell forms around the wounded area, much like a scab that protects a skin abrasion from further damage while the tissue underneath repairs. While this does help in reducing the hearts immediate vulnerability by blocking potentially damaging signals from causing further wounding, it also obscures the light at the centre of our being that would otherwise, like a flame, warm and illuminate the personality. Thus, with increased wounding, the protective shell that surrounds the heart becomes thicker and denser, and the light of our life becomes more thoroughly obscured. Since the light looks dim we can easily fall into thinking that it is dim. My contention to you is that the light in your being is not dead or even dying...it's simply obscured.

In practice then, it's easy to fall into the trap of identifying with this diminishing light as the basis of who we are. It is this identification that leads us to feelings of hopelessness and helplessness which manifests as anxiety and depression in our lives. Healing requires that we dissolve the protective shell of fear, anger, and depression, which has taken up residence around our hearts, so that we can once again (or in some cases for the first time in our life) be warmed and illuminated by our own natural light. In every client, I see a beautiful heart temporarily obscured by a tough protective shell. It is this fact that allows me to meet every human being with unconditional positive regard. My client will probably be convinced that that they are nothing but a dim light, and in some cases, a rotten worthless shell. I start out every person's therapy with the understanding that beyond their wounding, at the heart of their being, is a sun sized radiant warmth that can make them, and those around them, feel glad to be alive. If I can help them to dissolve the hardness and contraction that has accumulated around their wounding, they can then begin to feel once again the safety and expansiveness of their hearts own light and warmth.

THE ROLE OF LOVE

We are speaking metaphorically here. I am mindful of the fact that too much talk of "love and light" can be construed as airy-fairy talk with no substance. Before continuing, I think it's important to make sure we're speaking the same language. Where the word "love" follows, I'm not talking about some sickly-gooey-sentimental Hollywood-saturated ideal. I'm talking about something much grittier than that. When I think of the word love, it has a bit of fight in it. Love cares. Caring by definition doesn't automatically imply sentimentality. Caring is a positive response to being alive. Caring is intrinsically dignified. To care about something means that there is recognition of its value.

Love therefore is life's recognition and valuing of itself.

Since you are part of life, loving yourself means recognising and valuing yourself. Loving things external to ourselves, like other people and aspects of the world, likewise involves recognition and valuing. There is dignity in this. It's not gooey. If we care about something, we are usually willing to fight for it too. Love is about doing the right thing, even if it's not the easy thing. When you cultivate caring towards yourself, that is self-love. Loving yourself isn't always easy, but it is dignified. It is this quality, and this alone, that has the necessary power to dissolve the hard protective shell that has accumulated around any wounded heart.

As darkness is an absence of light, so fear can be thought of as the absence of love.

Take note of this statement and remember it. It may look rather romantic at first glance, but look without sentimentality and you will find a deep human truth here. One of the things we really fear, deeply, is the absence of love. Where we feel an absence of love, we usually find fear in residence. Why? Because an absence of love implies an absence of caring and valuing, and if something is not cared for or valued, then it is by definition left vulnerable to neglect, or worse still, abuse. Life recognises that neglect leads to systemic disorder (breakdown), and that the ultimate outcome of neglect and breakdown is pain. The formula simplified therefore is that love-less-ness equals pain, and we fear pain.

Caring feels safe, and maintains order. Neglect feels unsafe, and leads to disorder. Life fears pain so where there is no love (caring) there is the threat of pain, and fear exists to alert us to that imminent threat. Follow this logic and you will quickly arrive at the recognition that the limbic system becomes involved when pain is perceived as a possibility.

What this means in practice is that the unconscious mind, charged as it is with the task of keeping us safe, goes to great lengths to protect us from both pain and the absence of love. We experience fear in our lives wherever the possibility of running into pain or love-less-ness is perceived. How sensitised we are at any given time to the presence of this painful fate is largely dependent on our past experience, or put another way, how severely we have been wounded throughout our lives. If we have experienced life as being full of hostility and neglect, then our anticipation of experiencing more of the same in the future is likely to be amplified. The most extreme form of this perception is paranoia. Paranoia is the unshakeable feeling that the world is out to get you. Unfortunately, this perception can become a self-fulfilling prophecy. When you expect hostility, you behave defensively. Since the best form of defence is attack, there is a tendency then to exhibit a persona that is difficult for people to warm to. When this happens, the very thing you crave, caring and valuing, is the last thing you receive. This then leads your mind to believe that it's assessment of the world as a hostile place is in fact correct, and the strategy remains in place, leading to more of the same.

The expectation of negative outcomes usually leads us along paths which filter out alternative perspectives leading us mostly to experience exactly what we expect.

Why is the inclusion of love important then to our discussion about anxiety? Well it's simple. If loveless-ness generates fear, then it follows that love (caring, valuing, and attention) generates safety. When we feel safe, we don't feel anxious. This isn't just a nice theory. In practice it is true.

Consider for a moment. What are most people anxious about? There are the obvious things like money, bills, job security, our loved ones, health, and safety, but I can tell you from many years of experience as a therapist that the majority of anxieties are in one way or another about other people! Why? Because we care deeply about how we are perceived by others. We fear that love, in any of its forms, will be withdrawn. This fear has a biological basis. To be excluded from ones community may once have meant literal death. Survival has always been a joint effort, and if your community rejected you, the chances of surviving alone would have been slim in a hunter-gatherer lifetime. We now have the luxury of knowing that there are people to care for us no matter what our situation. We may understand that consciously, but two million years of evolution has taught our limbic system that what other people think of us matters!

So consider for a moment that it's illogical to perceive that other people will see you as valuable if you don't see yourself that way.

Personal wounded-ness manifests as not feeling good about yourself. That makes it much more difficult to believe that anyone else could see good things about you. They do of course, but you won't be able to believe that unless you see it in yourself. True healing includes therefore bringing love (caring and valuing) to the wounded (neglected and vulnerable) parts of our selves. It is this caring and valuing that creates a sense of safety that can dissolve the protective shell around a wounded heart, and allow the flame at the heart of being to burn more brightly, and be felt more clearly.

Love you see, caring and valuing, has a rather mysterious and magical effect upon life that has wilted due to wounding and neglect. No respectable physician should ever be heard speaking of such foo-foo of course! Wilted life? Magical effect you say? Mysterious you say? Yep. That's what I said! Science argues that for a thing to exist it should be "proven" to exist. When it comes to weights and measures that's perfectly reasonable, but love? How can you measure such a thing? I make no apologies. We could discuss the evolution of the brain. We could posit the theory that humanity as a species has endured through co-operation and that empathy is a biological pre-requisite for such cohesion. All of this is almost certainly true, but, what of our most simple experience? What of that simple experience when we have a moment of tenderness, where someone is truly listening; a hand on the shoulder, an empathetic smile, a true compliment given without ulterior motive? Are we contemplating our synaptic pathways in such moments? No. In such moments we are experiencing a moment of meaning that defies scientific definition. We are experiencing love. Our experience is primary. Regardless of what chemical reaction is taking place, or which neural pathway is being stimulated, our experience is what ultimately matters because that's where we actually live our lives; in experience.

One of the great wonders of our experience of existence is that we are occasionally touched by love, and the experience of being cared for, and valued, is naturally soothing and healing. I call it a wonder because it is at best a divine design of the highest good, and at worst a biological "trick" designed to encourage systemic co-operation for the furtherance of the species. In any case, in practice, in experience, love does exhibit great transformative power. To our simple sense of experience this is a rather miraculous fact, as well as being an extraordinary stroke of luck because we can harness this power to heal. Nowhere is this principle more relevant than in the way we approach ourselves.

We will return shortly in a dedicated chapter to looking at practical ways of harnessing loves healing qualities, but before we do, there is still some more to say about the foundations of healing.

You can take your hat off now.

THE ROLE OF SKILL

Love may be a vital component of true healing, but of equal importance is "skill". All the good will and compassion in the world may be wasted if our efforts are not directed skilfully.

Being emotionally healthy is not a moral issue.

The idea that we "should" be well and happy if we choose to be "good" or "nice" is too simplistic. In fact, we can recognise that being a good or nice person can often contribute to overloaded anxiety levels if our definition of what being a nice person involves is distorted. Being nice or good doesn't always mean doing everything that's expected of you. So the saying goes: the road to hell is paved with good intentions. If being "nice" becomes more important to us than making sure our needs are met, we can suffer as a result.

There are many skills we need to acquire in order to live full rounded lives. Communication, patience, discipline, assertiveness, confidence, courage (yes, this too is a skill that can be learned), responsibility, discernment, empathy, and social grace, to name but a few.

Wellbeing levels are improved with the acquisition of a good skill base. When we have acquired a good skill base we are more resourceful as a result. The more resourceful we become, the better our sense that we have tools that can help us to successfully cope with the demands of life. This in turn decreases our sense of vulnerability. If we feel less vulnerable, we generally feel less anxious or depressed too.

THE ROLE OF RESOURCES

Skills can be learned. It's a mistake to assume that what you are today is what you will be next year, or in the next decade. Anxiety busting is a skill. What you are reading here is a resource. Resources help you to get what you need.

Selling yourself the idea that you don't "have" courage, discernment, patience, social grace, or confidence, and then believing that it's a done deal forevermore is a pretty sure way to depress yourself. The fact is that all these skills and many more can be learned. Recognising this fact places you in a potentially empowered position because then you can stop telling yourself that things will be like this forever because it's just who you are. It's not. You are where you are largely because of the skills you possess, and of course, the skills you do not yet possess. You have options, and you can choose to acquire the skills you want or need.

Living life well can be thought of as living life skilfully. What we are seeking, is a way of living which offers maximum output or result (a strong sense of wellbeing), for minimum effort or energy expenditure. This doesn't mean trying to get something for nothing. Neither is it an invitation to become idle. It just means that we aim to streamline our activities so that we don't waste precious energy, either physically or psychologically. This can be remembered simply as the goal of "MiniMax". If you recognise that your life is proving harder than it needs to be, there's a good chance that you're lacking a necessary skillset. Being willing and able to do something about that is an important part of anxiety busting. When you decide to acquire missing skills to help yourself live well, it is an act of self-love because you are communicating to yourself that you value yourself enough to bother.

Remember that acts of self-love make us feel safer so choosing to help yourself by acquiring the skills you need reduces anxiety.

One of the problems with acquiring new skills is that it is often costly. Sometimes that means that there is a financial outlay, but just as often it's an energy issue. The question really becomes not "Can I get the skills I need?", but "Am I willing to pay the necessary price to get the skills I need?" Put another way, we need to ask ourselves how hungry we are for that prize. This can be remembered as the price and the promise. Is it important enough to us? The answer to that question can only be answered by the individual concerned. Nobody but you can decide what's truly important for you, and what isn't. This however is why self-love is such a vital part of anxiety busting because if we don't value ourselves, then our sense of what is truly important for us can be distorted. Why would we bother to go through the expense of acquiring new skills to help ourselves out if we don't think we're valuable enough to be worth the effort? The degree to which you decide that you are willing to do what's necessary to improve things for yourself is strongly related to how much you value your-self. If you doubt this, just consider for a moment what you would be willing to do for someone else that you value enormously if they needed your help? Is it more than you would do for yourself? Reflect on this.

We need to be really honest with ourselves here. Sometimes we're actually not that hungry for the change. That's fine. There is no "should" about it. It's not a moral issue. It's a skill issue. If the pain of being stuck where you are is worse than the pain of doing something about changing it, then it's un-skilful to do nothing. Without wishing to insult your intelligence, what follows is designed to get you thinking in formula rather than state the obvious. These are rather obvious examples, but the important point is to learn to recognise that few problems are truly intractable, and that the sense of being stuck is often related to either a failure to think the matter through to solution logically, or an unwillingness to pay the price to acquire the change we want. Many problems can be solved by acquiring new skills. Here then are some examples of how gaining new skills could improve a person's life, along with some suggested resources. The examples assume that the problem is recognised as mainly lying with the person seeking to make the change, and not with the World at large.

Problem	Skills Required	Resources
Repeated Failing Relationships	Communication Skills Listening Skills Assertiveness Skills Patience Recognising Self-Worth	Therapeutic Input Self Help Books/Internet Non-Violent Communication Course CBT
Repeated Debt Crisis	Prioritising Skills Personal Restraint Practical Money Management Delaying Gratification	Life Coaching Computer Software Paper Spreadsheets "Manage Your Money" Evening Class At Local College. Books/Internet Ask A Friend/Relative For Help In Organising Your Monthly Spend

Deeply Unhappy In Current Career	New "Trade" Skills	Self-Belief Apprenticeship University Placement "On The Job" Training. Private Education Open University Course Self-Education
Repeated Episodes Of Anxiety And/Or Depression	Understanding Of The Causes Of Emotional Disturbance Relaxation Skills CBT Skills Medication	GP Therapy Books/DVD's/Internet Friends/Family/Others Self-Development Courses Mental Health Charities

None of the above mentioned examples are exhaustive or definitive. Different people may need different skills acquired from different resources. The point is just simply to consider the role that resources play in acquiring skills, so that you can stop telling yourself that you've exhausted all your options. So the saying goes "Never give up...never give up..." Obtaining help should not be underestimated as a booster to morale. It can go a long way to have someone or something on your side. Knowing that you are working towards a solution to your problem will usually lift your mood considerably and create real hope. Things don't need to be perfect in order for us to feel better. They just need to be moving in a positive and constructive direction.

Even when looking for help though, we still need to be skilful. We need to invest in something that really is likely to help us solve the problem. Choosing a resource which ultimately leads us nowhere fruitful is an unskilful move that will lead us deeper into misery and hopelessness. It's no good climbing a ladder, if it's the wrong one. It's up to you to choose wisely when selecting a resource you need to acquire a skill. If it turns out that your first choice isn't fulfilling its promise, then switch to something that will. Don't tell yourself that you've tried and failed. That's just creating unnecessary hopelessness. We are all different. What worked for your friend might not work for you, and vice versa. Your first choice might not be fruitful. If it isn't, then try again. There is someone, or something out there that will be a good fit for you. Stay with it!

Of course, sometimes certain resources are genuinely beyond our reach for one reason or another. Then we need to look to what is within our reach. This may well be a step towards getting where we ultimately wish to go. So, we break down the process into smaller steps. This is referred to therapeutically as "chunking down". This means breaking the process down into manageable bite-sized chunks. If we find ourselves overwhelmed by the scale of an undertaking, it may well be because we're looking at going from A to Z in one giant step. This can sometimes appear, and often is, unmanageable, and so we feel overwhelmed, and become paralysed as a result. Then we don't act at all. That's analysis paralysis. Instead we need to consider which smaller steps will lead us to our goal, and then concentrate on the small steps one at a time, much like crossing a river by stepping stones. Saying "I want to lose four stones by Christmas" is a potentially overwhelming goal. It looks like such a long road ahead that we can easily feel overwhelmed and quit before we've started. Switching that to "I want to have lost 7lbs by the end of March" and then intending to review the situation seems much more manageable. The ultimate goal may still be to lose four stones but the pressure is removed from the situation, and we are more likely to act because the goal seems more manageable.

SUMMARY

Here then is a summary of the key points we've discussed in chapter two for easy recall.

* Your mental and emotional health is primarily your responsibility. The state may offer you some assistance, but relying on the state to provide you with ALL of the help you need can create the erroneous belief that you cannot be helped because the state's resources are limited. What the state is able to supply may not be sufficient to meet your personal needs. You may need to seek your own private solutions alongside whatever help the state can offer.

* Medication may be a part of the solution, but is only sometimes all of the solution. A therapeutic approach is often of equal or greater value than medication alone. Medication and therapy combined may be of greatest benefit, but many difficulties can be resolved using therapy alone.

* "Healing" is a preferable goal to being "cured" because healing works on the underlying cause of un-wellness rather than just being rid of symptoms, which are likely to return if the underlying causes of distress are not addressed. Healing is mobilised by positive commitment towards your-self, and offers a long term solution.

* Therapies and Therapists are well placed to help you with your difficulties. Seeking the guidance of a specialist is not a sign of failure. Nor does it make you weak, or less worthy, than anyone else. It is a practical matter of seeking out the tools you need to create wellness, in the same way that you might consult a mechanic when your car needs servicing. Trying to do it all on your own without using the appropriate tools is likely to frustrate you and make your journey back to wellness much more difficult than it needs to be. The cost is an investment in your wellbeing. Approached sensibly, it may be more affordable than you thought. Nobody is profiteering from your need.

* Flitting from one "cure" to the next will water down your overall approach and leave you full of knowledge, but lacking in practical

application. We need to understand what's necessary to achieve a reduction in anxiety and stick with it for long enough to master it. Your tools may already be sufficient, but it takes time to learn to use any tool effectively. Learning to bust anxiety is a skill. This book is a resource designed to teach you that skill. You can draw your skills from more than one resource, but do not abandon each resource you use because the next big thing looks better. It might be bigger, shinier, and more expensive, but every tool is only as good as the craftsperson using it. Having a vast toolkit is no good to you if you don't know how to use any of the tools effectively.

* Un-wellness (anxiety, depression) is not a signal that you are permanently broken. It is a temporary veiling of your natural wellbeing. Emotional and mental wounds cause this veiling effect, and by healing our wounds we can reveal once again the safety and light that has always been a natural inherent part of our being, at core.

* Anxiety is a response to feeling threatened. The absence of caring, or the presence of hostility is perceived as inherently threatening, and thus creates anxiety.

* Love is defined here as "caring and valuing". Love has natural anti-anxiety properties because caring and valuing implies safety. Therefore, replacing neglect (absence of caring) with caring and valuing reduces anxiety.

* Skill is of equal importance to love in anxiety busting. Skills can be acquired, so we need to remain mindful that we may not have all the skills we require yet to create solution, but that does not mean that we can't get them. We can!

* Acquiring skills uses energy and sometimes finances. We need to be honest with ourselves about the "price and the promise". Are we really willing to pay the price or put the work in to acquire the skill we want or need? If not, fine, but at least be honest about this instead of telling yourself that you "can't" when it's really a "won't".

 * We may not be in a position to acquire all the skills we want or need straight away, but we can approach our longer term goals in bite-sized

chunks, thereby taking small steps that lead us eventually to where we want to go, like stepping stones. It's important that we do not try to take on too much all at once, or we can become overwhelmed by the scale of a task, and wind up feeling deflated, and do nothing as a result. Taking small steps is obviously preferable to doing nothing at all to help ourselves.

* Resources are necessary to acquire skills. Being resourceful means finding the help we need. We should take care not to tell ourselves that there is no help available because it hasn't presented. We need to figure out what we need, and then go out there and get it. Not all resources deliver on their promise. Selecting resources skilfully can help you to avoid feelings of hopelessness if a poor resource fails to deliver. If, with best intention, the resource we choose does fail to deliver, don't blame yourself. It's unavoidable trial and error sometimes, so don't give up. Rest, regroup, and then look somewhere else. What you need is out there somewhere!

Starting out with the correct mental approach is of vital importance. Approaching any activity with an unrealistic expectation of what's required for the undertaking is a recipe for disappointment at the best of times. Since hopelessness and helplessness are key enemies of emotional wellbeing, the importance of being properly mentally prepared with a realistic expectation should not be underestimated. With that point I hope now firmly established let's move on to the practical business of constructing some solutions!

Chapter Three – Foundations Of Healing

Beating anxiety is something you *learn* to do. Here's what Wikipedia has to say about learning:

Physiology Of Learning

*"Thought," in a general sense, is commonly conceived as something arising from the stimulation of neurons in the brain. Current understanding of neurons and the central nervous system implies that the process of learning corresponds to changes in the relationship between certain neurons in the brain. Research is ongoing in this area. It is generally recognized that memory is more easily retained when multiple parts of the brain are stimulated, such as through combinations of hearing, seeing, smelling, motor skills, touch sense, and logical thinking. Repeating thoughts and actions is an essential part of learning. Thinking about a specific memory will make it easy to recall. This is the reason why reviews are such an integral part of education. On first performing a task, it is difficult as there is no path from axon to dendrite (**from one brain cell start point to other cells – emphasis mine**). After several repetitions a pathway begins to form and the task becomes easier. When the task becomes so easy that you can perform it at any time, the pathway is fully formed. The speed at which a pathway is formed depends on the individual, but is usually localised resulting in talents.* **Wikipedia**

Neural Pathways, Neural Plasticity

Neural pathways are habits of thinking. We can learn habits, we can unlearn them, and we can re-learn them. Addictive, anxious, depressed, and obsessive processes are at one level, negative neural pathways. These are habits of thought, triggering in a non-helpful context.

For much of the twentieth century, science considered that after initial development (0-20 years), the adult brain must be immutable and unchanging. New scientific research is revealing that the brain is in fact an ever changing living organism. The brain disconnects and reconnects neural pathways according to need. This is hardly surprising when you

70

consider that human beings are extremely adaptive creatures. Such adaptation would simply not be possible if the brain were truly inflexible.

The brain contains a vast matrix of complex connections. The number, and nature, of these connections dictate the way we perceive reality.

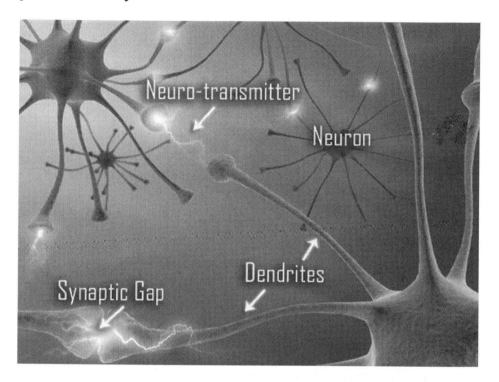

In the picture above we see the brain in action. Here's a quick explanation:

Neuron - A brain cell. The human brain is estimated to contain around 100 billion nerve cells. These are electrically/chemically sensitive hubs for the storage and transmission of information.

Dendrite - Arms of neurons, allowing for multiple complex connections with other cells, for the purpose of sending and receiving information.

Synaptic Gap - A small gap which sits between dendrites, across which, chemical/electrical signals flow.

Neuro-Transmitter - A chemical messenger, which transmits signals from one neuron to another, across the synaptic gap.

If you consider this picture of the brain in action, it's much easier to understand that our state of mind at any given time is the result of A to B connections. Consider that the synaptic gap is a gap! It is not permanently bonded to sister cells. It is free to move, and free to make new connections. Dendrite "A" does not have to connect to dendrite "B". A can go to C, D, E, Z! In terms of habits of thought and perception it's all a matter of what's connected to what.

This is great news for the anxious, angry, obsessed, or depressed person. It means that you can change the way your brain processes life. It may not happen on its own though. New input is necessary to get those pathways connecting in new ways. Research shows that on average, we can learn a basic new function in one to two days, change a habit in three weeks, and re-pattern a neural pathway in three to six weeks. A neural pathway is created when we use our brain repeatedly in a certain way. Neural pathways can be adaptive, like in learning a new skill, or maladaptive, as in learning a bad habit. We can now understand the battle cry of solution focussed brief therapy:

If you always do what you always did then you'll always get what you always got.

So it's like a muscle. We either use it or lose it. If we work on our triceps, they'll get larger. If we concentrate on our biceps, they'll grow. Similarly, if you concentrate on seeing the worst in life, then your "seeing the worst" pathways will increase, and you'll see more of that. If you concentrate on working out your "making solutions" pathways, then you'll start to increase your ability to perceive solutions much more quickly, as more and more of those pathways form and connect. In other words, with continued repetition, change becomes easier, and eventually it becomes automatic. The learning here is simply that over time you get more of what you focus on. Your brain simply makes more "positive" connections, or more "negative" connections, according to where you choose to focus your attention. The book "Buddha's Brain" explains "What fires together wires together". In other words when you consciously direct your attention towards solutions you can create new neural pathways.

It's all about what you "endorse", or "buy into" with feeling. Where attention goes, energy flows.

A nice metaphor for understanding how neural pathways operate is to think of a jungle. You have a number of paths through the jungle to various locations. It's easy to walk these paths because they've always been well trodden. These are your habits of thought. However, the problem is that these particular paths lead only to dried-up old swamps. You're sick of drinking dirty water. You know that somewhere out there is a new pristine clearing with a beautiful flowing waterfall. It's tough at first to start clearing a new path. You need to take your machete and hack at the strong vines to clear the way, but soon you're making headway and the path is clearer every day. Each time you walk the path there is less foliage to clear. After a time, the new path is as clear as the old ones were, just as easy to walk, and you are blissfully drinking clear fresh water once again. Out of curiosity you one day have a look at the old paths to find that they can hardly be found, since they're now all overgrown.

If you doubt the science of neuroplasticity, consider for a moment the case of Kate Allatt. On February 7th 2010, Kate suffered a massive stroke. The blood clot damaged her brain stem and she found herself unable to move or speak, a condition known as Locked-In Syndrome. The doctors said she would never walk, talk, swallow, or lead a normal life again. She ran a 20 metre run for charity on the first anniversary of her stroke. I heard Kate describe first-hand, how she had made the decision to find a way out, despite the doctors' damning prognosis. She understood that neuroplasticity is possible, and she was determined that she was going to use it. She knew that a part of her brain had been damaged, and set about instructing her brain to engineer new connections around the damaged material. She said that the visualisation she used was that of the fairground attraction of hammer and slider. If you hit the hammer hard enough, the slider will ring the bell. This became the metaphor for her attempts to rewire. She visualised the slider as new neural pathways, and reasoned that if she could get the slider to reach all the way to the bell she could eventually get it to ring the bell, and that would mean movement. Sure enough, after many attempts over a period of time, with conviction, eventually she was able to extend the slider to ring the bell, and she found she was able to move a finger. Then more fingers, and so on. Kate is perhaps a rare case when it comes to such extreme difficulty, but the important thing to notice here is that neuroplasticity is a reality. Her story can be an inspiration to us all.

ANXIETY DOES NOT DROP OUT OF THE SKY ON YOU!

I know it feels like it does, but if we settle for that as an explanation, we'll never get control of it!

It is in fact maintained on a daily basis. This may seem like a very surprising proposition to anyone who has suffered from a long-term anxiety related difficulty because it seems like we're just anxious all the time, with no rhyme or reason. Consider however, that neural pathways are habits of thought and behaviour, and you will begin to understand how a status quo of anxiety can be maintained on a daily basis. If those daily habits of thought lead repeatedly to negative conclusions, about yourself, the world, and other people, then your poor old limbic system has no choice but to continue to respond to those perceptions as though they are true. In practice this means that the limbic system responds to life with an increase in protective instinctive responses such as anxiety and depression because those habits of thought repeatedly assume that situational outcomes will involve pain or threat. This can be as simple as an **unconscious** expectation that yesterday was tough, so today will be too. Any pattern of behaviour or thought that's been around for a long time becomes normalised, meaning that it's accepted as "just the way things are". In other words, such alarming patterns of thought and behaviour go largely unquestioned, and are perceived as "true". The alarming perceptions are thereby continually endorsed, and as a result, the level of anxiety remains constant.

Anxiety busting involves identifying and altering the patterns of thought, and behaviour, which cause the limbic system to remain unnecessarily alarmed.

In order to understand how we maintain a daily level of anxiety, it's useful to use the analogy of a stress bucket. The idea is that we all have a nervous system, and that nervous system has a finite capacity for carrying emotional arousal. We know the saying "I've had it up to here!" This alludes to our stress bucket. Under ideal conditions we begin the day with a largely empty stress bucket. As any day progresses, our stress bucket fills. This is natural and normal. The nervous system does need to be rested and re-charged, and for this we have sleep. Our stress bucket functions best when it is no more than halfway full by the end of the day. Then we sleep, and while we are in the REM sleep cycle, the bucket is emptied throughout the night, so we then wake up ready to meet the new day with an empty bucket. When our bucket is only halfway full by the end of the day we're in a very safe position because we have plenty of spare capacity to deal with unexpected additional stress. When we know we have plenty of spare capacity to deal with unexpected eventualities, then we tend not to worry about such things occurring. We take things in our stride, and the sense is that we have enough reserves that we'll be able to cope with what life throws at us.

YOUR NERVOUS SYSTEM – THE STRESS CONTAINER AND THE IMPORTANCE OF SLEEP

"I've had all I can stand!" is how we express the feeling that we are close to overload. This is in fact a very accurate model of how we experience stress in the body and mind. Stress is definitely held in the body, and manifests as tight muscles, tight chest, discomfort in the solar plexus, tingly fingers, sweaty palms, headaches, and so on. Your nervous system can suffer with an accumulation of arousals which can overload the container. So here is a stress container belonging to a relaxed individual:-

The Stress Container

A non-anxious person has plenty of spare capacity to deal with unexpected stress and therefore feels safe!

Plenty of room for extra stress

Daily Stress

Unresolved "Issues"

REM Sleep

De-arouses daily anxiety.

In order to better understand the stress container, we need to consider the role of sleep in emptying the container. According to Joe Griffin and Ivan Tyrell (Human Givens), sleep, and lack of it, relates directly to our daily levels of emotional arousal. They tell us that there are two ways that emotional arousal can be discharged from the system; either by taking action (engaging the situation), or through the process of sleep. Since there are many moments in life where it is simply not possible to discharge an emotional arousal in the moment, then nature takes care of un-discharged emotional arousal through sleep. When we sleep, the mind metaphorically replays the theme of concern, and thereby discharges the associated anxiety "virtually" by playing the theme out to conclusion. This process we experience as dreaming. The content of dreams is estimated to be approximately eighty per cent negative. When we recognise that the brain is discharging yesterday's anxious moments this fact becomes less surprising. We can see in the diagram above that when a stress bucket is not overloaded, the REM sleep mechanism is

76

easily able to discharge yesterday's daily stress so that we awaken in the morning fresh and ready to meet the new day in a relaxed way.

Problems begin when the bucket becomes overloaded generally. Here's how that can happen:-

In the course of any night's sleep we cycle between Slow Wave Sleep and Rapid Eye Movement (R.E.M.) sleep. The graph below shows this process. We can see that we enter REM sleep periodically throughout the sleeping period. The most prolonged REM sleep takes place in the latter half of our sleep cycle with the deepest slow wave sleep taking place in the middle of the sleep cycle. On average we sleep about 25% REM to 75% Slow Wave under relaxed conditions.

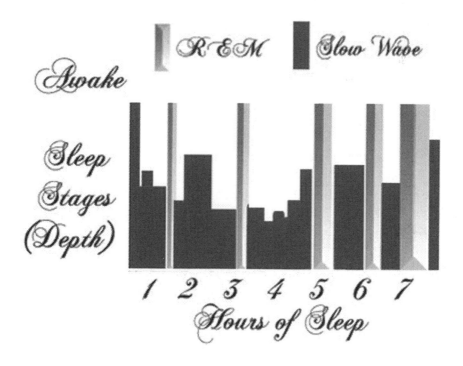

In a relaxed individual, approximately 75% of the sleep period will be spent in slow wave (recuperative, healing, relaxing) sleep, while 25% will be spent in REM (highly active) sleep.

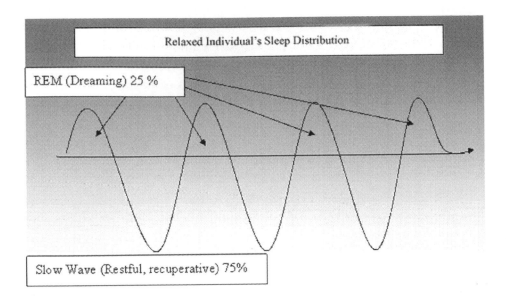

Studies have shown however, that in anxious, depressed, or obsessive individuals, this ratio shifts. This person spends more time in REM and less time in slow wave. In highly depressed individuals we can see the entire cycle invert so that only 25% of the sleep period is spent resting, while 75% is spent wrestling in the realms of the archetype, dreaming.

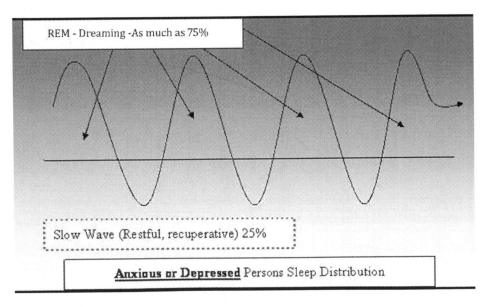

The really important point to note here is that REM is not recuperative. In fact, it's quite the opposite. The brain is working harder in REM sleep than it is during a waking period. We often think that if we've been asleep, then we've been resting, but this understanding highlights the fact that actually our brain may have been working very hard during the night. So, while a relaxed individual who sleeps eight hours a night may receive six hours of rest in the form of slow wave sleep, someone with an overload of emotional arousal may receive much less rest even though they are asleep for the same amount of time. This explains why anxious and depressed individuals often feel exhausted when they wake up, even if they've slept for a long period of time. It also explains why anxious people report more nightmares. They are dreaming more frequently and intensely as the REM sleep mechanism is overworked in an effort to discharge an overloaded bucket. It's not all down to how much we sleep. It's also about our quality of sleep. Most people who are anxious experience some sleep disturbance. Apart from the fact that sleep is less restful during periods of emotional disturbance, we also need to factor in that when we are anxious, we feel like we are in a warzone generally.

From an evolutionary perspective, it would have been dangerous to sleep too deeply while finding oneself in a potentially dangerous environment since the brains security system would recognise the possibility that one might come under attack while asleep. The solution then, would be to "sleep with one eye open", remaining very vigilant, even though asleep. This manifests as light or broken sleep, early waking, or even just not being able to go to sleep. Today, we respond in just the same way, but the world has changed. In many ways, this response is even more troubling to us today than it would have been to our ancestors as our modern day lives often demand that we need to be somewhere at nine a.m. Today's "dangers" can often be imagined, and here you have those recurrent intrusive thoughts and worries which keep one from going to sleep. The limbic system, which takes care of such natural functions as sleep, will respond to what is real and what is imagined (potential). All of that worry and replaying of negative scenarios (past, present, or future) in the mind's eye is tantamount to a real encounter with a tiger, as far as the subconscious mind is concerned. The mind and body, necessarily deliver a fear response to deal with those potential threats, and sleeping with a body primed to escape or do battle, a body full of adrenaline, is next to impossible. In addition to this, the brain inherently recognises that doing too much REM sleep is exhausting, and will actually prefer awakened rest to disturbed REM, causing frequent waking in an attempt to break the intense REM cycle, and conserve energy. It is rather damned if it does and damned if it doesn't!

If your sleep is disturbed:-

* Stop any mentally stimulating tasks at least one or two hours before bedtime. It takes time for your brain to wind down when it has been highly active.

* Don't "try" too hard to sleep! Trying implies effort, and gives you the opposite of what you need, which is relaxation.

* Don't watch TV in bed. The brain can learn to associate the bedroom with waking activities and become reluctant to switch off at bedtime. The rule is that the bedroom is for sleeping and loving only.

* Use relaxation recordings or soft music to ease you into a sleepy relaxed state which will help you to calm your thoughts, and drift into sleep easily.

* Avoid caffeine after 3pm. Caffeine stays in your system for twelve hours. Six hours after you drank that double cappuccino this afternoon you still have half the caffeine in your system. That's enough to easily disturb sleep for some people. Caffeine is not good if you're anxious full stop.

* Do your best to stop thinking when you go to bed. If you know something is likely to irritate you before you go to bed, be disciplined enough to leave it for tomorrow.

* Definitely never go to bed angry or in the middle of a dispute.

* Record your "to do's" on a piece of paper an hour before you go to sleep. That way you can convince your brain that it doesn't need to swirl them around while you're trying to sleep. You can take care of them tomorrow.

* Avoid vigorous exercise less than 2 hours before bedtime. This can leave your system "amped".

* Make sure you're doing enough in the day to finish the day a bit tired, and ready to sleep.

In any case, we know that sleep, like any other automatic function, will generally tend towards being naturally balanced when obstacles (such as anxiety) are removed. In other words, the more we reduce our emotional arousal levels, the better sleep will be.

Here we see the stress bucket revisited for an overloaded individual:

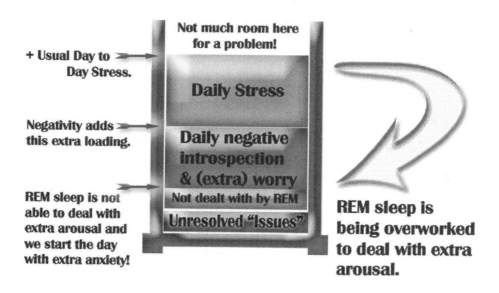

The Stress Container

+ Usual Day to Day Stress.

Negativity adds this extra loading.

REM sleep is not able to deal with extra arousal and we start the day with extra anxiety!

Not much room here for a problem!

Daily Stress

Daily negative introspection & (extra) worry

Not dealt with by REM

Unresolved "Issues"

REM sleep is being overworked to deal with extra arousal.

What we are seeing here is the REM mechanism failing to cope with the ongoing emotional overload. Firstly we see "Not dealt with by REM" in amber. This is the overspill from yesterday's emotional arousal. The REM mechanism cannot cope with the volume of anxiety, and fails to properly empty the bucket, meaning that we start the day with some of yesterday's anxiety still present. On top of this we have our "Daily negative introspection and (extra) worry". This is caused by the habits of daily negativity that we have fallen into, and the additional worry we feel as a result of feeling anxious. On top of this we have our usual daily arousal, leaving us little or no room for unexpected stress. What this feels like in practice is that we simply don't feel like we can cope with any (more) problems. Intuitively, we sense that we are close to tipping point. If our bucket reaches all the way to full and over-spills, then we experience feelings of panic, as the nervous system seeks to discharge some of its energetic overload through the last vent it has available to it.

You'll note that in both buckets we have allocated a small part of our bucket's capacity to "unresolved issues". This accounts for our long-standing wounds like grief, or lack of forgiveness. These are the things we carry. I included this fact in the diagram because I wanted to make the important point that only a minimal proportion of our daily stress truly relates to our unresolved issues. It is easy to blame all of today's woes on what has gone before, but it is unproductive in terms of recognising solution. Those events may well shape how we deal with things today, and therefore, may be indirectly contributing to our overload of stress, but they are not directly responsible for today's stress overload. The rule here is that, excluding massive events like deaths and serious traumas, if an event happened more than three months ago, then it is largely not directly affecting your level of stress today. We need to be careful here. I'm not suggesting that anyone just gets over a big loss or trauma in three months; far from it. What we're saying is that the massive utility bill you got last June may well be counted in your inventory of why you feel bad today, but it's probably nothing to do with it in actual terms. This is important because if we are to reduce the level of stress in our bucket, we need to be working on the real causes of our daily anxiety, and that requires that we identify those causes accurately. Solution focussed therapy recognises that the majority of ongoing anxiety is created on a daily basis. This fact is attested to because we know that when we are less emotionally aroused generally, we do not tend to focus so much on the past. If it were the case that emotional arousal related entirely to past events, then we would feel anxious all the time. Yet most anxious people experience periods of anxiety relating to feeling currently overloaded. We will cover how the past affects us in detail later, and for sure it has a place here in some cases. For now though, we need to acknowledge that the majority of our anxiety, which is what we need to work on immediately, is created daily as a result of ongoing negativity and worry. This means owning it, and recognising that it has a cause. The question which naturally follows is, "Why is my bucket overloaded?" Answer this question, take appropriate action, and you have a large part of the solution to your anxiety problem.

Why Is My Bucket Overloaded?

There is no such thing as a definitive one-size-fits-all answer to this question. The good news though is that there are a *finite* number of places to look. Another way of asking this question is what makes you personally feel stressed? Let's define stress.

Basic definition: Stress is a negative physical/emotional/nervous system response to feeling in some way overwhelmed. It is usually caused when the perceived demands placed upon us appear to outweigh our ability to cope.

Not all stress is bad. A certain amount of stress can help you to perform at your best. It's quite normal for instance to feel some stress when giving a public presentation, or interviewing for a new job. In short, low-intensity bursts, the stress response can keep us alert and sharp. It only becomes a problem when we feel stressed for an extended period of time, or so powerfully, that we then don't function well. Stress is therefore very subjective. What's easy for one person is stressful for another because stress rises when we feel out of our depth, or lack control. Our personal stress triggers are intrinsically linked to our beliefs. You are unlikely to become stressed when you have a strong sense of confidence that you can manage the presenting situation adequately. Here are just some of the potential causes of stress for modern humans:-

* Feeling conflicted because my Mother wants me to go to dinner with her and I already made other arrangements to see a friend. Who do I let down?

* My work requires me to work late for the next three months. I want to be home with my wife and new baby.

83

* Worrying that I won't have enough money to pay my bills and/or keep a roof over my head.

* Feeling like I'll never find a partner because (I believe) I'm too ugly.

* I'm not going to meet a business deadline no matter how hard I work.

* My elderly relative is ill and I'm not in a position to do more to help.

* I've gained twenty pounds in weight this year and I feel out of control.

* I'm in debt with no way of paying!

* I've been given 30 days to find somewhere else to live.

* I'm being made redundant from my job.

* I've been diagnosed with....

* I might fail my exams.

* I should....

Notice that in many of these examples the primary cause of stress is "obligation" and the feeling that someone will be let down in some way if we don't fulfil the obligation. The others centre on the possibility that life will be awful in some way if certain conditions are not met. So let's start at the beginning.

If you are reading this book because you've been troubled by chronic ongoing anxiety, then almost certainly the first thing to come under the magnifying glass is anxiety itself!

FEAR OF FEAR

In 1932, Franklin D. Roosevelt's inaugural address to the American Nation contained the historic quote, "The only thing we have to fear is fear itself." These are timeless words indeed. Is there anything more paralysing to us than the effect of fear itself? In psychology, this is known as secondary disturbance. The primary disturbance is the object that causes you to become anxious in the first place. The secondary disturbance is the experience of being anxious. In practice this secondary disturbance frequently overtakes the primary disturbance as the number one fear.

Maxine was travelling home from her Spanish holiday, and the aircraft experienced some turbulence. For an awful ten minutes Maxine became convinced that she was going to die. She hyperventilated, and even after the turbulence ceased she remained panicky and tense. The following year she could not bring herself to book a holiday abroad. All she could think about was how awful she had felt on that flight. She was terrified, and just knew that she couldn't cope with ever feeling that way again.

On returning from the flight she investigated turbulence, and discovered that turbulence does not cause crashes these days. Modern airlines are more than adequately strengthened to withstand all turbulent conditions, and advanced technology makes it possible to avoid severe turbulence anyway. Still, she just couldn't move past her fear. Consider this for a moment. Maxine is not afraid to fly actually. She is afraid of "feeling that way again". She knows that the turbulence caused no injury. She understood clearly that turbulence would cause no injury were it to happen again. The trauma here was not the turbulence itself, but Maxine's **anxiety** in response to the turbulence. She says it herself. "I couldn't bear to feel like that again...I couldn't cope". She can convince herself intellectually that the flight itself will be safe. It's much harder for her to convince herself that she won't be **anxious** on the flight. Here we have anxiety itself becoming the central problem. In practice this is true of most anxiety-related problems. We think we're afraid of planes, vomit, spiders, or napkins! What we're really afraid of is fear, and the loss of control that such fear threatens to consume us with. Sounds familiar?

So what's the antidote? Well, the antidote is to learn to recognise that fear can be handled. Fear does not automatically cause a loss of control. The problem is that the first few times we experience fear we can often experience the feeling that we have completely lost control. If you consider how conditioned responses are created (remember Pavlov's dogs?), it's easy to see how one or two experiences of loss of control are imprinted into the template library as **completely true**. We now have set a very negative precedent indeed. On the basis that our first experiences of fear were overwhelming we now believe absolutely that fear leaves us completely powerless. By extension, we endorse the perception (belief) that if we were to be overwhelmed by fear, that anything could happen, and right there is the core of any anxiety disorder. We become terrified that anxiety could strike at any moment and leave us completely disempowered. Beliefs seek to reinforce themselves by looking only for evidence that supports that way of perceiving. As Robert Anton Wilson said:-

"What the thinker thinks, the prover proves". I'll call it what the believer believes, the prover proves.

Here, the believer is the template library, and the prover is the limbic system. Now, in this example, our lady is relatively lucky. Her anxiety is safely confined to aeroplanes. Solution for her is simple. Never fly again, and there's no chance of feeling anxious like that again. The fear is contained in a nice little box. What about when anxiety strikes in the middle of an every-day event though? Worse still, what if the anxiety strikes while I'm sitting in my own home having a cup of tea and watching the six o'clock news, seemingly for no good reason at all?! Now I'm in trouble, right? The message that this sends is that anxiety just dropped out of the sky on me! This is frankly terrifying because if that were true, it would mean I could never feel safe again. If it's happened to you, I'm sorry. That sucks. However, it's not what it appears to be. It's not for no good reason at all. It *is* about something. While this may not be presently obvious, you can take it as fact that there are reasons that it's happened. It's almost certainly nothing to do with my cup of tea, or the six o'clock news. It's much more likely that my anxiety truly relates to the boundary dispute I have with my neighbours, or the MOT bill I don't know how I'm going to pay, or the fact that my daughter is being bullied at school, or that I upset my best friend last week because I couldn't get to her birthday celebrations, or that I'm exhausted because I've been working a sixty hour week for the past three months. We could go on. You get the point? This is *"context"*. Anxiety does not drop out of the sky. It is *about* something. Even with our turbulence-phobic lady this remains true. Did everyone on the plane develop a phobia in the ten minutes of turbulence? No of course not. The difference is that she was pretty close to the top of her bucket when it happened. While most people had been sunbathing and sipping cocktails for a week, she had been rowing with her husband daily, and worrying about going back to the job she hates on Monday. The turbulence, alarming as it was, accounted for a 40% rise in stress bucket levels and became the straw that broke the camel's back; the bucket overflowed. What is confusing is that sometimes anxiety that's been steadily building in the background can hit us at a moment when there's no obvious reason for us to be anxious. To further complicate matters, the limbic system can then make an erroneous assumption that there must be something about the situation we're in at the moment anxiety strikes that is threatening, and logs that as a template for future reference. If I happen to be driving on the motorway at the moment my anxiety bubble bursts, then motorways become my fear. If I'm in the supermarket, then it's supermarkets. What I really fear however is neither motorways nor supermarkets.

What I really fear is having an experience of fear that causes me to lose control when on a motorway or in a supermarket.

Now, let's consider motorways for a minute. Almost without exception, the people I have worked with for their motorway driving phobias have gone on to explain that one of their new fears is that they may faint while driving. They base this assumption on the fact they felt "really weird and spaced out" when they had their panic attack while driving, and in that moment they had the thought "What if I faint?" We've already covered the fact that anxiety produces light-headedness and feelings of being "spaced out", so we can look from the outside-in and see exactly what's going on here. Our poor client however has bought it, hook, line, and sinker. They are convinced that this is a real and likely possibility, and now avoid motorways like the plague. The very mention of motorway driving cause palms to sweat and guts to churn. Do you begin to see now how anxiety operates? It tells us convincing lies about how endangered we are, and we make the terrible mistake of unquestioningly endorsing what it tells us. Having now bought the story of a terrible trauma waiting just around the next corner we proceed to sell it back to ourselves with great conviction! With no one left to fight for a rational perspective the limbic system responds to all this threat in the only way it can. If I am being threatened then the correct response is......? That's right, anxiety.

So I now avoid motorways, aeroplanes, and supermarkets, but I'm still left with a sense of unease. I start to wonder. "What if I have an attack like that on the bus? I might not be able to get off! I might make a complete fool of myself in front of a bus-load of people!" So now I start to fear buses too, and then maybe the thought will spread to social engagements, or family arrangements. As I start to avoid more and more situations in case I have an anxiety attack, my life shrinks. Fear will take up as much space in your life as you're willing to give. So remember:-

Life shrinks or expands in proportion to ones courage. (Anais Nin)

In the above example we are focusing purely on specific concerns. Sometimes, however, the perceived threat is much less well-defined. Often we don't know why we fear feeling anxious. There's just a sense that our anxiety could leave us badly damaged in some way. Often people worry that they might be going mad. They worry that they won't be able to hold down their job. They worry that they might not be well for their children. They worry that they won't be able to cope. All of this is fear of fear, and this worrying alone contributes masses of anxiety to our stress bucket causing it to overload and create the very thing we are trying to avoid, anxiety. So how do we escape this cycle?

What sits as the core of this entire cycle is the unquestioned belief -"I can't handle fear".

Consider for a moment. If you knew absolutely that you could have fear in your life, and that your sanity would be just fine, would you continue to worry that you might go mad? If you knew that you could have fear in your life, and definitely hold down your job in spite of that anxiety, would you worry so much about the future? If you knew that you could have fear, and still be there for your children, would you still feel hopeless? No. You will of course prefer not to have fear, but if you knew you could cope with having fear, without having your life fall apart, you'd feel a whole lot less anxious about fear, right?

If you knew you could definitely cope with fear then fear would be seen as an uncomfortable inconvenience rather than a life shattering catastrophe.

So, this becomes the goal! We need to go from seeing anxiety as an uncontrollable juggernaut of destruction, to an inconvenient, uncomfortable, but ultimately manageable difficulty. "Hang on!" you say. "Isn't the goal to stop feeling anxious altogether?" Yes, it is, and in time that will happen. We cease feeling anxious when our stress bucket empties. We get there however by a series of steps. The first of those steps is to learn how not to fear the fear. There is a bit of hidden psychology here. Although our ultimate agenda is to stop experiencing fear altogether, we need to use the interim step of learning to accept fear because by ceasing to worry *about* fear we reduce the level of anxiety we carry generally, thus reducing limbic system arousal overall. This is a little counter-intuitive, but it is the overlooking of this step that causes anxiety to maintain its grip on us. We are using reverse psychology here. One way or another, our goal is to reduce the level of stress going into our bucket on a daily basis, and if your fear of fear is the number one contributor to that daily stress overload, which is the case for most people, then we need to start here.

Now, there is an obstacle here. The obstacle is simply, how can we convince ourselves fully that we'll never again be overwhelmed by anxiety, and really feel that to be true? In order to feel it is true we need to know it is true, and we arrive at a place of knowing through experience. So there are two central aspects to learning that we can handle fear. The first aspect is that we need to have an experience that shows us that we can handle fear, thus rendering it possible in the future. The second aspect involves understanding how we have disturbed ourselves with catastrophic thinking during past fear episodes, and learning how not to do that in future. So let's look at the practicalities of doing this emotionally, and then intellectually.

DEALING WITH FEAR OF FEAR

In the introduction of this book I promised to avoid relying solely on "technique led therapy". I also promised to put great emphasis on understanding. What follows will appear to be, on the face of it, a simple technique. However, in applying anti-anxiety measures it's not what we do that matters, but **how** we do it. Platitudes won't get us very far. We are basically dealing with our deepest selves. Intent and sincerity is everything here. The technique itself is relatively unimportant in the great scheme of things. The technique is simply the visible face of a completely new way of approaching your emotional wellbeing. It's what sits behind the technique that does all the healing work.

When you feel an anxious feeling, what is your first instinct? Run? Cower? Hide? Fight? Become frustrated? Feel hopeless? Try to ignore it? Go into despair? Distract yourself? Become hysterical? You already know that none of these responses make you feel any better. Some of them make you feel much worse. Consider for a moment that in any given anxious moment there are two forces involved. These are your intellect and your limbic system. We have examined how and why the limbic system becomes alarmed. As far as the limbic system is concerned something terrible is happening, or is about to happen. Then there is your intellect (frontal lobe). For the purposes of this particular example we're going to call your intellect "the rest of you". Think of the limbic system as a child, and the rest of you as an adult, the parent even. Now toddlers fall over sometimes. Your toddler (limbic system) is running across the playground and suddenly takes a tumble. There is a moment of silence, shock. Your toddler looks up as you approach and is looking for cues. Is this bad? Am I damaged? Should I be scared? Your response as the parent (frontal lobe) will dictate their emotional response. The parent that runs hysterically screaming "Oh my God! Are you okay?! Let me see!" will encourage a traumatised response in the child. Tears, tension, and fear will follow immediately. Such a traumatic response could even register in the template library and create a future fear of falling. Conversely, a calm parent will lend a gentle hand up and some warm words of reassurance. The child will brush themselves off and carry on their way towards the swings. This model is you and your limbic system. What kind of parent are you to your limbic system, hysterical or soothing?

It is quite natural to instinctively respond to the presence of fear with any one of the aforementioned responses, thoughts of escape, despair, frustration, alarm, etc. Don't be too hard on yourself. Most people do just that. You can begin to see though that it's not a very skilful way to respond because all of these responses send a powerful alarming message back to the limbic system. They all say "Something is terribly wrong", and you should by now be recognising that this message makes us more anxious.

There is actually only one correct response to the presence of fear, and it's utterly counter-intuitive, which is why so many people fail to achieve it without direction. It is in fact the very last thing you would think to do. Instead of running from it, hating it, being frustrated by it, being alarmed by it, depressed by it, or any other "*" from it, we simply be fully present with it. Now I am by no means the first person to say this. What I do hope to help you with here however is exactly how to do that effectively. One common complaint from people I have worked with is that they have been told that they need to "accept" their anxiety, but they have been given little more explanation on exactly why that is so, or how to go about doing that. Ultimately this has led to further frustration. Being told to simply "accept" your anxiety can border on insult if no further explanation is offered. The first question that arises when being told to welcome, accept, or sit with anxiety is: "Why on Earth would I want to do that?!" Before we get to "the technique" then, we need to take a detour to explore exactly why eight little words, and a bucket load of sincerity, can make the world of difference when we feel emotionally disturbed. Stay with me here, it's a necessary detour.

CONSISTENCY IS SAFE

Accepting anxiety is not primarily an intellectual task, though there is an intellectual component. It is primarily an emotional endeavour, and it is in fact, a labour of love. You will remember that we discussed earlier the role of love in healing, and it is here that we begin to put that understanding to practical use. You see, it would be easy to think of this as purely a technique, and indeed there is technique here, but there is also a much deeper opportunity. There is an opportunity to learn to self-support in an entirely new way, and what we are really talking about doing here is learning to be completely consistent with ourselves. If fear really is an absence of love (caring and valuing), then consistently

91

coming through for yourself with caring and valuing in difficult times, is the ultimate expression of safety. When we feel truly safe, there is no room, or need, for anxiety to persist. This word consistent is a very important one in this context. Consistent means predictable. Predictability is safe. I know where I am with consistency. I know that when X occurs, Y will be the result.

So, consistency is predictable and safe. Hold that thought. It's just one of the threads that we'll draw together in a moment. The next thread is unconditionality.

We live in a very conditional world. Very few relationships are truly unconditional, and with good reason. Conditional means: If X condition is met, then Y is the result. In practice this plays out as, "If you treat me with respect and caring (condition), I will do the same for you (result)". That's a reasonable condition. Conditionality however is very easily abused. Sometimes this occurs wilfully, and sometimes it occurs through ignorance or misunderstanding. The effects of deliberate or inadvertent conditionality are never more poignant than in our formative years. Children process their reality with themselves at the centre of the Universe. For a child, everything is about "me". So the messages that we receive as children inform our developing self-concept extremely powerfully.

One thing that every young human being craves deeply is love and attention. In our first few years of life we are completely dependent on the love and attention that our carers provide. If love is here defined as caring and valuing, then being dependent means that we not only want that caring and valuing, but that we actually need it. So for a child it's all about how to get that. The majority of parents/carers are painfully aware of this fact, and do everything they can to provide the right balance of discipline and valuing for their growing children. Parent-child relationships are the relationships which generally come as close to unconditional as possible. Many a Mother or Father understands the feeling of "No matter how my child behaves, I will never stop loving them". Parents often see beyond the behaviours of their children to their child's original innocence.

Children feel safe when they know they are loved "no matter what". Positive parents don't withdraw their love if their children misbehave, they withdraw privileges. If love is here defined as caring and valuing, then even discipline is a form of those qualities. Children know the difference between discipline and neglect. Negative parenting involves the withdrawal of love. This is neglect. Love-starved children learn to mistrust the World very quickly. It's simple logic. Our basic genetic conditioning tells us very clearly that our parents/carers are the people most likely to be available to give us what we need, in terms of valuing and caring. If we find that they are failing to do that, what hope do we have of ever getting that from anyone, or anything, else? If we can't trust our parents to deliver, then who can we trust? To a child, the unspoken answer is nobody. The assumption is quickly formed that the World will not meet our needs, and the World quickly looks like a very hostile place. What happens to a child who experiences neglect is that they quickly close down that vulnerable place within themselves. It's less painful to stop hoping for love than it is to hope for it and repeatedly experience the disappointment of love's withdrawal. That's too much to bear for human beings.

What this means in practice is that their innocence and open-heartedness hardens to form a protective shell. So what would have been a bright shining light is dimmed as we discussed earlier. Little light illuminates the personality, but at least what light remains is protected from nasty people with buckets of cold water. In addition to this protective withdrawal though, there is something else. Remember that children process their reality with "me" at the centre. What happens then, when the genetic instruction that "these people should care for me" is not met, is that the child arrives at a fundamentally damaging conclusion. The conclusion is "If they do not care for me, then there must be something wrong with *me*". From an adult perspective we can see definitively that the problem is with the parent. The parent is failing in their responsibility to provide caring and valuing for their child. The child doesn't see it that way though. The child concludes, "If I was better, then they would love me". By extension, the conclusion is, "I'm not good enough. I'm un-loveable". In practice, most of us have had a mixed bag of unconditional love and conditional love. Sometimes we've felt valued. Other times we've been made to feel worthless. While most parents do their best, few get it consistently right, if there is such a thing? So, even where great parents aim to be unconditional in their love, it's a difficult thing to master, and many of us are left with at least some small sense that we need to be more than we are if we are to receive the caring and valuing we crave. Sadly, some people receive more than their fair share of negative reinforcement. Some people have been sent a "you're worthless" message from the outset of life, and this can have a massively negative impact. This person is likely to enter adulthood with low self-worth which will manifest in every area of life, work, education, relationships, and social bonding, making success in any area much more difficult than it would have been if they had been taught how to value themselves, and others, in the beginning. What good parenting instils in children is the knowledge that people, including themselves, are inherently valuable. This is a great start to life if you are lucky enough to receive it. If you've been unfortunate enough to miss out on that, it can still be learned.

So that's a quick overview of our first taste of learning that there are conditions attached to receiving love. It doesn't end there though. After our parents, there is the World, and here there's a whole new set of rules to master. In most relationships there is a healthy need for a certain amount of conditionality. In a friendship for instance, there are unspoken conditions on how that friendship will develop, and maintain itself. The unspoken condition is simply that we agree to treat each other as well as we can. We make allowances for our respective flaws. We make allowances for the fact that sometimes our friends are stressed, and they treat us badly, let us down, or take their frustrations out on us. This is human, and the condition of such friendship continuing is that we need to know that our friends mean well even if they don't always get it right. We hope they will do the same for us. If however, our friends show no positive intent towards us, repeatedly letting us down, or disrespecting our boundaries, then the conditional nature of our friendship may mean that the friendship withers. This is healthy. It then is a lesson to the other that if they want friends, they need to treat people with a basic level of care. In terms of learning how to be a member of a community, similar rules apply. If you treat the community space, being, and property with respect, the community gives you the same consideration. If you act with malevolence towards the community, then you forego your right to be part of it. The ultimate expression of this is prison. So, we live in a naturally conditional World. Conditions help us to know what's acceptable, and what isn't.

CONDITIONALITY IS UNSAFE

Early life is a minefield, and conditionality is present in many other ways. Even with the best parents in the world we can find that school and community offers further challenges when it comes to receiving positive reinforcement. In fact, it seems there's no way to avoid a certain measure of negative self-image at some time in life. It's part of our learning. I learned an interesting lesson from a young man I worked with a few years ago. He presented with depression. It is true that he needed a little help in tidying up generally but when we traced the roots of his depression and feelings of failure, it all rooted back to losing a competitive event at twelve years of age. Up until that point he had never experienced significant loss, and that particular loss, which he had deemed as highly important, had been experienced as catastrophic. He literally didn't know how to handle failure. His parents had done too good a job of instilling self-worth into him. It's not uncommon for grown children to feel that their parents left them ill-equipped to deal with the harsh realities of life because they were wrapped in cotton wool. Tricky, isn't it? Even if we go through life believing that we are good enough, we are likely to encounter some event or experience at some point that shatters that certainty, and if we are ill-equipped to handle such change, it can be emotionally damaging. In many ways feeling not good enough sometimes is a part of life's experience. It teaches us to accept imperfection and occasional failure as part of the human condition. A little of it can motivate us to work harder, and achieve more. Some degree of recognition of imperfection therefore is a healthy thing, but feeling like we're fundamentally not good enough most or all of the time, no matter what we do, is the biggest scariest joy killer around!

Next, we have culture. Culture is the worst of all offenders on the conditionality list. It's a really big problem for human beings, especially in the West. Feeling not good enough, and moreover being constantly told we're not good enough, underpins many emotional and neurotic disorders. Take Anorexia Nervosa as an example. Anorexia rates are currently higher than ever by a wide margin in Western Society. What drives this disease? Well, we know that it's a complicated picture involving obsession, compulsion, anxiety, depression, neurological atrophy, hormonal imbalance, fear, and the need for control. All of this is true, but when you come back to the root of the symptomatic display of the disorder, what underpins the whole thing is one simple culturally promoted belief. "I can only be good enough if I am skinny because skinny is beautiful. If I am skinny then I will be loveable". I hardly need to point out where such messages are coming from. What you have here is a conditional statement around what it takes to be "good enough", and what it takes to be "loveable". If I am skinny then I can feel I have worth. If I am skinny then I can be loveable. What is longed for here is not really about being ultra-thin. It is the desire to fit in - to feel good enough, valued, and loveable. We see the same psychology manifest in many other areas.

Some examples:-

If	Then
I am the best lawyer in town	People will respect me.
I get plastic surgery	People will see my beauty
I do everything that's asked of me	People will love me
I am better than him at tennis	I'll know I'm not a failure
I am rich and famous	I'll be worth something
I please my parents	Maybe they'll finally love me

If I am perfect	I'll be loveable

When you look at the above examples you're looking at people who need to achieve something in order to feel okay about what they are. This might be thought of as the need for esteem as opposed to the need for worth. It's worth understanding the difference. We might say that esteem relates to the ego, and worth relates to the self. The problem with esteem is that it tends to be insatiable. The more we have, the more we want. Feeling fabulous is very addictive. So you're a B–list Hollywood star. It's an amazing achievement, but you're still not happy. It's not enough. You need to be A-list. Two years later and you're finally on the A-list, but guess what? You're still not happy. Now you're obsessed with the shape of your nose. Two surgeries later and you're worrying about your wrinkles. On it goes! Those who do achieve their goals are rarely satisfied. This is the insatiable nature of the ego as it chases some unattainable idea of perfection.

Meanwhile, somewhere off the coast of Cornwall, there is a fisherman hauling in his nets. He looks up at a clear blue sky and a wave of contentment washes through his being. He's never had much, and though he works hard most days, he doesn't want for much either. His skin is weather worn and he carries a few extra pounds around his middle, but he's happy. He knows he's not Brad Pitt and never will be, but he has the love of a good woman and a warm cottage to return to in the evening. It's a simple life, but he knows he will look back with few regrets.

Western Culture has become very confused on this issue. Our media is particularly culpable when it comes to conditionality. We are constantly bombarded with messages telling us that we're not good enough unless we are thinner, richer, harder working, better looking, wearing the right clothes, the right accessories, living in a bigger house, owning a better car. We all know it. What we don't know necessarily is just how deeply that stuff affects us, even if we think we're wise to it. It's very insidious. The motive behind all of it is primarily financial, but its net effect is pretty damaging to our collective and individual sense of worthiness.

What culture does is it shows us "perfection" and then asks us to be it by selling us stuff that promises to make us into that. The implication is that if you're not it, then you're not good enough. What's really scary about this is that many of us buy into this idea and propagate it amongst ourselves so that we now are the ones doing the judging. This means that we place enormous pressure on ourselves and others to meet unattainable standards. According to culture, we all want to be fabulous and extraordinary because we're told that's what we need to be if we want happiness, and yet the truth is, very few of us actually are extraordinary. Then we wonder why we're so stressed and unhappy. It's a simple case of being out of touch with the reality of the situation.

Challenge: Go to your local shopping centre. Sit and watch the people go by. Count the ratio of "perfect" people to "imperfect" people. You will find that for every one person that appears to be young, fabulous, well dressed, slim, and gorgeous, there are in fact forty other people who aren't that!

So what's "normal"? Perfection, at least in the way that the media and culture portrays it, doesn't exist. Most people now know that magazine models are airbrushed so that they have no cellulite, slimmer tummies and legs, more perfectly defined features, and glowing skin. This was not public knowledge for some time though. We, the adoring public, have historically seen these images and concluded that there must be something wrong with us because we do have crooked noses, imperfect teeth, bulges and cellulite. This is particularly worrying as it infects our teenagers to a growing degree year on year. Culturally, we are becoming increasingly obsessed with perfection, which can only mean one thing; that more and more people will feel dissatisfied with themselves as they fail to meet the unrealistic expectation. I'm not suggesting that we should not seek to make improvements, only that there is a point at which the obsession with being "better" becomes unhealthy.

So, we can see that conditionality can be healthy to a point as motivator, but that there is a line which is all too easily crossed that makes self-worth and happiness almost impossible to attain. That line is best summarised as "I can only be happy if..." or "I can only feel good enough or loveable if..." This level of conditionality makes us all feel very unsafe.

From every side, the message from culture is "You're not good enough as you are". Perhaps it's time for us to decide for ourselves what true value is?

So, our detour brings us neatly back to why learning to "be fully present" with an anxious feeling is the correct strategy.

WORKING WITH "PARTS"

It's rarely "all" of us that is scared. We may feel fear in our guts or chest, but at the same time we have another "part" of us saying, "This is ridiculous! What do I have to be frightened of?!" Although clinically we have talked about anxiety being a response from the limbic system, we can also work with our anxiety in a very human way. The mistake we are making in approaching anxiety as an enemy to be destroyed is that we are not recognising that we are actually dealing with a frightened part of ourselves who is feeling unsafe. We see anxiety as a beast attacking us from the outside-in. We need to shift away from this perspective. That just makes us feel like we are being victimised. Instead, think of it like this:-

Anxiety, at one level is a part of your-self experiencing distress through the feeling body and calling out for attention with the message "I'm frightened. I feel unsafe"

Now, we can make a helpful distinction here. We can think of it like this.

There is an anxious feeling, and then there is a part of you that is experiencing that anxious feeling.

This is a very important distinction to understand because it's the piece of information that helps us to shift away from the position of feeling that we're being attacked by an alien outside force (anxiety), towards a clearer understanding that:-

Anxiety actually signifies that there is a part of us in need of attention and/or support.

99

What constitutes support? Well, let's look firstly at what doesn't constitute support. Running, cowering, ignoring, becoming angry, frustrated, alarmed or depressed, by the part of you that is in need of support, is no support at all. In fact it's quite the opposite. It's actually adding insult to injury. When you respond to anxiety with any of these responses you are indirectly sending at least two messages back to the part of you that needs your support. Those messages are: "I cannot handle your presence", and, "I have no intention of supporting you. Given the chance I would destroy you". What effect do you think these messages have upon the part of you that is in need of support? These responses tend to make things worse, not better. These responses simply alarm us more deeply because the assumption is that if no support is forthcoming then things will therefore **never** get better. The limbic system does the only thing it knows how to do under such circumstances, and turns up the heat. We get locked into a stalemate summarised by:-

"I cannot be okay while this feeling is present."

In CBT this is known as low frustration tolerance, or in plain English, an inability to tolerate difficult feelings. Notice how conditional the above statement is. The condition here is "I can only be okay, IF this feeling goes away".

We need to recognise that our anxiety cannot go away until the part of us that is feeling like there's nothing consistently safe in the World receives the support that it needs!

It is this stalemate situation which keeps us locked into anxiety. Clearly, with many people, this can persist almost indefinitely because the way out of this situation is simply not obvious. Neither side can move until the other side does something differently. Usually it doesn't even occur to us that we could actually welcome, and care for our anxious parts, but this is actually what we need to do. I know it's a radical message, and it might not make sense yet so let's examine how exactly we can supply the support that is necessary.

SELF-SUPPORTING CONSISTENTLY AND UNCONDITIONALLY

Consider that feelings are like messengers. If we are "open" to receiving the message then the messenger can deliver the message and leave. If however, the messenger arrives and the door is bolted shut, then the messenger has a problem. Now the messenger starts knocking ever more persistently at our door.

"Go away!" we shout.

"I can't" says the messenger, "I am charged with the duty to deliver this message to you".

We peer through the curtains and see that the messenger is carrying a big black box. We're quite sure there's something nasty inside.

"I'm not leaving until you open the door!" shouts the messenger, and the knocking gets louder.

"Look, just bugger off! I'm not opening the door and I don't want to know what's in the package. Just leave me alone and stop worrying me will you?!"

Time passes. Then everything is quiet for a while. It seems the messenger has left. We hope he won't return. Sometime later though, there's another knock at the door. Now we are wondering what's in the box? That messenger is pretty persistent. It must be important but it looks so menacing. No! Opening the door is simply not an option.

"Look, just go away. I don't want the box!"

By this time we're sure that the box contains something unthinkably awful. Our alarm is growing. The messenger is still knocking. A stand-off ensues. We are trapped in our own home by this awful messenger. We can't go out because we'd have to deal with the message. We are going stir crazy staring at the four walls. We have convinced ourselves that receiving the package is simply not an option, and so we resign ourselves to our fate…alarmed, trapped, frightened. Hopelessness follows.

Then one day, a postcard arrives in the doormat. In the message are just a few words. It reads:

"Courage is not the absence of fear, but rather the judgement that something is more important than fear." (Ambrose Redmoon)

We are startled by the simplicity of this message. Oh? Well, perhaps we've never really thought of it that way. What could be in the box that's so awful that it's worse than being prisoner in this house? Is the fear of what's in the box really more important than freedom? More time passes. It takes a while. Peering out of the window, the box still looks pretty menacing but we consider...the box...these four walls...the box...four walls? In a moment of madness (for this is how receiving the package feels), courage, and resignation, we stride up to the door and wrench it open.

"Okay, okay! Give me the damn box!" At that very moment we're expecting the end of the world. The messenger hands the box over without a word, turns and leaves. Wow. That's weird? We were expecting some kind of confrontation, but nothing, so matter of fact.

With trembling hands and trepidation we pull open the string tied around the dark menacing box and a puff of dust shoots out of the top and rains down all over us like some terrible cloud. We watch in horror as the dust falls all around. The worst has happened. The box **is** loaded, just like we thought it would be. Bracing ourselves, for the very first time, we feel it...we **really** feel it. Then, there is a pang of awfulness. We know exactly why we didn't want the box. It's almost unbearable. But, this lasts only a moment, and then suddenly it subsides, and something amazing happens. Like a grace, we suddenly relax. The resistance is over. The fight is over. The story has reached its completion. The worst has happened. We opened the box...it was awful...but we survived! Suddenly there's nobody knocking on the door. The house is quiet again. The door is open, and the sun is shining in. There's silence...and an empty box on the table.

So this begins to paint things in a slightly different light doesn't it? We know that our experience is relative and subjective. When you can actually welcome difficult feelings as a part of life, then your subjective experience of them becomes something to be embraced rather than something to be rejected or avoided. Why would we welcome them? Well, if we can recognise that we've learned from other difficulty, and eventually overcome it, we can reason that the same will happen again, which in fact it does when we work with it instead of against it.

"Your pain is the breaking of the shell that encloses your understanding. Even as the stone of the fruit must break, that its heart may stand in the sun, so must you know pain." Kahlil Gibran

Actually, difficulty helps us to grow. When we are challenged, we are asked to become more than we were. That means creating new perspectives and acquiring new skills. In other words we have to expand our understanding in order to be able to overcome the obstacles facing us. When we welcome this as a fact of life, then we can see that there is something in it for us to welcome difficulty. It doesn't necessarily make difficulty comfortable, but it does help us to become more comfortable with the discomfort. Thus we avoid raging against "what is". So finally, after much metaphor and foundation building we arrive at the practical work.

THE ACCEPTANCE APPROACH

First, sit comfortably and quietly in a safe cosy space. Take a few deep breaths, releasing any immediate tensions from your body, and then allow your breath to return to a normal steady rate. Just close your eyes and spend a minute or two simply noticing your breath as you breathe. Keep it simple. The idea is simply to turn your focus inward.

You have been struggling with difficult feelings, and up until now you've been using strategies of one kind or another to get away from them. Now, we're going to do the polar opposite. So bring your attention to the inside of your body. What do you feel? Do you have tension in your jaw, your chest, or shoulders? Do you feel hollow, empty, tense, or sick in your tummy? Do you notice grief, or fear? Is there anger or frustration present? Just scan your body and notice whatever feelings are present.

Then, being courageous, and with the intention of being willing to tolerate the discomfort, you simply take your awareness to the area in your body where you feel the most fear or discomfort, and you give every bit of your attention to that feeling. You focus on it wholly and completely, and you simply sit with it, quietly. Even if it is really uncomfortable, you simply sit and feel. You are giving complete permission to yourself to fully feel the feeling. In practice this is much less scary or difficult than it sounds because actually not doing this is what makes the feeling so intense. It's worse when you don't do this. So even though you may fear being overwhelmed by the feeling if you give your undivided attention to it, the truth is, it's already worse than if you were sitting with it. Right away you have changed something. You're not fighting it. You're not running from it. You're not cowering from it. You're not trying to "work it out". You have no agenda, other than to give those feelings your full attention. Just simply by "sitting with it", as neutrally as possible, you are changing your relationship to that feeling. This is opening the box. You are doing something differently. The laws of relationship remind us that we are like actors on a stage. When you change the lines you deliver, then you expect that the response will also be different. Right away your subconscious mind (limbic system) sees that you are much less bothered by these feelings than you have been, and begins to re-appraise the situation. Your willingness to "sit" with those feelings sends a message back to that protective mind that even though that mind is convinced that there's something terrible occurring, you are sending a very clear message that you will not consider it as dangerous because you are willing to be with it. If you are willing to be with it, it can't be that dangerous can it? You will find that simply sitting quietly with those feelings will put them into a much more manageable perspective for you. Most people will report that the feeling immediately diminishes, and quite often they will say it has disappeared completely! You should be able to begin to see that it's "just" tension in your stomach. Uncomfortable yes, but not the monster you had it marked up to be. The metaphor that springs to mind is that in all the running and cowering, we only ever glimpse distorted views of the monster, as in a quick peep over the shoulder, or through the fingers. Then the imagination fills in the terrible details. It's like a mouse's shadow in the candlelight on the wall. It appears to be 10 feet tall. The imagination has done its worst, but when we turn the lights on we find it's just a mouse. We can go further too. As you become accustomed to sitting with these feelings, you can begin to feel into a clearer definition of the feeling/s. There may in fact be many feelings jostling for attention. I like to think of these feeling as "parts". "Parts" refers to components of the personality. We all have parts of our psyche which are stubborn, warm, gentle, hostile, young, old, happy, scared etc. Part of our job as human beings is to balance as best we can the needs and relative influence of these parts, and sometimes for reasons often complicated, we can decide to ignore or disown those parts of our personality which are deemed to be threatening or undesirable. Essentially, we attempt to keep those parts of ourselves at arms-length, outside of ourselves. Unfortunately, this is enormously painful for those parts of our-selves which are being held at arms-length, since the one thing that these parts desire more than anything else is our attention. The human psyche seeks integration. It's a natural process. So, one can begin to see that feelings are like "parts" trying to be heard, and ultimately integrated. So if there are parts of us desperate to be heard, and we push these parts away by labelling them as undesirable and unacceptable (we refuse to answer the door to the delivery man.), then we create more tension. We find that these parts actually shout louder in an attempt to be heard, and this shouting we hear (feel) as an increase in the volume or intensity of these unpleasant feelings. So one can see then why fighting, running, and cowering from these feelings are ineffective strategies because in those strategies we are not listening, and when we don't listen, then feelings have no option but to shout to be heard. This can be easily remembered with the helpful phrase, "What you resist...persists". By extension then, also, "What you accept...diminishes". Try this exercise at least five times on five different days. Remember what you learn. If for any reason it's too uncomfortable, then you should discontinue and read on. Most people however, will learn that taking focussed attention to a difficult feeling produces much better results than trying to get rid of it! If that's you, keep up the good work. Your journey back to health has now begun!

Learning To Self-Soothe With Empathy

So that's step one. You have learned that you can be present with a difficult feeling without being destroyed. If all has gone well in your practice, you've also learned how to use a valuable, practical tool for reducing the intensity of your feelings.

Now let's take this understanding further. We've started by simply learning to "sit with" difficult feelings. We can go further though. Now we want to enquire more deeply into the specific nature of that discomfort so that we can go about meeting the need. Once you have mastered sitting with a feeling, it's time to learn how to tune in to the needs of the feeling. Here's how I do it.

* Locate the anxious or depressed feeling in your body. Is it in your chest, your arms, your head, your neck, your shoulders, or your belly? If possible describe it. Does it have a shape, a texture, a colour? Is it gaseous, liquid or solid? Big? Small? Moving? Still? Warm? Cold? Spikey or smooth? Not everyone is visual so you might find you are vague on this point. That's fine. It's just helpful to have a visual lock on it if you can. Just feeling it is perfectly adequate.

* Next, feel into that feeling. Imagine you could dive inside it and feel it from the inside. Be "curious" about it. If it could speak, it would say "I feel...(what?)..." Anxious? Tense? Afraid? Sad? Frustrated? Angry? Desperate?

What will happen for most people is that various layers of the feeling will come into focus. So let's suppose that you identify that the tension you are focussed on is "fear". Your difficult feeling tells you "I feel afraid".

If those parts of us that are carrying negative emotion need us to listen, they need even more to know that we care how they are feeling. So we can simply send an affirmation to those parts that communicates that we are listening and that we do care. This is a very powerful tool. We can bring about great transformation in a relatively short space of time using this technique because it is that essentially human emotion, which does all the healing here, compassion. This is where all that foundation laying we've done so far suddenly comes into use. We need to connect with that part of ourselves which really knows how to care. A good way of connecting with this is to remember a time when you saw someone suffering, perhaps a friend or loved one, and you felt that feeling of truly understanding their suffering, perhaps in a way that no one else would. If you did something to help, or wanted to reach out, then that is even better. That feeling of empathy, and the action that springs from that, is compassion. Compassion is empathy and understanding coupled with a desire to act, to alleviate that suffering. The goal is to connect with this feeling of empathy to the best of your ability, and then bring this to the part of your-self which is suffering, and offer it. The real change will happen when you can really offer that emotion sincerely, and with heart, to yourself. It's not pity. It's not sympathy. Neither is it feeling sorry for yourself or wallowing. It is simply the extension of empathy and judgment-free understanding towards our-selves.

So as an example, using our "anxious" feeling, we will go and sit with that part of ourselves which is experiencing the difficult feeling and offer that sincere compassion. Imagine sending it like a river from your heart to the hurt, and while you are doing this you say these eight little words exactly as they are written here:-

"I hear and accept that you feel scared"

For absolute clarity, the principle is the same no matter what feeling you are working with. If the feeling you had tuned in on had said, "I feel sad", then you use "sad", instead of scared. That would look like this:-

"I hear and accept that you feel sad"

If it was frustrated, you use frustrated:-

"I hear and accept that you feel frustrated"

This may seem like I am labouring a point but I want you to make this understanding your own. I have had clients who have said "I feel nothing...I feel numb". Using this understanding, we can class "numb" as a feeling. Then it will be "I hear and accept that you feel nothing/numb". It's all about hearing what's actually going on, no matter what that is.

So, now you are really "hearing" the message from your feeling body, and you are communicating a genuine, caring response. This is true support. This is not pity. Pity says "That's awful. I'm glad it's not me -

poor wretched thing!" There is something slightly condescending about pity. It looks down upon the pitied. Empathy however is different. Empathy stands shoulder to shoulder and says "Yes, I know how that feels. I have felt it too". There is solidarity in empathy. It is sincere. We are dealing with our deepest selves here and we need to be clear that we are not merely going through the motions.

We need to bring sincerity and an adult mind-set to this. We are being a safe parent to our frightened inner-child. Now is the time to step into your biggest self. You just keep repeating these statements either out loud or quietly inside, but *feeling* the words deeply as you say them and *meaning* them. Really feel what those words mean. Sincerity is everything here. Keep sending that empathy to whatever part of yourself you happen to be comforting and supporting at the time. If you feel other words of support that intuitively need to be spoken then speak them too, but keep it positive and keep it simple. We do not want this to become complicated. Nor are we encouraging a dialogue. You do this for as long as it feels real. In practice we'll usually experience a short period of time in the moment where the support feels poignant and sincere, and then once the acknowledgment has taken place deeply, we may find that the focus (and often the feeling) seems to fade somewhat. This is normal. Don't force it or fake it. You will know intuitively when it's time to bring the exercise to a natural close.

Isn't This Just Wallowing In Self Pity Though?

This is a relatively tough understanding to communicate on a page, in a book. Often, in the practice room, it is a moment of real magic to watch somebody apply this understanding as I guide them through the process. Sometimes I need to add clarification as we go along. They may have felt these feelings a million times before, but it may be the first time they've ever allowed themselves to really acknowledge these feelings with acceptance and self-support. In the consulting room we have the luxury of being able to watch, calibrate, and check understanding as we go through. Here, we don't have that luxury. The atmosphere we are aiming to cultivate is quite specific so let's clarify. Wallowing in self-pity will not help. Being stuck in "poor me", feeling sorry for ourselves, is seen therapeutically as a major obstacle to wellness, and one which we are striving to overcome as part of our wellness agenda. There is a clear distinction between acknowledging/accepting, and wallowing. Wallowing can go on endlessly. Acceptance and acknowledgment takes a few moments. Wallowing is full of self-pity. Acceptance is supportive, patient, unconditional, and encouraging. Wallowing is hopeless. Acceptance is hopeful. Wallowing is fearful. Acceptance is courageous. Take some time to understand the difference. This may be a very new way of thinking about things. It may take a little time and practice to identify these new feelings of unconditional support and become familiar with the perspective of acceptance. Please do not assume that it's not there if you don't connect with it immediately. Be inquisitive. Be sincere. Be interested. And, practice patience. With perseverance you will almost certainly have a moment of breakthrough. There is an opportunity here to learn something of great potential value.

WHY ARE EIGHT LITTLE WORDS SO IMPORTANT?

First of all "I hear" or "I acknowledge" (which can be used instead of "hear" if you prefer) communicates that we're listening. If we're listening, our feelings don't need to shout at us. Naturally the intensity decreases. "I accept" communicates that we're not in resistance. If we're not sure we do accept then the statement can be softened to "I'm learning to hear and accept that you feel X". Then "that you feel". One thing to remember here is that we do not substitute the word you for I. You don't say "I hear and accept that *I* feel anxious". When you say "I" it implies "all of me" - If that's the case then who's there to do the supporting? The whole idea behind this is that you are learning to step back from your feelings and assume a kind of witness or observer position. Beyond this, you are cultivating the position of becoming a supporting carer to a distressed part of yourself. Although the distressed part is recognised as being a part of you, we are addressing only the specific feeling rather than the whole of our-selves. It is therefore correct to say "I hear and accept that *You* feel X". This has cognitive implications because it re-frames the way we are looking at the situation, and it helps us to recognise that feeling scared is a feeling, and not an absolute fact. This point is further clarified by the use of the word "feel" as opposed to "are". If we were to say "I hear and accept that you *are* anxious", it implies a fixed permanent state. When we use the word "feel", as opposed to "are" it implies that the state is fluid, flexible, and passing. This is an important change in perspective, and although it is subtle, it is also very powerful. In many ways its subtlety is its strength because it can slip underneath the radar of the unconscious mind's protective mechanisms. In this instance that's exactly what we want since the unconscious mind is being overly protective with its unnecessary anxiety.

Then if you want to continue, move on. One feeling may diminish, or disappear, and we may find another layer reveals itself. Now what is the feeling? Repeat the process. Little and often is good. On occasion the transformation in the way you feel may be an immediate relief, may bring tears, and can be massive because perhaps for the first time ever, you are being truly heard. On other occasions it may be hardly noteworthy. In most instances, you will literally watch that part of yourself brighten up as it receives this love. Other times there may be little discernible shift, but where this is so, it becomes even more important to continue the practice of sitting with the difficult feeling with empathy.

When you sit with a difficult feeling with empathy and find that it still feels difficult, that is not the time to throw the towel in! It's the time to love more deeply.

We talked at length earlier about how inconsistency and conditionality feels unsafe because both leave us without any certainty. Here is where that understanding becomes imperative. What kind of support says "I'll love you only IF you go away"? Or, worse still, "If you don't go away I will withdraw my love!" Take a moment to understand this. If you are not willing to give your support **unconditionally and consistently**, then what hope does that scared part of you have of ever feeling really safe? It is not true support, and the unspoken threat is that the support could be withdrawn at any moment. In fact we could go further. Giving oneself this unconditional support and then attaching conditions like "I'll only keep caring for you if you go away" is actually bordering on manipulative. This is likely to deepen your self-estrangement, not heal it! Acting inconsistently, and conditionally, when it comes to self-supporting is really no support at all. We need to understand that we are

110

dealing with sometimes genuinely frightened parts of ourselves and it's all about cultivating trust between those frightened parts and the rest of ourselves. Trust is earned. You may have been at war with yourself for a long time, labouring under the misunderstanding that you're a useless bag of muck because you're anxious or depressed. This is exactly what we are working to counteract here. So, suddenly coming forward and saying basically "I love (care for and value) you even though you're carrying an anxious feeling" is a very novel message, and one which an anxious part may well regard with suspicion initially!

It is only by being consistent with our support that we re-establish trust. Trust is really important here. So we need to be very patient with this process. I made the point earlier that the "technique" is just the visible face of a much deeper process. One big mistake I encounter again and again in the consulting room with clients is that they are thinking of this as simply the application of a technique, and failing to appreciate its deeper implications. These deeper implications are a difficult thing to communicate because in many ways those deeper implications are felt, not thought. It is in the **doing** that intellectual understanding forms as **felt** understanding. It reminds me somewhat of the Eastern principle that deep knowledge is not transmitted by words but by the presence and example of a person who holds that knowledge. It is said that the "Dharma" is transmitted directly in this way. It is subtle understanding. It's possible to miss it if we don't look carefully, or apply ourselves properly. Be aware of this. Mastering this understanding may take time, practice, and diligence. The swiftness with which you start to feel the deeper benefits of this approach will depend largely on how estranged you have become from yourself, and how deeply you are able, or willing, to engage with this process of self-communication. Those benefits become increasingly evident as we start to trust ourselves deeply once more, or maybe even for the first time ever. If your self-estrangement is considerable then expect that it could take some time, but this is a sure fire way to get it done!

Learning to trust is sometimes a slow process. We cannot force it.

We can only be consistent, and allow our wounded parts time to get used to the new supportive arrangement at a pace which is organic. Where we meet with resistance in this process we are being invited to love more deeply. We may find ourselves tested. Parts of ourselves that have been let down before may well understandably test us to see if we're going to fold at the first sign of difficulty. This again is why consistency is so important here.

Like I said at the beginning of this chapter, acceptance is a labour of love.

Obstacles To Progress

An important consideration here is that some people, for various reasons, find this "unconditional support", or even just "sitting with a feeling" to be a very challenging request. If that's you, don't worry! It's not a black and white situation. Support comes in many forms and part of this process is being okay with what is, even if what is, right now, is that it's too challenging to be completely unconditional with your-self. There is much else to do yet and we'll be moving on to some very different understandings shortly. Though I would want to encourage those who can to break through this obstacle, we cannot force such a process. Think of a relationship with a friend that has suffered a breakdown in communication, or even a minor betrayal. The beginning of any reconciliation might begin with "I want to trust you again, but right now I just don't know how to do that". It's a start, right? The same principle exists here. If it's too much to say "I hear and accept that you feel X" you can begin instead with "I'd like to accept your presence but I'm not sure how to do that right now, and I'm working on it". The important point is that connection is initiated. Note that the communication remains sincere, and most importantly, not hostile. While not ideal, it's better than no connection at all, or an entrenched position of hostility. We can think of it as process involving degrees. Instead of thinking I either can, or cannot, be unconditional towards to myself, we might think of it as "I can be unconditional with myself in some ways, some of the time", or if you prefer "I am learning to be kinder to myself". If using these words is uncomfortable, then perhaps just try "sitting" with your feelings (without hostility), without saying anything at all. Even this can be therapeutic, as it communicates in itself an "okay-ness" with the feelings as covered earlier. By all means, if you have your own words, providing they are not hostile and make you feel better, then use them. The words, the technique, are less important than the connection. It is the connection, the attention and the caring that counts!

For any readers who found any of the techniques difficult, worry not, there is much else to do yet! I want this book to be used safely. You should definitely not "force" yourself to undertake these exercises. If they are uncomfortable for you, then simply don't do them. If you feel that it's an important aspect of your healing to resolve, but are unable to do this on a self-help basis, then I would recommend seeking the help of a professional. Taking this principle further in the pages of a book is almost impossible, and potentially messy because there are so many possible variables as to why you may feel unable to offer yourself this particular kindness, self-punishment being one, feeling unworthy, or lack of self-forgiveness being obvious others. There will be reasons why such internal positions may have become so entrenched. Such reasons really require one to one exploration. Good therapists can act as guides and mediators in this process of internal reconciliation. I do believe that internal harmony is a very important part of anxiety busting, but I would also add that I have met a few people along the way for whom this "hear and accept" approach just was not a good fit. On occasion we explored it and resolved it. In one or two cases we simply agreed to move on to other approaches like CBT, and found that we were still able to resolve their anxieties. With anxiety-busting we don't ever want to be conditional with our approach. I would never go so far as to say that it is absolutely essential to be consistently caring and valuing towards ourselves to stop feeling anxious. I just say that it will help most people enormously, and is definitely the preferred option given the choice. We don't want to say "You can only feel better if you follow these steps". That would be very conditional, right?! In practice, different approaches fit well for some people and not so well for others. For those of you who find this approach a good fit, it will be an extremely powerful and useful tool. It is a fast and reliable way to stop fearing fear, or indeed any emotion. You will learn through mastery of this practice that you have a tool with which you can nearly always improve the way you feel instantly. Mostly, you can expect to feel an immediate improvement in your sense of wellbeing by practicing this understanding. Knowing that you have a tool that can do wonders for your sense of control is powerful anti-anxiety medicine because it means that you're not at the mercy of your feelings any more. And here is the crux of the matter. By restoring control, you can stop the "what if's" because you already know that you can do something to help yourself. If you've done your homework properly, you will have learned that fear won't destroy you. It's just some part of you that needs reassurance, and when you give that part of you what it needs, then peace is restored, and perspective returns.

Another obstacle that sometimes presents here is uncertainty about who is saying what to who and why. Some people have the feeling "Why should I say that I accept my anxiety? I don't!" It's an understandable sentiment. The distinction I would ask you to make here is the one between the anxious feeling and the part of yourself that feels the anxious feeling. Consider that we are saying "I hear and accept that you feel anxious".

Essentially, you may not feel like being kind to your anxiety, but you can at least be kind to the part of yourself that is feeling anxious.

That part of you feeling the distress is not the problem. The distress is the problem. Be clear about this distinction. We're aiming to accept that there is a part of ourselves feeling anxious and by extension we're accepting, not rejecting, ourselves. Keeping a clear perspective of this distinction should help considerably with being able to be kinder to your-self.

APPLICATION

So, with a clear understanding of the approach established, it's now time to put it into practice. Practice, here, is an important concept. Although I am keen to ensure that this book remains free of religious implication, it's worth considering that the techniques of prayer and meditation are fundamentally techniques for cultivating inner peace. One could think of this concept of sitting with ones feelings with acknowledgment and acceptance, as a kind of meditation. It's a well-established, scientifically recognised fact, that meditation has health benefits for many who

114

practice it. With this in mind we can consider that the word practice implies repetition with the agenda of improving ability. Acceptance of one's feelings is a skill of sorts, and can be learned through practice. I'm often asked "how often should I do this?" To put it into some sort of perspective, I still personally use this technique regularly after many years. I need to do it formally much less these days because I have been doing it for so long that the message it cultivates has become established as a clear and automatic part of my being. I do experience difficult emotions and feelings sometimes, but what is different for me is that I don't feel bad about feeling bad. I simply recognise that I'm having an emotionally turbulent day or week, and I just sit with it. Sometimes I do this formally with eyes closed, but more often than not I'm able to just "know" that all is okay even if it's not 100% comfortable. So the first part of the answer is that you use the technique on an as-needed basis. Further to that though my advice is, that providing you are comfortable enough with the approach and its application, I'd say ten to thirty minutes a day is a pretty good practice. If you do ten minutes and would like more, then by all means, stay with it for as long as you feel it's benefitting you. What will happen over time is that this consistency of message will be absorbed by your deeper self as a true sense of ongoing support, and this will ultimately flower to become an ever-present feeling of safety. It is in fact an auto suggestion, that is, an idea which becomes truer with repetition. This is the longer term goal. The message is "Whatever happens I'll be able to cope because I always self-support". For me personally, after many years of practice, this feeling has become deep and profound. I do experience hardship in life still, but that message remains deeply established, and it is a great comfort in times of difficulty. Little, often, and consistently, is the answer to the question of how often? It's a practice. You are "learning".

CHAPTER FOUR – USING YOUR HEAD

THE IMPORTANCE OF CRITICAL THINKING SKILLS

So, we now have a better grip on the emotional component of handling fear. When thinking about head and heart we might say that's the heart. So, what of the head? Does that play a role in anxiety? You bet it does! Your intellectual brain, the frontal lobe, deals with logic, reason, planning, and control. You will remember that we were discussing earlier how the intellect can be overwhelmed by signals from the limbic system and function less well as a result. This leads to a loss of frontal lobe control, but we must remember that the overload, and subsequent loss of control, is only ever partial, not total. With the application of our learning so far, we will find ourselves less overwhelmed by emotion, and thereby in a stronger position to have our frontal lobe working for us!

We understand that the limbic system can easily get the wrong idea and respond to inappropriate triggers, but the frontal lobe can still influence our emotional mind to a much greater degree than we recognise. It's not something that necessarily occurs naturally when we've been overloaded emotionally. We do in fact need to **consciously** engage the frontal lobe to bring about clear thought and flexible perception.

Your emotional mind hears every negative thought you "buy into" with feeling as though it is an absolute fact.

...which quite often, let's be clear, it isn't! It's an "assumption" that comes packaged with a feeling. We need to learn to differentiate facts from feelings. To say "I feel it therefore it must be true" is a serious mistake. Every negative-introspection you entertain is like a small anxiety explosion for your brain.

Ruminating makes you anxious. Never entertain it as a pastime!

You cannot afford the luxury of consistently thinking negatively. So...

S.M.A.R.T. – (S)TAY (M)INDFUL (A)ND (R)EORGANISE (T)HINKING

Did you know that an overload of emotional arousal can stupefy the brain? That's not of course meant to be disrespectful to anyone. The polite way of saying it is that emotional arousal hijacks our intelligence. When we become angry we "throw our toys out of the pram", when we're depressed we sulk, and when we're fearful we want our parents. In other words, we behave like children. That's not to blame anyone so please don't misunderstand. We're just making it very clear what we are up against. Researchers tell us that's because the emotional mind has the average emotional age of a seven year old child. When we are in the midst of an emotional arousal, we revert into a childlike mode and feel powerless, which, of course, we are not.

So, how do we avoid the emotional mind trap? Well we need to get S.M.A.R.T. (S)tay (M)indful (A)nd (R)eorganise (T)hinking when dealing with emotional arousal. When we're anxious, angry, or depressed, we're working with a handicap; namely that we're temporarily less intelligent than we would otherwise be because arousal is blocking access to the solution creating areas of the brain. When we're anxious, it's all too easy to forget everything we know about solutions and go into helpless mode. In plain English, we can temporarily "lose the plot". We lose intellectual control, and we don't think straight. If you've gone temporarily "stupid" as a result of too much emotion, remember you can get SMART!

These states are the most powerful of all trances (a trance implies being firmly fixed upon one thing only), and we can be temporarily locked into these states, where we forget to get SMART. Forgetting to get SMART can leave you feeling a little bit caged!

Actually getting SMART isn't only about staying mindful, and reorganising thinking. That's just an easy way to remember that you are not powerless. It's actually about remembering everything you need to know about busting anxiety.

You see there is a rule in psychology that says you'll need to hear something multiple times (some people say eleven) before you really absorb it. Buddhist wisdom says that on average, we'll make the same mistake seven times before we learn to do something differently. We are slow learners apparently. Slow we may be, but eventually we get there.

Cognitive Behavioural Therapy (CBT)

In life, we are taught to wash daily, brush our teeth, wear clean clothes, and keep a tidy home. This is our personal hygiene, and most of us take pleasure in it. We accept it as a given that it is something which requires maintenance. So what of "mental hygiene"? Who teaches us that this is important? Mostly, nobody!

Think about it. Your brain is also your home. You live there consciously for sixteen hours a day. Do you devote the same level of maintenance to your mental processes as you do to your teeth and armpits? If you think about things this way, you can begin to see that it is unreasonable to expect your house to be bright and tidy, a nice place to spend time, if you never clean it. Likewise, negative thoughts are like cobwebs, weeds, or dirty socks in the mind. They obscure, constrict, and leave a bad smell.

The mind too therefore requires maintenance. Of course once a house is clean, it's much easier to keep clean.

Habitual negative thinking can be both the cause of anxiety, and also the result of anxiety. Spending any length of time feeling anxious or depressed will wear a person down, and this naturally leads to the formation of negative thinking styles because the outlook can begin to feel hopeless. So anxiety causes us to think negatively, and negativity causes us to feel anxious. A negative feedback loop is created.

It's actually a mistake to believe that the outlook is hopeless, and accepting that the future is truly hopeless is the surest way to remain anxious or depressed. For someone in the midst of anxiety however, it is often very difficult to see a way out because the feelings of impending doom are so convincing. A negative lens tends to see the worst in things, and then we feel "unsafe" because everything looks threatening or unsatisfactory, and we forecast (naturally) that things will remain this way. Unfortunately, the habit of thinking negatively can develop as the result of short illness, a traumatic experience, or just a short period of anxiety or depression. Just like any bad habit, it's easier to acquire than it is to shake off. Most people will bounce back from life's temporary difficulties, and reinstall positive thought patterns quite naturally. But, equally, sometimes negative thinking styles are so insidious, and easy to fall into, that we won't even notice that we have adopted them. We often hear people say "I've never been the same since...." While there is much that can be said about life's experiences changing us forever (and they do for sure), it is always worth considering whether we have also simply fallen into the bad habit of automatically assuming the worst? This will account, in many cases, for at least some part of our continued anxiety. You can pretty much take it as a given that if you are experiencing anxiety and/or depression, then you will definitely be experiencing a negatively focussed world, which may appear to you as an objective reality. Rest assured a worldview is always subjective. It can almost certainly be improved.

The formula: Negativity creates anxiety. Anxiety is converted to fear. Fear must have a focus... And there is your problem.

So part of the solution then is to cease the negativity. The good news is, it is possible to change these patterns of negative thought, and this will improve the way you feel. Changing old patterns of negativity does however take effort. There are a number of reasons why we might fail to address this. Let's explore some of these:-

* The benefits are not immediately apparent – One can easily decide it's simply not worth the effort. Negative thinking may lead us to conclude "Don't bother. It won't help....." One has to be willing to press on regardless of such feelings and to hold some trust that the benefits will become apparent through time.

* Negative thinking has become a friend. Believe it or not, anger, and raving about how terrible everything is for us can feel good in the moment. Anger can stimulate the production of opioids (the same chemical family as heroin) in readiness for battle/wounds. These are the body's own natural pain relief chemicals, and we can easily become psychologically, perhaps even physically, addicted to this rush. Unconsciously, we enjoy staying angry or depressed. Unfortunately, although this presents as a workable strategy in the short term, it

creates more anxiety and low mood overall, and is never a successful strategy for long term happiness.

* Overcoming negative thinking is like breaking any habit. We need to continually think and behave differently, making adjustments. Imagine being asked to do anything differently in your life. Even zipping up a new jacket from the opposite side takes mental effort. Initially it takes mindfulness and effort to create a new pattern. This can feel like work. It is however, work that is essential if we are to create, and maintain, a state of good mental health. Once a habit is broken, it becomes easier over time. We have to work hard initially to break the habit, but when you've zipped up your new jacket a few times, it quickly becomes automatic.

Staying SMART means remembering that your emotional mind needs your input, logic, and clarity, when it comes to working out what is worth worrying about (not much actually), and even more importantly, what is actually true (fact versus feeling).

Having established what is/is not true, or worth worrying about, you can now dispute that which is erroneous when it arises in your mind/feeling body and stop buying in. We need to continually challenge habitual negative assumptions. We also need to work on finding positive ways of viewing situations. Continuing to bombard your emotional brain with high-powered negativity explosives will make your emotional brain highly aroused, in all the wrong ways!

Your emotional brain hears everything you say to yourself.

KEEP YOUR LANGUAGE CLEAN

This is a true story. I once knew a lady who used to say "I've had a gut-full of it…." "I can't stomach it when such and such happens.", and "No…really I am…I'm sick of it." She told me she went through a period of vomiting every morning before coming to work. Many are the stories of hypnotherapists helping people to resolve their skin conditions by resolving what is actually "irritating" them. These things really can be linked. Have a look at this list of words:

Dirty, Bitter, Angry, Impatient, Guilty, Ashamed, Gutted, Hopeless, Abused, Worthless, Despairing, Helpless, Trapped, Unloveable, Incompetent, Useless, Irritated, Despised, Hated, Threatened, Failure, Misery, Frustrated, Enemy, Unforgiveable, Inferior.

Read these words five times (if you can bear it!) What happens in your feeling body? What happens to your mind?

Now, try this list, again five times.

Clean, Joyful, Calm, Patient, Innocent, Proud, Delighted, Hopeful, Valued, Valuable, Excited, Capable, Free, Loveable, Competent, Useful, Peaceful, Adored, Cherished, Safe, Success, Happiness, Contented, Friend, Forgiven, Equal.

Now what happens in your feeling body? What happens in your mind?

Notice that the second list is the polar opposite of the first, word for word. Think about this. How much of your internal monologue contains words from the first list? How many times a day do you hear those words (or similar), in sentences, inside your own head? If you see a pattern there, it's time to make some changes!

Your unconscious mind really does hear everything you say to yourself and sometimes it responds quite literally.

There's no blame to be apportioned. We recognise that negative thinking, as well as being a **cause** of anxiety and depression is also a **symptom**. At one level, it's simply those habitual negative neural pathways we spoke about earlier firing automatically. The good news though is that you have the power to stop them. In time it will become easier to think positively and avoid habitual negativity, but it takes practice and effort. That begins by becoming aware of the patterns, recognising them, and then deciding to do something about it. Don't expect that it will happen overnight. It won't. You need to be willing to put this effort in. It's an unaffordable habit which you'll need to get yourself out of!

If you're having a hard time with anxiety, ask yourself what you are telling yourself about life or yourself that's scaring your emotional brain so badly that it has to stay anxious?

If you look carefully, you will almost certainly find some areas where you could think smarter. There is always something you can do to improve things. Naturally, the question now becomes "how?" Luckily for us, people have been asking this question for as long as anyone can remember, and there is a very well defined body of knowledge available to answer it - Cognitive Behavioural Therapy. For reasons already explained, I'm keen to avoid this book becoming a technique-led workbook, so we'll be stopping short of a full exploration of the techniques used in CBT. With that said, no anxiety related help-book would be complete without at least an explanation of CBT's aims, and a few important teachings. We will be looking here at the central technique of keeping thought records, and later we will inevitably arrive at an exploration of some other important CBT-related concepts. For the purposes of gaining a basic understanding, we'll just say as much as we need to for now. There are many resources available in the form of websites, and books, which offer an in-depth look at CBT. Further exploration can bear fruit for you if you are willing to apply what you learn from them.

Rather interestingly, the now hugely complicated field of CBT was developed from a very simple idea. Following the trauma and loss of the second world-war, there were many people in need of fast therapy. Need hugely outstripped supply, and CBT was the therapy of choice because it is fundamentally simple, and easily applied. Perhaps most importantly, once learned, CBT could be self-applied without the need to have a therapist present. It has been referred to as three minute therapy. Today, the medical orthodoxy generally recommends CBT as the number one treatment for anxiety and depression. This is because CBT performs well in randomised trials and is relatively speaking an extremely safe form of therapy. It does not involve re-visiting traumatic material or psychoanalysing oneself. The principles can be learned and easily applied by anyone willing to learn them. Though there is much to be said for employing a CBT therapist as a guide, CBT can be successfully undertaken entirely on a self-help basis.

CBT Explained

Cognition (to cognise) means "to possess knowledge or information about". Re-cognise therefore, means to know again. In practice, the word cognition is also used to mean "to think", or to perceive. The way you cognise something is the way you perceive or know it. Cognitive Behavioural Therapy therefore, is a therapy based on cognition (knowing), and behaviour. Human beings can think, feel, and behave, irrationally and inflexibly. Here, the word "inflexibly" doesn't imply being difficult or awkward, but refers to perceiving in a fixed or rigid way, without the possibility of using alternative perspectives. The word "irrational" doesn't imply hysteria either. It just means "not properly considered". Having irrational beliefs, thoughts, and feelings, can lead us to perceive the world through negatively skewed, fixed, perceptual filters, and the resulting distorted cognition can make us feel (mistakenly) awful about ourselves, the world, and other people. In the same way that we can see things through "rose tinted spectacles" when we're overly optimistic, we can also see things as being more threatening than they really are if our perceptual filters are negatively focussed, or distorted. Irrational and inflexible thinking creates disturbance at the emotional and mental level because perceiving negatively means that we find the World unnecessarily threatening, leading to inappropriate activation of the fight and flight mechanism. This emotional and mental disturbance can lead to symptoms of anxiety, depression, anger, sexual dysfunction, phobias, social anxiety, loss of confidence, fear of the World, low self-esteem, perfectionism, irritation, jealousy, obsession, compulsion, impatience with others...the list goes on. Cognitive Behavioural Therapy might be thought of at core then, as learning how to be aware of anxiety causing perceptions, and how then to use this awareness to maintain on-going positive mental hygiene. The outcome of this strategy is a reduction in anxiety and all its associated symptoms. Once learned, it will be with you as a tool for life.

CBT does not talk about good and bad, or right and wrong thinking/feeling/behaviour. In fact, CBT is deliciously free of such thinking. It is not a "moral" therapy. It doesn't ask whether it's "right" to think or believe a certain thing, or not. It simply looks at whether it's helpful to feel or believe a certain thing, or indeed, to behave in a certain way. This is known then as adaptive (helpful), or maladaptive (unhelpful) perception. It can deliver a much more balanced approach to assessing one's thoughts and feelings more accurately.

THE HISTORY OF CBT

Although CBT has been influenced by Buddhism and Science alike throughout the years, perhaps the most notable individual historical contributors are Marcus Aurelius, Epictetus, and Immanuel Kant.

Marcus Aurelis (121-180AD) was a Roman Emperor. He was the author of a classic philosophical text called "Meditations". Centrally, he is quoted as saying "If you are distressed by anything external, the pain is not due to the thing itself, but to your own estimate of it; and this you have the power to revoke at any moment". This idea that we can choose how to respond to situations and events is central to CBT.

Epictetus (55-135AD) was a slave and endured great hardship. His "master" would often torture him, and on one occasion, during a leg twisting torture session, Epictetus warned his master that the leg would break. The message was not heeded and the leg broke, leaving Epictetus lame. Epictetus is quoted: "Some things are up to us, and some things are not. Our opinions are up to us, and our impulses, desires, aversions, – in short, whatever is our own doing. Our bodies are not up to us, nor are our possessions, our reputations....that is, whatever is not our own doing". Although this message is perhaps less relevant to most people's situation today, the central theme, that being that there are factors in life beyond our control, such as illness, or other people, and their opinions, remains highly relevant to CBT. In essence, there are many things we can't control in life, but he notes we can choose to control how we respond to those things.

Immanuel Kant (1724-1804) – Immanuel Kant basically proposed that objectivity (the real world) is ultimately imperceptible to the individual. He explained that all experience is filtered through subjective mental/emotional filters, named schema. This also is central to CBT. In understanding that what we experience is an "interpretation" of events rather than a "fact", we can easily find our way back to the CBT-based

125

understanding that what we "feel" (our filtered interpretation) about something doesn't always match the "facts" of the situation.

How Does Negative Perception Cause Emotional Disturbance?

Essentially, we, as human beings, naturally tend to believe that if we feel something, or think something, then it must be true. It's simply not questioned, especially if our experience has told us that our perception is correct. If we live with a certain belief, we then go on to act and behave automatically as though that feeling or thought is absolutely true. In other words, we assume that feelings and thoughts are facts, when in actuality they are often subjective interpretations of the facts based on our own personal beliefs and perceptual filters. Put simply, perceptions are by nature highly subjective (i.e not everyone would feel the same way about it). If it just so happens that the thought or feeling we are experiencing is negatively focussed, then it usually creates fear, tension, worry, and stress. Though there may well be some truth to our assessment of the situation, a more objective evaluation will often reveal to us that a situation or perception is rarely as absolute as we perceive it to be. We actually have more options available to us than we recognise. These options can take the form of behaving differently, or thinking differently. Often we don't perceive these options because in a stressed or un-resourceful state we can mistakenly "buy into" or "endorse" the feelings/thoughts/belief/s exactly as they present to us. This can cause us to react rather than respond. Reaction is instinctive. Response is thoughtful and deliberate. Reacting can leave us feeling as though we had no other choice, and this in turn can leave us feeling very stuck or emotionally/mentally disturbed.

As an example we know that depression, for instance, is triggered partly by a feeling of helplessness. If our thoughts tell us "There's no way out", then this perception can contribute to, or sustain, a depressed state. The assumption that there's no way out is clearly only a perception, not a fact, and yet it can feel very true when there appears to be no evidence to the contrary. Obviously, believing we are eternally stuck in an unpleasant world will be a very disturbing perception when we believe it absolutely, as if it were a fact. If we can become aware of contrary evidence then, we're on our way to finding a way out!

CBT sets out then to look for this contrary evidence. Practiced properly, it doesn't seek to wow us with unrealistic, and therefore unbuyable, positivity. Instead It looks for evidence, both for and against the negative cognitions, and then offers tools to go about integrating that evidence, so as to think more critically (rationally) about our perceptions, thus reducing the level of disturbance such perceptions can cause. We then go on to learn to behave in accordance with our new more adaptive understanding, which over time, through repetition and continued thought/belief/behavioural adjustment, helps us to feel less stuck or disturbed.

THE INSIGHTS

Paraphrased, Albert Ellis's insights (part of the foundation of CBT) state the following:

Insight 1 – How you feel is mainly determined by the way you think. – This notes that the beliefs you carry and action with feeling, become your living emotional reality.

Insight 2 – You become distressed when you endorse your own irrational beliefs – This notes that those beliefs which create unpleasant feelings will distress you when you "buy in" to them (endorse) without challenging the assumptions by recognising different options of thinking and perceiving.

Insight 3 – Be kind to Yourself. You, like many people, can think irrationally, so don't judge yourself too harshly – This notes that CBT is not a self-blame exercise. Everyone thinks irrationally sometimes. It's not right or wrong. So you can be kind to yourself, while adjusting thoughts and behaviours appropriately for easier feelings.

Insight 4 – You have to make a sustained effort to recognise and challenge your irrational thoughts - This notes that effort is required over a sustained period of time to make the above adjustments. Years of ground-in negative perceptions take time to adjust! Patience and persistence is necessary, but there is a pay off!

With CBT a sustained effort on the part of the user is necessary for results. CBT is a conscious mind therapy, and that means we need to consciously adjust negative automatic thoughts, and challenge errant negativity. Ellis tells us that a "protestant work ethic" is required. With this said, when people engage with the CBT process, they are often delighted with the results because with application an entirely new framework of thought, and belief can be established which can last for the rest of a persons' life.

As with all good therapy, CBT is goal oriented, reflective, methodical, evidence-based, and time-limited. In plain English this means that we want to see the results, and we want to reflect as we go on, measuring and recording each stage of the progression towards wellness and understanding. This measuring and recording of progress involves using worksheets, which ideally, will be kept in date order, so that you have it in black and white that things are improving as a result of your efforts. You can think of it as moving methodically towards symptom resolution in stages of understanding and application. CBT is very much a learning and brain re-training process. Central to the CBT approach is the understanding of exactly how we go about thinking irrationally. When we can identify skewed perceptions as they arise within us, and have ready some counter-perspectives (evidence against), we are then much better equipped to stop any internal endorsement (buy-in) of irrational, disturbing perceptions before they occur. CBT recognises that you can't necessarily stop negative thoughts coming in, but you can learn how to handle them.

For clarity, let's remind ourselves, that negative automatic thoughts will reduce naturally as we lower our stress levels generally. With less limbic system arousal, you will find CBT to be more effective.

Thought Distortions

The following describe some of the best known perceptual distortions that occur in thinking:-

All or nothing thinking

This is "absolute" thinking. Here, if something is less than perfect, then it's seen as all bad. If we can't do it/have it all, then it's perceived as having no value at all. This can create feelings of being overwhelmed. We need to recognise that things are rarely absolute. There are a million shade of grey between black and white. Life is not a pass/fail scenario.

Over-generalisation

Characterised by using the words "always", or "never", this thought distortion creates feelings of being consistently defeated, and maintains a negative feeling about the World, Self, and Others. It is rarely based on fact. To overcome over-generalisation we look for exceptions to these internal assertions. Is it actually "sometimes"?

Mental filter

This distortion involves filtering out whatever doesn't fit ones beliefs, and looking ONLY for evidence that supports your way of seeing things, even if that's purely negative. Usually this means dwelling on a single negative detail, and excluding all else. Extreme fundamentalism is an easily recognisable symptom of this kind of thought distortion, and good evidence to remind us how deep it can run in some people!

Discounting the positive

Can you accept a compliment? Can you give yourself a pat on the back for something you did well? This one involves being able to discount the twenty people you helped today because one person had a complaint (justified or not). You reason that the rest don't count because anyone could have done your job, and they were just being nice because they felt sorry for you anyway.

Jumping to conclusions

A well-known saying is that "to assume makes an ASS out of U and ME". It's a useful phrase to remember. Assumptions are prone to inaccuracy. This is the "mind reading trick", and it's what happens when we assume that people or events have a particular meaning without checking whether that's actually true. CBT will encourage communication rather than assumption, and recognises that someone with a distorted filter is in danger of making all kinds of disturbing assumptions, such as "I know what they meant with that look!" or "She said she can't make it to my party, but I know she doesn't really want to be my friend". CBT asks for evidence first.

Negative Forecasting

Forecasting that the future (events and general) will be awful is a massive cause of stress. Since your brain is the most powerful future experience rehearsal machine in the World, your poor old (not so logical) subconscious mind becomes very worried indeed when you negatively rehearse the future as a frightening destination! When you tell yourself that things will turn out badly, you create fear and stress. Then because you're so stressed and fearful, your performance drops; everything turns out badly, and you say "See! I told you so!" Then the whole cycle begins again, but reinforced because it did in fact go as badly as you imagined. Ironically, that's because you imagined it going badly first!

Magnification or maximisation

Exaggerating your problems and shortcomings so that everyone (and you) knows how helpless or useless you are. If you're already useless then at least you can't fall any further, right? Magnifying your negative qualities is the surest way to stay in self-judgement and out of learning to love yourself...warts and all. We all do it. It's a continued area to work on. Also, magnifying your problems makes your life look completely unmanageable, and creates feelings of hopelessness.

Catastrophising

This is like magnification but comes with a whipped cream topping of drama. Catastrophising means seeing negative events, people, or mistakes as absolutely and quite unbearably awful. It is often also therefore called "awfulising". This is a very important distortion to understand in CBT because how we "choose" to see events will dictate how we feel about them subjectively. We all have to deal with unpleasantness sometimes. It's easier if we can learn to deal with it courageously and with dignity. Catastrophising is perhaps the most direct way to ensure you directly and needlessly disturb yourself. Being a drama queen/king will upset the limbic system!

Minimisation

Playing down your strengths – No matter what the evidence is that you have good qualities you just can't/won't see/believe it!

Emotional reasoning

I feel it therefore it must be true. "Feelings are facts and to hell with the truth!" Or, "I've made up my mind, don't bother me with facts."

Inflexible language - Mind menace talk.

Should, must, ought to, have to etc statements are known as "Mind Menace" language. When you say something "should" be a certain way, you are guaranteed to feel disturbed when it's not! The same goes for have to, ought to, must etc. This language can be directed towards yourself and is even more powerfully disturbing when directed towards the world or others! "Should" is the surest way to ensure you don't! "Should" is also the surest way to get someone else into a defensive stance when you throw it at them. People don't like to be told what they should or shouldn't do. "Shoulds" can be easily replaced with "I'd prefer", or "I'd like to" or "I could". "I can't" can be replaced with "I could try".

Negative labelling

This refers to labelling self or others as exclusively negative. So rather than knowing that no-one is perfect, we can over-generalise a person's behaviour or thinking as bad, and label that person a failure or a jerk. This is inflexible thinking, and can also be directed towards one-self, creating terrible feelings of low self-worth!

Personalisation and blame

We personalise that which is often outside of our control. When an event happens that is beyond our control (illness, redundancy, someone else's actions), we blame ourselves. This makes you feel rotten about yourself! Perfectionism can also fall into this category. Blame is the opposite of personalisation. Here, we are unwilling to assume responsibility for our lives and behaviour, and thus never arrive at a place of healing. How can we heal it if we don't own it? Blaming also makes you mad at everything (creates anger), and blocks solutions in a big way!

We are often in the habit of thinking in these distorted ways without conscious awareness of doing so. CBT uses many different techniques to bring a new awareness to these patterns. A central technique is known as a "Thought Record". A thought record asks you to record exactly what's happening at the moment that your mood shifts from positive to negative, and then to write down your thoughts exactly as they occur at that moment. We are then able to identify how the situation, and more importantly, what we think during that situation, causes us to feel distressed. Having identified those central "disturbing, maladaptive" thoughts, feelings, and beliefs, you can go about replacing those perceptions with more adaptive perspectives. So, let's take a look at the central technique of keeping thought records.

UNDERSTANDING "THOUGHT RECORDS"

Ellis's Insights (Reminder)

Insight 1 – How you feel is mainly determined by the way you think.

Insight 2 – You become distressed when you endorse your own irrational thoughts.

Insight 3 – Be kind to yourself. You, like many people, can think irrationally, so don't judge yourself too harshly.

Insight 4 – You need to make a sustained effort to recognise and challenge your irrational thoughts.

Based on the above insights we can recognise that thoughts themselves can be a source of emotional disturbance. Perhaps the most important word in all of the above is the word "endorse" in insight two. To "endorse" means to "approve of or agree with", and/or "to support". Insight one reminds us that the way we feel is determined by the way that we think. Insight two tells us that we can become distressed when we agree with, or support, unpleasant thoughts. Although we can't always necessarily change the thoughts that enter our minds immediately (remember that negative automatic thoughts are a symptom of an overload of emotional arousal), we can choose how we will respond to the presence of those thoughts. If we make the mistake of "endorsing" disturbing thoughts, that is, behaving as though they are true, then it follows naturally that we will increase the level of disturbance that we experience.

An obvious example of such a thought that might occur as a response to making a small mistake at work is: "Oh my God!! They think I'm an idiot. I'm going to get fired!"

Here, there are a number of assumptions that underpin the thought which are obviously emotionally disturbing. Primarily they are:

* Oh My God!! - There is a crisis (Catastrophising/Awfulising – Alarming your mind).

* I'm an idiot. (Globalisation/Negative labelling – applying a small mistake to everything).

* Everyone thinks I'm an idiot. (The mind reading trick – assuming what others think).

* I'll lose my job. (Jumping to conclusions).

* My life will fall apart. (Globalisation - Making a small problem apply to "everything").

Clearly this is an overblown response to the small mistake, but it is typical of the kind of feelings and thoughts an anxious person might experience. The problem is your limbic system doesn't know that what you are telling it isn't completely true, and so it provides feelings that mirror the level of alarm created by those thoughts, and behaves as though you are in a true crisis, providing you with plenty of emotional disturbance.

It is our job to minimise the level of emotional disturbance we experience, and so our therapeutic agenda is to interrupt the pattern of automatically endorsing disturbing perceptions. When you successfully challenge a negative automatic thought, and stop endorsing it as if it is absolutely true, you naturally decrease the level of emotional arousal (disturbance) you create and experience.

"Thought records" are powerful tools which can be used to provide evidence against automatically occurring disturbing thoughts, thus providing you with a new, more flexible perspective that can also be shown to be true, and believable. We actually want to find evidence against the disturbing perceptions. It's your job to fight for these other more flexible perspectives. It has been said that if you fight for your limitations, then you get to keep them. If you feel the need to play "Devil's Advocate", then remember which side you are on!

When looking for evidence against negative automatic thoughts, you are asked to imagine that you are a barrister in a court of law. It's your job to convince the jury that the case for the negative automatic thought is weak, while the case against the negative perspective (thought) is strong. You are looking to provide as much evidence as you can.

Let's have a look at a Thought Record, and explore how it works.

What has happened? (Activating Event)	What emotion/s has this event left you feeling? (Include intensity %)	What negative automatic thoughts have arisen alongside the emotion/s?	What evidence do you have that show those thoughts are definitely true?	What evidence do you have against those thoughts being completely true?	Using your evidence for and against those thoughts, now create a rational and flexible assessment of the situation.	Now re-rate your emotion/s. (Include intensity %)

You can see that there are a number of columns that are to be completed from left to right. The idea is that we are looking to "catch" the thoughts which create emotional disturbance at the point at which our mood shifts. So you might be going along just fine one day and then an event occurs which negatively shifts your mood. Normally, this process is quite unconscious, and it's easy to get swept along with "feelings" without any real awareness of exactly what just happened. Sometimes, for example, I might suddenly become aware that I feel a bit low, perhaps over the course of an hour. I then start wondering. I was fine this morning. What's happened? I trawl back through my inventory of today's events and I can't put my finger on anything in particular. I went to the shops. That was fine. I spoke to my Dad. That was fine. Then suddenly, bingo! I remember that I was thinking earlier about a friend who is unwell. At the time I'd been busy painting a door and I'd been daydreaming. My thinking had barely consciously registered because I was focussed on my task. Here, my emotions crept up on me. That's an example of creeping disturbance. More often than not though, it will arrive in a moment of obvious alarm. You put down the telephone to your Mum and suddenly you feel like crap!

So, we're looking to analyse exactly what just happened, and why it created disturbed feelings. More importantly, we're looking to see whether there are some assumptions behind our assessment of the event that might be creating a distorted view of the situation. For simplicity we'll stick with our earlier example. Have a look at the completed thought record below and the accompanying description of how we completed it.

Situation Who? What? Where? When?	Mood? (One word with percentage)	Automatic Thoughts (What are you thinking as your mood changes?) Circle the "Hot Thought"	Evidence That Supports The Hot Thought.	Evidence Against The Hot Thought	Alternative Balanced Thought. How strongly do you believe the new perspective?	Re-Rate Mood
Boss tells me I've made a mistake by sending a customer letter to the wrong address.	Worried 90% Useless 70% Depressed 80%	"Oh my God! I'm an idiot. ⟨I'm going to get fired⟩ "I'll never live this down." "There goes my promotion." "I always screw everything up."	We are in a recession. I got fired from a job in 1998 when I messed up customers' orders. Jill Spires was fired in 2006. My boss asked me to be more careful in future indicating she still thinks I have a job!	Jill Spires was a repeat offender and received multiple warnings. It would cost the Company more to re-train someone than let me keep my job. I do a great job most of the time, and received a commendation in my one to one interview. People don't get fired for one small mistake. I am a much more mature employee now. I didn't care in the job in which I got fired. Things are very different now.	Everybody makes mistakes sometimes. My boss knows that too. I will be more careful in future. The evidence reminds me that I am safe in my job. I can relax and put it down to experience. I'm a good worker and they know that. My boss simply asked me to be more careful in future, and that is fair enough. In a few days it will be forgotten. The customer probably called just to let us know that another customer didn't receive their letter. 80% believed.	Worried 20% Useless 10% Relieved 90%

138

* _Situation. What just happened?_ - My boss came over and explained that the she'd just received a call from a customer who'd received someone else's letter in the same envelope as her own. She asked me to be more careful in future.

* _Mood_ - In CBT, mood is usually described with just one word and a percentage to show the intensity of the feeling. I felt therefore: Worried 90%, Useless 70%, Depressed 80%.

* _Automatic thoughts_ – At the moment my mood changes I make a note of what I am actually thinking at that moment. Here it is necessary to record the thoughts as accurately as possible, as if you record them from memory, they may be edited or inaccurate. You may remember it as "I "might" get fired, when in fact what you were thinking was "I WILL get fired". There is a difference, and we can see that "will" is a lot more disturbing than "might". I accurately recorded my thoughts as: "Oh my God!! I'm an idiot. I'm going to get fired. I'll never live this down. There goes my promotion. I always screw everything up!" I then circled the "Hot thought". This is the thought that most strongly alarms me, and that relates most directly to the shift in mood. In this case it was the "I'm going to get fired" thought.

* _Evidence that supports the hot thought_ - I actually don't have any evidence that I'll get fired or that I'm an idiot. These are assumptions without any actual evidence. Remember, I've got to convince a jury, so just "feeling" that something might be so, is not "evidence", and upon inspection I find that I actually don't have any evidence that strongly supports my "feeling". I do have evidence that the company does occasionally fire people because I know that Jill Spires was fired in 2006 for misconduct. I might also reason that we are in a recession and this makes me more expendable. I once lost a job in 1998 because I continually messed up the customers' orders. Although these may be compelling reasons to feel that I will lose my job they do not actually constitute evidence.

* _Evidence AGAINST the hot thought_ – Now here's where we need to start fighting our corner. Remember you are the barrister representing the case against the hot thought. The hot thought claims that you are an idiot, and that you will get fired as a result of your mistake. It's your job to find and present the evidence that this is not so. Use the list of questions below to look for perspectives that show your hot thought might be disputable.

Questions to help you find evidence against hot thoughts.

* If my friend or loved one was having this thought, what would I tell them?

* Have I had any experiences that show that this thought is not completely true all of the time?

* If I told my friend or loved one about this thought, what might they say to me? Would they suggest evidence to the contrary? If so, what might that be?

* What would I think about this situation if I didn't currently have an anxious or depressed feeling?

* Am I overestimating the degree of control I have in this situation, and if so, am I blaming myself for something beyond my control?

* Am I underestimating the degree of control I have in this situation, and if so, is there anything I can do practically that will allow me to exercise that control?

* What have I learned from previous experiences of being in a similar situation that might help me to think more flexibly right now?

* If I was a barrister, how might I convince a jury that this thought does not stand up to scrutiny when examined?

* Are there any strengths or positives in this situation that I am not seeing, or choosing to ignore?

* Am I discounting any relevant information that could help me to see this situation more flexibly/positively?

* If I am "assuming" that this situation will turn our badly because I had a previous experience where things went pear shaped, am I noticing what's different about this situation that makes a more positive outcome more likely?

* Do I have additional skills today to influence the outcome in a way I never had before?

Having applied these questions we arrive then at the following conclusions:-

* My boss asked me to be more careful in future, indicating she still thinks I have a job!

* Jill Spires was a repeat offender and received multiple warnings before she was fired.

* It would cost the Company more to re-train someone than to keep me employed.

* I do a great job most of the time and received a commendation in my one to one interview.

* People don't generally get fired for one small mistake.

Alternative Balanced Perspective – Here we are creating a more positive perspective that is nonetheless believable, and can be shown to be true enough. We may not be 100% certain that it is absolutely true but here we have managed to deliver a verdict on the situation that sways the jury strongly enough to vote for the new perspective.

* Everybody makes mistakes sometimes.

* My boss knows that too.

* I will be more careful in future. The evidence reminds me that I am safe in my job. I can relax and put it down to experience. I'm a good worker and my employers know that. My boss simply asked me to be more careful in future, and that is fair enough. In a few days it will all be

forgotten. The customer probably called just to let us know that our other customer didn't receive their letter. 80% believed.

Re-Rate Mood – Having established a more positive, rational, and considered perspective we then ask "If this event occurred now, and I thought about it with this alternative balanced perspective, how would it make me feel? What would the mood be?"

Here we find then that we still have a little bit of discomfort, but that discomfort is reduced considerably. We have the addition of "Relieved" as a mood, which replaces "Depressed". Having not berated ourselves for being an "idiot", we are now in recognition of the fact that everyone makes mistakes sometimes. In any case, we can see that the result of this exercise is to significantly reduce the level of emotional disturbance we feel in response to the event. Having "learned" new, more positive perspectives through this exercise, we find that this "knowledge" is quite rightly transferred to situations and events containing similar elements.

Outcome

This reduction of discomfort is a realistic outcome within CBT. We don't expect to completely eliminate all negative feelings or discomfort in a single fell swoop. It is much more about gently re-designing our response patterns so that we are learning to "respond" rather than "react". Reaction is automatic. Response is thoughtful and deliberate. We make long term changes by continually applying these principles. Please remain mindful that just one application probably won't be enough. We need to keep at it. Remember, there will be a limited number of "repeat visitors". These repeat visitors are the thoughts and feelings that keep returning in various situations. Though they may vary in terms of the presentation, you will find that the themes themselves are finite. In most cases there will be fewer than ten themes. In many cases there will be just one central theme. You can identify the trigger points, and then set about methodically disempowering each negative perception using this format. With practice and repetition you will learn that you do have some control over these thoughts because they simply cannot thrive as emotionally disturbing visitors without your endorsement.

Armed with your new evidence you are in a much stronger position to refute automatic negative perceptions, and replace them with more positive perspectives. Be patient. It does take time for your feelings to adjust, and remember too that negative automatic thoughts are a symptom of an overload of emotional arousal. This exercise will not necessarily "fix" your negative thinking or stop automatic thoughts arriving. It is one tool in our armoury designed to minimise the level of emotional arousal you experience. Please be as rigorous as you can be in applying this understanding and do relax into it too.

Behavioural Adjustment – Challenging Avoidance

So, we've placed a lot of emphasis there on dealing with the automatic negative thoughts, but CBT looks at cognition, and behaviour. It's recognised here that behaviour also sends a powerful message back to the limbic system. What you do in response to a feeling is really as important as what you think. Consider the following scenario:

You are invited to go shopping with a friend. You arrive at the designated meeting place and decide that you can't cope. You text your friend an excuse, and catch the first bus home.

What message have you just sent to your limbic system? The message you sent yourself by withdrawing is that the anxiety, and the situation, was unbearable. Your "behaviour" has reinforced the negative thought pattern that argued you couldn't cope, and this makes it more likely to recur in the future because...if you remember? "What the believer believes, the prover proves!" The goal with CBT then is to use clear thought and an increased tolerance of anxious feelings to go into challenging scenarios, and then see them through, even if there is anxiety present. The idea is that by repeatedly seeing your way through situations that you may previously have avoided you begin to a) Gain confidence. b) Prove to yourself that you're more resourceful than you thought you were. c) Convince your limbic system that the situation is not as dangerous as it appears. d) Accrue evidence that your actual experiences are generally more positive than your negative imaginings, which can be used to create more realistic future expectations.

As a general rule then, it's true to say that routinely avoiding challenging situations will deepen anxiety and depression because avoiding situations tells your brain that you agree with its erroneous negative assumptions of threat. Such endorsement reinforces those perceptions as though they are absolute truths. Deliberately entering challenging situations and seeing them through to completion does the polar opposite. There is however a caveat to this rule.

Let's assume that on a scale of one to ten, your anxiety about a specific situation is a ten, with ten being the highest anxiety you could experience. If this were the case, then forcing yourself into that situation with willpower alone is not likely to lead to a positive reduction in anxiety because it will be genuinely overwhelming. What we want to do is start with the situations that are maybe a five or six out of ten. Then staying in the situation is challenging, but ultimately bearable. This is basically a form of systematic desensitisation. In CBT we use a format known as a "Behavioural Experiment" worksheet to document your beliefs and expectations against your actual outcomes. In this way we can learn in safe incremental experiences that we are able to handle challenging situations. Usually your outcomes will be more positive than your expectations. Keep a diary of what you expected to happen versus what actually happened, and refer back to it when you're entering challenging situations. We're still here!

The Tyranny Of Rules – Mind Menace Language

Our lives are governed by "rules". There are the obvious ones that we all know about, like don't kill or steal. Then there are our subjective and personal inner rules. A devout Catholic for instance may live by the rule of chastity before marriage. Our inner-rules create order out of chaos because rules provide a framework of acceptability. Rules inform our sense of how to be in the world, and are therefore largely a positive organisational asset to us. Rules however can also become a claustrophobic prison when defined and applied without appropriate flexibility. In practice, rigid rules can become problematic because when an internal rule is broken, our emotions respond with some form of negative arousal such as stress, shame, anger, guilt, worry, or panic.

Inflexible rule systems are usually identified when they are prefixed with imperatives such as must, should, ought-to, and have-to. Can't, always, and never, are also inflexible words. These rules, if followed to the letter, are likely to be a cause of great stress for any person trying to live by them rigidly because if the rule is not fulfilled, then the emotional response which follows is that something is "wrong". That "wrong" feeling is a major culprit for emotional disturbance, which could include anxiety, depression, deflation, poor self-image, frustration, or anger, to name only a few.

Now we'll take a look at how we can make these "rules" much more flexible, and accommodating, to a peaceful mind. You will remember that we were discussing earlier the hardwired need to remain positively connected with our community? This can manifest as the rule:-

"I must be liked or accepted by every important person in my life for everything I do"

There's nothing wrong with the sentiment. It's human to want to please, but there's a problem with the way the rule is worded. It's far too rigid because it uses the word "must". What happens for us emotionally when we discover, or even just conclude, that someone doesn't like or accept us? If we do not meet those standards, emotional disturbance, the strong feeling that something is terribly wrong, will follow as sure as night follows day. We may conclude that we're no good or that everyone secretly hates us. It's an irrational position which forces us towards ongoing disappointment because the condition of pleasing everyone all the time literally cannot be met. It's the "must" that is causing the problem here. This may seem at first glance like simple semantics, but it is not at all. It is actually a very important piece of understanding. So, we need to understand that we can endorse the spirit of the moral position, which we may well wish to continue with, but it needs to be re-worded to be applied more flexibly. Here's my example of a positive re-word of this particular rule.

"The first rule of CBT is that I cannot control what other people do or think. I may be able to influence them using clear communication, but I cannot ultimately control their perceptions. I would like to please those people who are important to me and I will do so wherever possible. I recognise however that it's simply not possible to please everyone, all the time because different people are pleased or displeased by different things according to their own moral compass, and their own life experiences. Sometimes, even when I behave impeccably, it may displease someone because it could reflect back to that person something that feels out of control in their own life. My success, or willingness to experiment, may make them feel inferior or envious, causing them to show displeasure towards me. I will therefore aim to please, and be accepted, but not to the detriment of my own path. I have the right to make my own choices and to learn from my own mistakes if necessary, as do others. Nobody really has a right to judge me providing that I am acting within what I believe to be the best of my integrity at the time. I cannot live entirely for other people because that dishonours my own path, which is unique. That includes making mistakes. Nobody is perfect, and everybody is learning. If someone is displeased with me for something I do or don't do, then I can and do feel okay about that".

The idea is to write what is meaningful and believable for you. You may not believe a re-written statement entirely. That is fine. In CBT we use percentages as a measure of belief. Initially we are simply bringing awareness to other possible perspectives. We work on feeling their truth, increasing our belief, with practice and repetition.

The important point is that you identify inflexible (stifling, stress-provoking, disempowering) terms like "must, should, have-to, always, never, can't, only" etc, and replace them with flexible "room to breathe" language. This may include the words "prefer, like to, may be able to do some, sometimes, could, will, try, maybe, may be, can, okay to" etc. Note the use of the word "cannot" in, "I cannot control how others perceive me". Here the use of the word is *appropriate in context*. Likewise, sometimes "should" is appropriate. If you are ill, you *should* go to the doctors. If your friends insist that you should get a better looking girlfriend, it's none of their business! You'd be wise here to get better friends, and disregard their "should". This exercise is designed to get you thinking about *inappropriate* use of inflexible language.

146

CATCHING INFLEXIBLE RULES IN ACTION

Inflexible rules are amongst the key culprits when it comes to ongoing chronic anxiety. It is one thing to understand this as a principle, but it's quite another to actually put it into practice in your life. The presence of inflexible rules often goes un-noted. While we may think or feel that we're doing all we can to alleviate anxiety, closer examination of our thought patterns can be quite revealing.

The following exercise will help you to be better informed about how much inflexible anxiety-provoking thinking you do, and subsequently, endorse. It's not always possible to pull out a notebook at work and start writing, but the idea is to "jot" down the thoughts as they occur, and note how they make you feel. Failing that, just remember them and write them down later.

Thought: "I'll always be anxious".   **Mood/s**: Afraid. Desperate. Helpless.

These can be put through the CBT machine later when you have more time. The kinds of thoughts which support anxiety are those which could be called absolute. That is, inflexible, like the statement above. "Always" is a pretty alarming thought given the context. How might we soften this to something a) more honest and realistic b) less arousing? Answer: "I am having a wobbly moment. Tomorrow may be better. I know how to sit with this. I have learned in the past that these feelings can settle when I create the right conditions for that to happen."

The thoughts that are most likely to disturb you emotionally are ones beginning with the following:-

I am, I will be, I can't, I'm always, I'll never, I should, I must, I ought to, It is, I feel, He/She/They think, I know, I have to, What if, I'm only. All "absolute" statements.

If you are physically able to do so, jot down recurring thoughts you have which could be called inflexible or absolute. This may sound like a lot of work because there may be many thoughts. However, as noted earlier, there are really only a "top ten" themes at most. Though the thoughts may differ in their actual wording, you'll find that they are mostly about the same thing/s. The key is to identify the themes which are playing out, and sum up what they are telling you. Do this for a few days. You will see a pattern emerge.

Example Thoughts:-

"I am miserable. I can't see how I'm ever going to feel right again" "Everyone else looks happy, why can't I feel okay?" "My life is always screwed up" "What's the point? It will only go wrong".

What's the key theme here? Basically the theme is that "Life is hopeless". This is being promoted and endorsed as an absolute. Though there's no disputing that the person having these thoughts may be feeling this strongly at this present moment, the point here is to recognise that this assessment is not completely true all the time, and that we are needlessly disturbing ourselves by endorsing it. Now we go about looking for exception and counter evidence to this crippling belief.

Why do this? It's so that you are learning to recognise these thoughts when they arise (being mindful), and also so that you can remind yourself that there is a reason that you feel anxiety. All the while you are having such thoughts and discounting them as a cause of anxiety, you are effectively telling yourself that your anxiety is a mystery, which then makes you feel more hopeless because solution looks ever more unlikely. In fact, bringing awareness to the presence of disturbing thoughts puts us back in a position of power to start doing something about them!

So, while there is much more that could be said here, if you want to investigate CBT in more depth that's someone else's book I'm afraid, at least for now. I just wanted to share enough here to give you a little bit of understanding. Then, you may choose to learn more in your own time.

I want to move on now from our discussion of head and heart to look at the practicalities of how we can make our whole lives a fear-free space to be in.

CHAPTER FIVE – SOLUTIONS - THE IMPORTANCE OF HAVING NEEDS MET

PRACTICAL MATTERS...NO...PRACTICAL...MATTERS!

We've talked about how to handle fear both emotionally, and intellectually. We have looked at becoming better equipped to deal with the presence of difficult feelings. We've looked at how negative thinking can disturb us emotionally, and we've provided the necessary understanding to counter those disturbing thinking styles.

The next important area to investigate then is what has caused us to become fearful in the first place? If we can identify what's been making us anxious, we'll be in a much stronger position to eliminate those stressors, and create some peace. One area that warrants particular attention is the landscape of our lives generally.

When we open our eyes in the morning, what do we see before us? Do we open our eyes to another day of boredom, drudgery, workplace stress, and hopelessness? Or do we open our eyes to a day of fulfilling activity? Though CBT is quick to labour the point that our emotions respond to what we make of situations rather than the situations themselves, we can see that there is a limit to how far most of us are either able, or willing, to take this understanding. It's all very well putting an hour a day of CBT into practice, but if the circumstances of your life are miserable, you're probably trying to use a bucket of water to extinguish a two storey fire. It's not always about adjusting your responses to situations. Sometimes, you need to change the situation itself!

Joe Griffin and Ivan Tyrell are the authors of "Human Givens: A new approach to emotional health and clear thinking." They point out that human beings do have certain basic needs, and when these needs are not adequately met, emotional disturbance is much more likely. Their book must surely be recognised as one of the most important recent contributions to modern psychology, and indeed, many of their insights contribute significantly to the picture presented here. Their flagship book is entitled "Human Givens" because, they say, certain things, like the basic need for security, human interaction, intimacy, purpose, and problem-solving, are a "given". Though not a new idea in and of itself, their exploration of the theme is somewhat ground-breaking, and presents to us clearly just how important it is that we have our lives in basic order as a strategy for avoiding anxiety and depression. Having one's life in order, having one's needs met, is the principle that underpins Solution-Focussed Brief Therapy.

SOLUTION FOCUSSED BRIEF THERAPY – WHAT'S IT ALL ABOUT?

Solutions, sweet soothing solutions! Solutions are like magic ointment which can soothe emotional arousal. Usually they're available if we take the time to look for them. We're back here to skills and resources, but now we'll explore the application.

Solution Focussed Brief Therapy (SFBT) is simple. Solution-Focussed means focusing on building solutions to current difficulties. Brief Therapy means that it is time-limited, and doesn't go on indefinitely. "Brief" here means comparatively brief. In older forms of therapeutic intervention one might expect to undertake hundreds or in some cases even thousands of hours of therapy to sort out one's neuroses' over periods of years using an often painful introspective process of analysing emotional wounds, dysfunctions, and personal relationship dynamics. This is unnecessary, and possibly ineffective. Solution focussed brief therapy recognises that with the exclusion of really serious traumas or bereavements, we are generally unaffected emotionally by anything that happened more than three months in the past. Our disturbance today is generated on a daily basis. The past may continue to affect us, in so much as the patterns of behaviour and thought that were created by past events may continue to cause on-going anxiety today, but the recognition here is that the actual stress we feel on any given day is being generated now. It has not been "carried over" from a long distant event. This may well feel quite difficult to believe because looking back it's easy to see the time line as one long period of stress. It appears to be the case that the cause of today's anxiety is in the past. In fact, with a clearer perspective we can see that many people do go through difficult times and bounce back naturally because they re-establish positive

150

patterns of activity and thoughts once the situation has passed. If we haven't bounced back, then it's largely because negative patterns have taken hold which continue to generate on-going stress long after the original difficulty has passed. Ivan Tyrell and Joe Griffin even go so far as to suggest that theoretically we can solve depression in a twenty four hour cycle by ceasing negative rumination. They do go on to acknowledge that the practicality of actually dealing with the causes of rumination will take much longer to resolve, but the principle remains relevant. If you could magically stop ruminating in a single moment, your anxiety or depression would theoretically disappear within 24 hours. Anxiety and depression eats rumination and worry to sustain itself!

Personally, I don't subscribe entirely to this view. If you measure the levels of cortisol and adrenaline in a stressed/anxious person you will find that those levels are elevated. This is no secret. One theory suggests that with prolonged stress, the adrenal glands, which produce epinephrine (adrenaline) can become overworked leading to a condition known as Adrenal Fatigue. To the best of my knowledge this is currently not well-recognised by the orthodox medical profession, except in conditions where adrenal dysfunction is a known symptom, such as Addison's disease. The good news is that even if it is a valid condition, we know that when stress levels are reduced over a period of time, and attention is paid to good diet, then adrenaline and cortisol levels tend to drop back to normal levels. Whichever way you look at it, the solution is to reduce your stress levels and give your adrenal glands the rest and recovery time they need. In my experience, anxiety and depression don't heal overnight. It takes time, but not years when the conditions are right for healing to occur.

It is now widely understood that when you actively work on solutions you are stimulating the left pre-frontal cortex of the brain which is the part of the brain most closely associated with executive-function. If you remember the importance of this part of the brain in maintaining feelings of control then it's wise to give it a regular work out as often as possible.

A large scale study undertaken by the US Government Agency for Healthcare Research and Quality (AHCPR) into the most effective treatments for mild to moderate depression found that therapy:

* Should be an active process.

* Should be time-limited (and not go on indefinitely).

* Should focus on solving current problems (and not on rehashing old issues).

* Should specifically aim for symptom reduction as a goal (rather than assuming the symptoms will disappear if some deeper abstract personality issue gets resolved).

These are nice clear guidelines for successful therapy. The AHCPR does not go so far as to spell it out explicitly, but we can see that these are essentially the components of what is now commonly known as Solution-Focussed Brief Therapy (SFBT).

Solutions create hope. Hope makes a brain happy. There's nothing a brain likes less than feeling all hemmed in. So when your brain gets snagged or stuck on an obstacle, the very best thing you can do is build a solution. When you find a solution to a problem you get a little "feel good" chemical reward from your brain to let you know you did a good job. This is evolution again. Life rewards problem solving. Solving problems gives you a buzz. When you are in problem solving mode you are inviting yourself to step out of the emotional mind and into the left pre-frontal cortex. The left pre-frontal cortex is the part of your brain which enjoys the greatest degree of "control". When you are in control, there's no need to be anxious because being in control means that you are less vulnerable to powerlessness. When you're less vulnerable, there's less to avoid, so the fear response is increasingly unnecessary. We can choose to use our problem solving brain. Unfortunately, when anxious, it can be so easy to simply forget we ever had one! If we don't use our problem solving brain, then our emotional mind will try to figure it out all by itself using emotion alone, and since our emotional mind tends to see the worst in things when anxious, we're not likely to feel too great about what it comes up with - usually more negative emotion!

If you are feeling bad or hopeless, ask yourself what "problem" you are snagged on right now, and switch the focus from why do I have a problem, to how can I create a solution?

Avoid asking yourself "why" there is a problem in response to a momentary anxiety. This is different from educating yourself as to the rationale of anxiety and enquiring into solutions. That's why you are reading this book. That is a healthy "Why?" I'm referring here to an urgent moment of "I have to know what's wrong!" An urgent need to have an immediate answer to an anxious feeling will encourage a flood of internal dialogue that actually has the opposite effect of solving your problem. We're back to "I **must** have an answer...." and we know where that leads. What it gives you is an increase in intensity of thought relative to your sense of urgency. Much as this masquerades as problem solving, it is anything but. It actually has the effect of simply stirring up confusion, racing thoughts, and emotional overload. Stop asking "why" in your internal dialogue. That question has been well and truly answered at this point in the book. You now know why people become anxious. For everyday anxiety-busting you need to stay focussed in your everyday life on "how" to create solution. Solution-focussed therapy asks instead: How would you like things to be?

The miracle question is: "If we could give you a miracle tonight and when you wake up tomorrow you are a nine or a ten on your one to ten well-being scale (i.e things are great), what is different when you open your eyes?"

This question asks you to step into a solution-focussed mode of thinking. It asks you only to think of solutions and move away for a moment from your perceived problems. It shows us what our goals are, and highlights which areas of our lives are currently unsatisfactory. Interestingly, in practice, some people actually struggle quite a bit when considering the miracle question. I've often seen people become visibly upset by it. This fact alone is very telling. Though no blame is implied, it does highlight just how far we've wandered from supplying our poor old limbic system with anything resembling hope! Without such input, the limbic system quite literally has nothing else to work with. Though it may seem impersonal, and perhaps unfair, that our limbic system is quite so void of intellect, we need to recognise that this is the way it is. If we are to lead a positive anxiety-free life, we need to at least consider the possibility of how that might look for us, even if it is a bit scary to start hoping that things could be better. We need to start thinking in solutions. If we focus only on problems, the limbic system has little choice but to respond accordingly. The help of a good therapist, or even a good friend, can be invaluable here. If you're really unsure of where to begin, ask others for their input. Perhaps someone else can remind you, or help you to see more clearly where your joy, ambitions, and strengths lie.

Of course we can't necessarily supply the overnight miracle, but we can take steps that will bring us closer to the type of lives that we would like to be leading. Every step towards that lifestyle will create an improved sense of well-being. It's absolutely not about having everything in our lives perfect. It's simply about movement, building solutions, creating hope, and taking action. Failure to change unsatisfactory circumstances creates emotional arousal, and leaves us feeling trapped. Our work here is to overcome any emotional or mental obstacles which are stopping you from creating the life you want. Usually that's fear itself. Bearing in mind that our job is to reduce your levels of emotional arousal, there are some very obvious circumstances which can often be contributing to the continuation of anxiety, depression, or anger, which should not be overlooked. The following is a list of obvious emotional arousers, but is certainly not exhaustive:-

Allergies/Medical Problems/Medications. Too much/not enough responsibility. Involved in a negative relationship. Ignoring your own needs. Alcohol misuse. Drug misuse. Lack of exercise. Caffeine misuse (Caffeine is a powerful stimulant, and can aggravate anxiety).Poor diet/dehydration. Disempowerment - A lack of power or influence over one's life. Poor sleep (Also a response to stress as well as a cause). Victimisation (Being bullied). Losing a loved one (Bereavement, or the loss of a relationship). Family difficulties (Children, sexual difficulties, divorce, lack of intimacy). Boredom/lack of direction in life. A lack of time to do everything that needs to be done. Poor self-image/lack of self-worth. Guilt, blame and shame. (Punishing yourself). Financial difficulties (Debt). Work pressure. Illness. Loneliness. Etcetera

In Solution Focussed Thinking we recognise that there are three main areas we need to have working for us. They are:

Job (or vocation).

Our relationships.

Our self-concept.

If any one of these areas is seriously compromised or feeling out of control, it will contribute to high emotional arousal levels. The rule is that it's never about just one area alone. We cannot attribute more than fifty percent of our overall anxiety levels to any single area because you simply don't have a fantastic job and a terrible self-concept, or for that matter, fantastic relationships and a terrible self-concept. Control, we say, is a constant, meaning the level of control you have in one area generally you have in every area. Though maybe not completely true in all situations, it's true most of the time. Part of anxiety-busting is making sure we have the practical everyday stuff in order too. It might seem obvious, but if we really hate our job, and it's not that we're just being negative, but that we are really being bullied at work (as an example only), underpaid, or are just bored to tears, then we will need to change our job, deal with the bullies, or ask for more varied work and a pay rise. Something has to change. It's unlikely that we'll tackle our anxiety fully without addressing the cause of misery.

This understanding can be broadly summarised as ensuring that our needs are being met. The above understanding reminds us that we have needs in all of these areas. For instance, we "need" to have a reason to be. This will be covered by our job or vocation. It's our vocation that gives us our feeling of purpose. Purpose motivates us to get out of bed in the morning. We operate most effectively when we are driven by a sense of purpose. Our vocation can cover anything from having a hobby, to volunteering, to being a mum, or being the CEO of a multinational corporation. You don't have to be culturally classed as "successful" in order to be satisfied with your vocation. It just means that what you do, you are happy with. You could be being paid nothing, but if you like it, then that counts as satisfied. Not having any sense of purpose can feel rather depressing.

Our relationships feed our "need" to be loved, acknowledged, and wanted. Our ancestors were not solitary. They survived as a "pack". For our ancestors, to be ousted from the pack would have meant probable death because it would have been almost impossible to survive alone. Today we are still hard wired to seek acceptance from others. When relationships are not harmonious therefore we can really feel quite anxious about it. Self-concept is important. There are a number of implications here. Put simply though, it is important that we like ourselves...warts and all. It's fine to have aspirations for self-improvement, but in the meantime, being at war with oneself is another sure way to be emotionally unwell. Unfortunately, being at war with oneself is much more common than you'd think. In therapy we often discover that there are serious conflicts between "parts" of ourselves. We frequently see this in anxiety or depression. One part "feels terrible" and another part hates the part that feels terrible, as discussed earlier. When we step into the part that feels terrible and then receive what it feels like to be hated for feeling terrible, we begin to get some insight into how we can easily end up at war with ourselves. You now have some insight into how to be kinder to yourself in such situations. If you are still practicing your acceptance exercises, try this:-"I hear and accept that you are feeling terrible. I'm sorry you have been struggling. I'm working on making things better."

Also, if we are not taking control in the areas which are troubling us, we can end up hating ourselves for drinking, eating, smoking, spending too much etc. Self-forgiveness is another important area to be aware of. Apparently, we are our own harshest judges, and we will dish out relentless self-punishment if we feel it is merited. Usually this is an unconscious process. If we can bring these battles into the light of consciousness with kindness, we can begin to heal the rift that has developed, and ultimately change the situation.

So, solution-focussed thinking involves identifying how we want things to be, and then using that information as a compass setting for our lives. While it is fair to recognise that huge changes may feel somewhat out of reach immediately, we can start with simple things, and they too will help. In fact often, these small changes will bring about enough change in the landscape of our lives that what we were seeing as a huge intractable problem can actually fall away quite naturally, and simply be forgotten about. If you think about what you've learned so far this will make sense. By improving wellbeing and reducing negative emotional arousal, we naturally shift away from limbic system rumination towards frontal lobe control. Since nine tenths of any anxiety related problem is limbic system related it follows naturally that when we're using the solution-creating frontal-lobe brain we're no longer "stuck" in our perceived problems.

There is a lovely story called The African Queen of Milwaukee, often told about Milton Erickson, one of the grandfathers of modern hypnotherapy. Milton had just one day to visit with a lady in Milwaukee, who he had been told, suffered from terrible depression. As he walked through her house he noticed that the house was in great disorder. They soon arrived at a room full of cuttings of African Violets. These were her pride and joy. He remarked that it must be nice to share these plants. "Oh no" she said "I don't give them away". Milton, seeing an opportunity continued, "Here you are with all this money, time on your hands, and a green thumb. And, it's all going to waste. What I recommend is that you get a copy of your church membership list and then look in the latest church bulletin. You'll find announcements of births, illnesses, graduations, engagements, and marriages in there, all the happy and sad events in the lives of people in the congregation. Make a number of African Violet cuttings and get them well-established. Then re-pot them in gift pots and have your handyman drive you to the homes of people who are affected by these happy or sad events. Bring them a plant, and your congratulations or condolences, whichever is appropriate to the situation." Though the statement made the lady bristle, she agreed as a good Christian she could be doing more.

When she died ten years later there was an article published in the local Milwaukee newspaper entitled – "African Violet Queen of Milwaukee Dies, Mourned by Thousands." The article detailed her life, and paid homage to her trademark flowers and charitable work within the local community in the ten years preceding her death.

When Milton was asked how he knew what was the right thing to do he explained that he knew he had only one day to help this lady. He said that it would not be possible to root out her depression in such a short time, so he reasoned that he could perhaps help her to "grow" the areas of her life that could bring joy and satisfaction. This story illustrates perfectly the principle of solution focussed thinking.

SALAD DRESSING

Consider a bottle of oil and vinegar dressing. When at rest, the two liquids separate, and the olive oil will float to the top of the bottle while the vinegar sits at the bottom. Let's imagine that the vinegar is everything that's okay in our lives, and that the olive oil is everything that we perceive as not okay. From a solution-focussed perspective there is only so much room in the bottle. If we start to pour more vinegar into the bottle, the vinegar will sink to the bottom and will displace the oil which will naturally spill out. If we keep pouring, eventually there will be no space left for oil, and the whole bottle will be full of vinegar. This is really what solution focussed thinking is all about. There is no space left for depression or anxiety if our lives are already filled with stuff that's working. So, logic dictates therefore, that if we continue to make progress in filling our lives up with things that make us happy, we will eventually simply displace anxiety and depression. In practice this is generally true.

THE MIRACLE QUESTION EXPLORED

"The Miracle Question" underpins the whole solution focussed-enterprise. Though it can be adapted to pretty much any situation, it assumes that the problem has been solved, and then works backwards from there. It asks how that would look/feel/be. So the question, again:-

The miracle question is: "If we could give you a miracle tonight and when you wake up tomorrow you are a nine or a ten on your one to ten well-being scale (i.e things are great), what is different when you open your eyes?"

So let's look at a fictional but typical Miracle Question response:-

158

I wouldn't be worrying all the time. I'd be drinking less alcohol. I'd be getting more exercise. I'd have a girlfriend. I'd re-train as an electrician. I'd have things to look forward to. I'd have more fun stuff in my life. I'd lose ten pounds in weight. I'd be appreciating what I have rather than focusing on what I don't have. I'd feel proud of who I am and what I've achieved.

I'd like you to be the therapist for a moment. How can we help this person? What needs to happen here? If we achieved just one of these goals how might that affect the others? What suggestions could you offer for how to take small steps towards achieving some of these desires? Please do take a few moments to stop reading and just give this some serious consideration. If it helps, write down your answers...

Done it? Good!

Are you surprised by how much good solution-focussed thinking you can bring to the table? So, as the therapist you then set about sharing your insight with your client. What happens next? Your client says "Yes...but....." and explains why there is no way they can meet that need. No doubt you will meet with the same resistances when you attempt to create solutions for yourself. So here's a tool.

If you find your thinking is somewhat plagued by "yes...but" then keep the following in mind. If you are in the habit of saying "I know I could do X but...I'm too scared", remember that the word "but" is a deletion word. The word "but" deletes everything that went before it, making it seemingly irrelevant or impossible. Try using language that's structured as follows. "I know I could do X and...by the power of flowers, I think I will!" Alternatively, you can switch your sentences around so that the word "but" deletes the disempowered part. For example, "I'm really scared to change my job *but* I'm sure I can make it happen if I stay positive." Be mindful of this. It can make a big difference to what seems possible!

When creating solutions use the word "and" instead of "but", or switch your phrasing so that "but" deletes disempowering statements.

159

Now it doesn't look quite so impossible does it? Challenging it may still be, but no longer impossible. So, what would happen if we gained some control in just one of these areas? Do you see how that control would invariably feed into all of these other areas? You could start anywhere here and make an improvement. Does this person really need therapy to make some of these changes? Let's take as a starting point. "I'd be getting more exercise". With some simple adjustments this could happen. Maybe our client could park further away from work and build in an hour a day walking. Maybe we could find out what sports he likes, and encourage him to allocate one or two nights a week to visit the local sports centre with a friend. This alone would solve a number of points on the list. He'd be drinking less, losing weight, and doing more exercise. Making arrangements to meet a friend at the sports centre would make him feel more motivated to actually go because he now has a social contract which he wants to honour. He'll be feeling proud of himself because he's being constructive, and maybe, just maybe, he'd meet a nice girl at the badminton court! With his new fitter self, his confidence would improve, and he might actually find the courage to ask her out for dinner. Small changes can lead to massive improvements in life and wellbeing. While we know that realistically it doesn't always pan out quite as neatly as that, you can at least see the value in taking a solution-focussed approach to improving your wellbeing. However you frame it, it is lot more constructive than sitting at home ruminating on how terrible everything is and wondering why we're remaining so anxious!

If you're feeling "hemmed in" by your circumstances ask yourself honestly what you could be doing differently.

The principles of solution focussed thinking are as follows:-

* Become aware of repetitive patterns.

* If it's working, do more of it. If it's not working then do something differently.

* Small steps can lead to big changes.

* Developing solutions requires a different language to describing problems. Learn to speak "Solutionese!"

* You are not the problem. I am not the problem. The problem is the problem.

* Focus on what you want in the future, and how you're going to get it, instead of ruminating on what you don't want. Worrying is simply praying for what you don't want!

* Stop ruminating about the past. You cannot solve today's problems by feeling bad about past events.

* Describe how things are different when the problem is resolved, and then work backwards to today from that point. How did you get there?

* The future has not yet happened. It is not set in stone and remains negotiable. By defining clear goals and taking steps towards those goals, you massively increase your chances of leading the life you want to lead.

* You are not a victim of circumstance. You can create your own future starting today.

* Focus on what can be changed. Do not focus on what cannot be changed right now.

The Frontal Lobe Revisited – The most fabulous object in the World! Apparently the human brain is the most highly organised matter in the known universe. There is a popular urban myth circulating that we only use 10% of our brain's capacity. This myth has prevailed for over 100 years despite clear evidence to the contrary. We do in fact use all of our brain.

Phineas Gage, who we mentioned earlier, gave us our first scientific insight into the role of the frontal lobe. We've since learned a lot more about the frontal lobe and a good way of thinking about what it does is to think of it as a "future experience synthesizer". If you think about it, it's a pretty advanced piece of kit. You can have an experience before you have it. Imagine please...

So there you are. It's December. You're on the seafront and you're wondering whether you should take off all your clothes and run naked into the sea/mud? You don't actually need to do it to know it's probably not a good idea. You can run the process "virtually" in your frontal lobe and "imagine" what that experience will be like. If your virtual frontal lobe simulation of that experience tells you it will be a fantastic experience, then you'll throw caution to the wind along with your clothes and get wet. But if your simulation says otherwise, you will receive a feeling, courtesy of the limbic system, which tells you to avoid that situation.

Now consider. What kind of future experience simulations do you run on a day to day basis in your frontal lobe? Are you running simulations of solutions (which supply feel-good feelings), or of problems? When you consider how immediately your feelings respond to those mental event simulations, note how important it is to use your frontal lobe future experience simulator positively. Imagination is a wonderful tool, but misuse of the imagination can cause unnecessary emotional arousal. We'll say more about this in a bit.

LEARNING TO BE MORE COMFORTABLE IN THE PRESENCE OF DISCOMFORT

Getting comfortable with discomfort is possibly the most important skill a person can learn in life. In some ways we have spent our whole lives learning how to do it well. How many things which were once uncomfortable for you do you now accept without difficulty? As children we are bored if we are not entertained every minute of every day. As you have grown up you have probably learned to value/make use of your quiet time. What child welcomes being asked to clean their room? (If your children do then you are a very lucky parent!) And yet, as you have grown you have learned to appreciate that cleaning can be therapeutic. Exercise can be uncomfortable, painful even. Have you learned to welcome exercise and feel good about doing it anyway? I for one have had to train myself to eat vegetables. It never came naturally for me. Do you now eat foods you once disliked? Sure, taste buds change, but you do what's healthy first and foremost. What else that may be considered essentially uncomfortable have you learned to accept as comfortable in your life? Work? Having to be somewhere when you might prefer to kick back for the day in the sunshine? Having children screaming and making a mess in your house? Bureaucracy? Taxes? We could go on. The point is though, not everything in life is naturally "comfortable", is it?

You have a natural ability to desensitise yourself to discomfort.

You have been doing it your whole life. You are reasonably expert in the art of being comfortable with discomfort. Do people still live "happy" lives despite having to work, look after children, pay taxes, eat sprouts, go jogging, and fill out forms? Yes, of course many people do. In fact, studies have shown that many people who live disadvantaged lives are just as likely to feel "happy" with their lives as those apparently advantaged by wealth etc. Apparently, people synthesize happiness when they are happy with their circumstances, regardless of what those circumstances are. We all know that there are many disadvantaged/disabled people who lead truly fulfilling lives. One case in point is Nick Vujicic, a gentleman born with no arms or legs, who runs the "Life Without Limbs" project. He is a now an international motivational speaker, and if you web search him you will find video footage of him bringing rooms full of people, including children, to tears. He wrote the book Life Without Limits: Inspiration for a Ridiculously Good Life. He may be an extraordinary person, but he's a living example of the power of a positive outlook, and our ability to adapt when we choose positivity. If we know people do it, then it is shown to be possible.

So the assumption that the presence of discomfort in our lives means we cannot be happy is fundamentally flawed.

What happens though if you don't learn to be okay with the everyday discomforts of life? Stress is what happens. Raging is what happens. Feeling trapped/cheated/anxious/angry at life is what happens. We resent the kids, hate our boss, get angry in traffic, eat too much, drink too much, manage our money badly, feel irritated, impatient, irrational, emotional, and out of control. We're certainly not happy when we're not okay with discomfort. We'll be even more deeply unhappy if we believe that life should be consistently comfortable because now we feel cheated too. If we're expecting life to be completely comfortable in every moment, we will be constantly disappointed when life does not meet our expectations. We'll look at everyone else and say "Well they seem happy...why am *I* having such a hard time?" (They're okay incidentally because they are good at being comfortable with discomfort, not because they don't have any!) Feeling constantly disappointed that life isn't meeting one's expectations feels very much like something is "wrong". The "wrong" feeling is read by the emotional mind as a threat, and as you know, being threatened creates anxiety. In fact it's clearly a cognitive mistake to believe that life should, or must be comfortable at all times because it's just not.

To be happy, it is not necessary to have a life free from discomfort. To expect life to be free from discomfort is the surest way to remain unhappy. True happiness in life is created by accepting discomfort as an inevitable part of life, and learning to be comfortable in its presence.

A common occurrence with anxiety and depression is the presence of negative and disturbing thoughts. In a worldwide survey approximately 80% of the Worlds' population said that they experience disturbing thoughts sometimes. What is particularly interesting about this study is that the results are the same across cultures. It doesn't matter where you ask the question or who you ask, 80% of us say we are sometimes troubled by negative and disturbing thoughts. So it seems that negative thoughts are simply part of being human and owning a brain. Owning a brain that is currently overloaded increases the prevalence and intensity of these thoughts. So you can stop being alarmed that you had a wicked, alarming, or unpleasant thought now ok? It doesn't make you a bad person. It doesn't make you damaged. It just means you have a brain. Though we can't necessarily immediately stop negative thoughts happening, we can clearly learn to relate to them as a by-product of having a brain. Then we can stop becoming so emotionally aroused by them, while continuing to practice critical thinking. It should by now be clear to you that the same is also true for feelings. Everybody has difficult and uncomfortable feelings to deal with sometimes. The trick is to cultivate an ability to be comfortable with them. I guarantee you that you will have negative feelings to deal with in life, but you can become so expert in dealing with them that, like eating sprouts and paying your taxes (you know I really don't like sprouts) they will cease to be a significant problem.

SYNTHESIZING HAPPINESS – IT'S NOT "OVER THERE" APPARENTLY!

A relatively little-known fact is that we are apparently cursed with a very poor ability to predict accurately what will make us happy. Dan Gilbert, professor of psychology at Harvard University, and author of the book "Stumbling on Happiness", has some very enlightening information for us. I thoroughly recommend his highly entertaining TED talk on the subject available on You Tube. Though his idea is still considered somewhat contentious in certain circles (though I don't really know why?) his basic premise is that...

...more choice makes us less happy with what we have. Apparently, it's really true that the grass is always greener on the other side.

He makes a very good case for this, quoting statistics that show that after one year, groups that became paraplegic (wheelchair bound), and groups that won big on the lottery, were relatively speaking, equally happy. That doesn't imply that both groups are bounding with joy. Much as we might think winning the lottery would make us extremely happy, we know in fact there are, believe it or not, downsides to doing so. Equally, there are up-sides to becoming wheel chair bound. These are not of course apparent to our future-predicting hardware. Given the choice, who would not choose the lottery win? This is really the point that he makes. We assume that more or better will make us happier. Thus we may never really take the time to settle into where we are, and never be truly comfortable with it. Constantly reaching for more or better will often make us fundamentally unhappy. His research data collected through tests of satisfaction versus choice shows very clearly that those given more choice tend to be less happy with what they have, whereas those with little choice tend to feel relatively happy with they have. It can explain certainly why today we have so much, and yet tend to be so unhappy. My Grandmother really did say that the war years

165

were the best years of her life, despite living in London while it was constantly bombed, owning little, and having to work for next to nothing. I saw her eyes light up as she spoke to me about the good things that were happening in those days, amongst all the difficulty. She clearly remembered them with great fondness, and clearly she managed to synthesize happiness somehow, despite the dark circumstances. Earlier, we talked about the folly of chasing status and esteem. Understanding that we synthesize happiness rather than win it by completion of some grand plan explains this rather nicely too.

Now it doesn't go un-noticed that this data conflicts somewhat with much of what's been said so far with regards to solution-focussed therapy, which is all about improvement in circumstances. I think we have to exercise common sense in interpreting this data. The centrally important message here is not that we should not want, or choose more choice, but that we can be more aware that it's easy to make the mistake of thinking that we can only be happy if... When it comes to discomfort, the best strategy is really to make the best of it for now while keeping solutions in focus. We really do need to change what's fundamentally not working for us, but we also need to learn to appreciate "what is" in the meantime, even if some of it is challenging. Happiness is potentially right here, right now, even if there is some discomfort present too.

DEALING WITH CURRENTLY INSOLUBLE PROBLEMS

Sometimes of course, a problem is, for the time being, insoluble. Sometimes things occur in life that we can't have an answer to, or assurance of, immediately. How do we synthesize positive expectation when we can't know how something will turn out? Then we need to be able to put the problem to one side (to compartmentalise) so that we can get on with our lives without undue anxiety. If we can't think something constructive about a situation, then once we've thought it through as far as possible to solution, we need to stop thinking about it at all, for now. This isn't easy, but it is necessary. Remember that life usually has a way of working out. With the exception of permanent conditions, problems rarely last indefinitely. Most of the time they resolve with less fuss than we'd anticipated and things move on. How many times have you been in a position where you felt like your World was ending only to have forgotten about it a month later following resolution?

The real problem as far as emotional disturbance is concerned is that we feel like we must know how resolution will come about. When we tell ourselves we must have an answer, the emotional brain is then compelled to obsess in an effort to know the unknowable, and control the uncontrollable. Sometimes however, this feeling is occurring simply because we're not thinking things through to solution, and are mistakenly becoming snagged only on the problem. Here is a short exercise which can help you in such situations. It seems like common sense as you read through it but be aware that the value is in the doing of it. It's one thing to understand an approach intellectually. It's quite a different experience to actually do it.

SITUATIONAL ANXIETY – WORRY VERSUS SOLUTION BUILDING

The subconscious mind seeks closure, and doesn't do very well with ambiguity, particularly when we are feeling stressed or anxious generally. As you'll no doubt recognise by now, as stress increases we lose a certain amount of access to our frontal lobe functions which are: Logic, Reason, Planning and Control. What this means in practice is that we are more easily disturbed or "sideswiped" by "irrational" and disturbing conclusions about the likelihood of a disaster occurring. Since the limbic system is easily aroused by future projections of negative outcomes, this is not at all helpful when we are seeking to reduce anxiety.

The problem with ambiguity, or a lack of closure, is that the subconscious mind can embark on a background mission of "What if?!" We may not be fully aware of this process consciously, but we will feel the anxiety in a big way if we leave that process unchecked. The antidote to this situational anxiety therefore is to define the problem more clearly and find solutions. Remember that anxiety blocks solution, so it's a mistake to assume that we'll be able to just "know" what our options are unless we sit down and map them out formally. If we don't do this, what will happen is that the problem will remain vague and undefined, and knock around in the background of our awareness, creating chaos as it unfolds a million scenarios of how things might go wrong, without any reference to solution. This leaves us with an emotional sense that we are helpless or hopeless, and this of course creates feelings of anxiety and depression. In order to minimise our anxiety in the presence of such ambiguity it's necessary to ask the right questions.

The following questions will help you to deal with this runaway process and recognise more clearly what options are available to you. By clearly defining your options you are much better placed to see that things are probably not as bad as you feel they are. The worst case scenario is probably not as "stuck" a position as it currently feels. Having it written out, and addressed, will usually give you a much greater peace of mind.

* Define the "vague" worry. What exactly do you perceive might happen? What is the worst that could happen?

* Realistically, what is the likelihood of this occurring? (Use a percentage i.e 40% likely)

* What other more positive outcomes might or could occur? (Define the percentage of likelihood of each outcome).

* Are there any steps you can take right now, or in the near future, that will decrease the likelihood of the worst case scenario occurring? How could you implement these? Create an action plan.

* If the worst case scenario were to occur, what options would be available to you to move through to solution? ("Freak out" is not the right answer...try again with something more constructive!) Define your options clearly. Do not list only options that are comfortable. Define ALL your options. Though some of them may not be comfortable, they may still be much less anxiety-provoking than your worst fear, which is the current worry!

* Will the situation eventually be resolved? If so, how, and when?

If you use this method, do take a pen to paper. The temptation may be to scan the questions and answer them in your mind, but writing has a solidifying effect emotionally, and leaves you with a physical symbol of clarity that you can return to if you need to. Be methodical and rational in your thinking, not emotional or cyclical. Think it through to solution even if the solution is to know that right now, you can't know. Then you must put the problem, for now, to one side. Clear thought is tremendously empowering. By using clear thought you can stop those vague worries you've been having. Contingency plans are great anxiety busters. This is really as much as we can do in a situation like this. If we really can't see a resolution, then we're back to being as comfortable as we can be with the way things are.

There are some problems we just can't solve immediately, some things we can't know, and certain things we simply cannot control. This is never pleasant because we are creatures who like certainty, but we know that's not always possible. Raging against this fact can cause all kinds of problems, particularly obsessive ones. The way out, is to learn to accept that some things cannot be guaranteed, known, or changed. Uncertainty is a fact of life. We either meet that fact courageously or we suffer at the hands of ourselves by raging against the way things are".

Lord, Grant me the serenity to accept the things I cannot change, the courage to change the things I can, and the wisdom to know the difference.

You may already be familiar with the above poem/prayer. It pretty much sums up everything we've spoken about so far. It's little wonder then that these words resonate so powerfully with so many people. What we haven't really looked at in any detail yet though is the wisdom to know the difference. This is another way of asking what is or is not within my control.

CONTROL - HOW MUCH POWER DO YOU REALLY HAVE?

Take a moment to think about how important it is to assess the amount of control you have in any given situation before throwing yourself into it. In research, it has been shown that the strongest predictor of a depressive or anxious response is a lack of control over negative stimulus. Depressive episodes are driven by feelings of deep disappointment, or hopelessness and helplessness. We usually experience feeling helpless when we feel like something is, or will be, outside of our control. If it turns out that we have more control than we realise at first glance, then it follows that we may be feeling unnecessarily depressed by a sense of hopelessness. With a greater awareness of our options (control), we can challenge helplessness and take back our power. Similarly, if we believe that we have more power than we actually do in any given situation, we will end up frustrated and disappointed when things don't turn out the way we believe they "should", which also can create feelings of helplessness. Therefore, assessing "controllability" is another important skill to master for emotional wellbeing. There are two ways in which our sense of control can be distorted.

* *Believing that you have more control than you actually do in a situation – the illusion of control.*

* *Believing that you have less control than you actually do in a situation – the illusion of helplessness.*

Let's look at how these can disturb you.

* *Believing that you have more control than you actually do in a situation*.

This is called "The illusion of control". There are certain factors in life which are largely outside of our control. These include but are not limited to:

Other People. World Events. Illness. Ageing. Economic Uncertainty. Accidents. Reputation. Fairness. Death. Heredity. Job Security. Traffic. Weather. Our Childhood. Bureaucracy. Birth Status.

Many of these seem obvious, but still some people spend a lifetime bemoaning how awful it is that they are ageing or were born to poor/imperfect parents. I heard of a story of one lady dying at the age of ninety six who asked her physician "Why me?" Sometimes the obvious is not so obvious to everyone.

Believing that we should have control over uncontrollable factors is guaranteed to create emotional disturbance, and yet most of us do it in some form or another. Factors that are outside of our sphere of influence are naturally uncomfortable for us, but remember that CBT focuses on the simple premise that we become emotionally disturbed when we "endorse" or "buy into" irrational thinking. It's our job to become clear about what is really outside of our control, and then stop telling ourselves that we should be able to change things in these areas, or worse still, that things have gone wrong because we did or didn't do something. Sometimes "stuff happens" and it's nothing to do with what we did or didn't do. It just happened. Next then, the other side of the coin:-

* *Believing that you have less control than you actually do in a situation.*

The illusion of helplessness. Very often we have choices/options, but we don't realise that we do. Sometimes those choices are uncomfortable, or look too difficult to make. Then we can become paralysed, and we tell ourselves that there is nothing we can do, and believe it. What follows naturally then are feelings of helplessness, which in turn, can create anxiety and/or depression. There are many situations in which we can create the illusion of helplessness, including but not limited to:-

Working Situation. Relationships. Self-Healing. Finances. Addictions. Relationship to Food. Home Life. Social Status. Skill Levels. Confidence. Love-ability. Social Skills. Compulsions. Anxiety. Depression. Anger. Stress.

In every single one of the above situations there are steps you can take to improve things. The question is not really whether we "can" do something to improve things, but much more whether we "will"? When we talk about digging deeper, we're not really talking about working harder, although that may be necessary too. Really we are talking about not settling for the first explanation we give ourselves about how stuck we are. When we challenge our "stuck" assumptions, we can usually find other choices. Making changes requires courage, and it can seem that the price is too high or unaffordable but often our assessment of the price is based on a "feeling" rather than "facts". Sometimes that "feeling" is based on past experience, so before we go any further let's just remind ourselves of the power of past experience to limit our perception of what's possible today.

LEARNED HELPLESSNESS

Dr Martin Seligman carried out some famous research on learned helplessness. What he discovered is that when an animal (including some people) learns that a situation is inescapable, it simply stops trying to change it, or escape it. That's sensible enough it seems, but when the circumstances are changed so as to allow solution, no effort follows. Effectively, the subject has "learned helplessness", and makes no attempt at solution even though it is now possible.

Consider then that your assessment of what appears to be "hopeless" may in fact be based on outdated information. It is often the case that we are simply not seeing the potential solutions which are unfolding before us because we have "learned helplessness". One thing you can be sure of in life is change, and what seemed hopeless yesterday may well be soluble today. Just because you feel helpless, it doesn't make it a fact. Sometimes, to escape helpless, we need to think the unthinkable, or do the undoable. Remember the old CBT distortion of "emotional reasoning" that tells us with tongue in cheek that "Feelings are facts and to hell with the truth". So it is too with helplessness. One of my teachers said "If your client fights for their limitations then they get to keep them". This means simply that if you're determined to remain helpless, there is nobody in the world that can "control" that factor except yourself. It's up to you to understand that you do have choices, even if they are unpopular with you, and to recognise that the real enemy is "helplessness" itself, not the challenge that you are faced with. We will of course concede that there may be some situations where this is not true, but most of the time, it is.

LEARNED OPTIMISM

Dr Seligman also went on to publish a book in 1990 entitled "Learned Optimism". He points out that there are genuine health benefits to cultivating an optimistic outlook in life. He explains that pessimism is not by definition a fixed state. Instead he challenges us to recognise that it is possible to learn optimism as a skill set, by focusing primarily on explanatory style, that being how you explain the things that happen in life, to yourself. We can see immediately that there is a direct parallel here with CBT. The cornerstone of this understanding is as follows:

* **Permanence**: An optimistic outlook takes the view that negative events are transient and temporary, and perceives that good things happen for permanent reasons (i.e Kindness is a fact of being).

* **Pervasiveness**: To what degree do positive or negative events colour our entire lives? Optimistic people are able to pigeon-hole negative events so that they do not seep out into their lives as a whole. Therefore, a failure in one area is not seen as pervading life generally. Conversely, positive events are allowed to colour life generally positively. Pessimists allow isolated negative events to pervade their whole sense of life causing hopelessness to thrive, and create further pessimism, while seeing positives as mostly meaningless in the context of life as a whole.

* **Hope**: When explaining life's events, optimists will generally explain negative happenings by pointing towards temporary causes while pessimists will see negative causation as permanent and fixed (i.e The World is a bad place).

* **Personalisation**: What does this event say about me? An optimistic outlook sees a negative event as originating externally (circumstantially), whereas pessimists may blame themselves for all negative events.

In summary then, an optimistic outlook sees negative events as unlucky setbacks to be overcome while working towards goals, and positive events as evidence that life (eventually) rewards engagement, persistence, and trust. A pessimist sees negative events as inevitable failure waiting to happen, with no hope of any lasting success in the future. Positive events are considered meaningless moments of relief between inevitable catastrophes!

BLIND OPTIMISM

Blind optimism is my idea of a Monty Python'esque deletion of the negative (it's just a flesh wound!). When applied to real suffering, not only is this kind of optimism insulting to the human condition, it is also very unskilful. Life really does have a gritty, uncomfortable side to it, and endlessly-positive shiny people do no service to our quest for comfort. They simply make us feel like there must be something wrong with us if we're not endlessly positive. The truth is, life is sometimes very unfair. The truth is, as Scott-Peck points out, "Life is hard". Wellbeing demands that this fact is firmly faced and integrated. However, this is not reason alone to expect the worst as a matter of course.

The degree to which we may choose optimism over pessimism is strongly related to our early programming, and our subsequent ethical and philosophical outlook on life. Arguably, an optimistic outlook on life can be said to be a failure to look at the facts squarely. Pessimists take the position that "If you're not pissed off you're not paying attention!" However, there is a middle way, and blind pessimism is equally damaging. If you find yourself choosing pessimism, there is an important question to be answered. That question is this. "Is your pessimism damaging your sense of wellbeing and positive engagement in the World?" So goes Ghandi's quote "Be the change you want to see in the World". You are at your best when you are positively engaged in life. When you are at your best, you are also at your most effective.

I would argue that pessimism is philosophically well-intended but ultimately unskilful as a strategy for life.

The pessimistic assumption is that if we see the worst in things we are a) prepared, and b) better placed (motivated) to act. Intuitively this seems true, but in practice we find the opposite is so. Since a pessimistic outlook damages emotional health and wellbeing, we are in fact less well prepared, and less able to act, as a result. Pessimism also misses opportunity because expecting the worst quite literally blinds you to opportunity. An optimistic outlook is therefore the logical choice for best results in life. Just remember that there is a distinction to be made between blind optimism and an optimistic explanatory style. We can look realistically at the facts and still explain these facts in an optimistic way which encourages us to feel hopeful about ourselves, the World, other people, and the future. Often, this means that we feel inspired to take action. The assumption that optimists fail to act is flawed. In fact, optimism, by definition, looks for solution, and therefore encourages action. Optimists are not head in the clouds rose-tinted-specs-wearing lefties. They are people that figured out that continually seeing, and expecting the worst in things is a poor strategy for a good life. Optimists learn that looking for the best in things makes you feel better, and increases your chance of befriending opportunity.

LUCK

Professor Wiseman of the University of Hertfordshire set out to examine "luck". He asked for people who believed they were naturally lucky, and people who believed they were naturally unlucky to apply. In the experiment, he asked the two groups to count the pictures in a newspaper, and inside the newspaper he placed a large message saying "Tell the examiner you have seen this message and win £250". Many of the people who presented to join the "unlucky" group simply missed the message, despite the fact that it covered half a page! They were only looking for what they expected to find, pictures. The majority of those who considered themselves "lucky" spotted it and won their bonus payment. Optimism, it seems, really does help you to be more attuned to the presence of opportunity.

CHOICES AND RISK

"If what you are doing is working do more of it. If what you are doing isn't working then change it." This is the battle-cry of solution-focussed therapy. Changes however, require courage, and remember that courage isn't the absence of fear, but the determination that what you want/need is more important than the fear. If we are to be successful in our goals to change, they need to be S.M.A.R.T. That is Specific, Measurable, Achievable, Realistic, and Time Limited.

One of the main reasons that we don't implement change is that we fear that we either a) can't do it b) will make things worse c) will be too uncomfortable when making it happen. That's basically fear. Do remember that fear-based decision making is not a very productive way to live, and being afraid that we'll make things worse can often, though not always, be an emotionally based perception rather than a rational one.

If we're suffering because we're not making changes, and those changes are necessary for solution, then we need to cultivate courage.

In summary we're likely to suffer more if we don't change a pattern that's causing us distress, so it's a no-brainer when you put it to the rational assessment test. If we made all our decisions based on fear alone, we'd never achieve anything! As a colleague of mine recently said when asked how he knew what was the right thing to do in life "I figure out what fear tells me I can't do, and then I do that". This may not be good advice for everyone, but the spirit is admirable.

Change therefore does involve risk, but risk isn't intrinsically a bad thing. **Unexamined** risk is what causes problems because if we fail to accurately assess the risk of going into a given situation, then we can easily fall into the illusion of helplessness, or the illusion of control. Either way, the outcome is likely to be emotionally disturbing. Remember, we're asking right now "How much control do I really have?" Risk is intrinsically linked with control because the amount of control you have over the outcome of a given situation determines the level of risk you are taking. The more control you have, the less risk you are taking, and the more confident you can be that you are doing the right thing. The less control you have, the more risk you are taking. So, to more accurately assess the risk in any given situation, ask the following questions first. Write down your answers:

* What is the situation you wish to deal with?

* What factors are likely to determine the outcome?

* How much control do you have over each of these factors (list them with percentages)

* Add all of the percentages and divide your total by the number of factors for an average percentage of control.

* Use this figure to assess how much control you have over the outcome of the situation.

* Make a decision on whether to proceed with action, which takes into account how willing you are to enter a situation over which you do, or do not have, a great deal of control.

By using this risk assessment process you can come to a clearer understanding of:-

* Your options.

* The likelihood of those options succeeding.

* The reasons they might not succeed.

There is no right or wrong way to proceed. The intention here is to create understanding about what you're getting yourself into. You may decide to proceed with a situation that is risky. The trick is to know that it's risky. Then, if it doesn't work out, you don't beat yourself up or feel depressed because you knew beforehand that you were choosing to take a risk. Since you chose it, it doesn't make you feel helpless. You just say "Oh well...I knew it was risky...onwards and upwards then!" Obviously it's not wise to take big gambles with important things. Betting your house in a poker game is pretty foolish and asking for upset, but here we're talking about smaller stuff like "Should I ask Amy out to dinner?" The risk here is rejection, but if you're lonely and you like Amy it might be worth the risk of rejection even if she's a super model. Perhaps she likes quiet guys?! Conversely, you may choose not to go into a situation that has very little risk. Again, this is fine because at least you are now aware that you do have options should you wish to pursue them. You have simply chosen not to at this point. Knowing you have options will also stop you from feeling helpless. Learn to assess your level of control accurately, and you will experience much less upset in life.

CONTROLLED WORRY PERIODS

It has been said that worrying is praying for what you don't want, but worry is also part of the brain's vigilance mechanism. Obsession is worry taken to an extreme. One way to combat worry is through the use of controlled worry periods. This is so simple that you'd be forgiven for thinking that it couldn't help, but it can be very effective indeed for reducing worry. You simply arrange a time with yourself which you will devote wholly and entirely to "worrying". So you might say that between six and six thirty this evening I will give myself a whole half an hour to worry as much as I want, about all of the things that are worrying me. Then, if worries arise through the day you simply defer them to your allocated time. On the face of it this may sound like poor advice, but there is logic to it. Worry is an effort to come to solution. We sense when there is no promise of solution, and that uncertainty is what disturbs us emotionally, and worrying is the result. The promise of time allocated to solution later, can be enough to rest the mind. Of course, when you do your "worry" period it may seem rather absurd, which is again a great thing because you may just realise that worrying doesn't achieve much. However, we all worry to some degree, so be gentle with yourself. The best use of that worry period at six o'clock would be to implement some of the strategies presented above!

Chapter Six – Dealing With Obstacles

Having now understood some of the ways in which we can definitely make positive progress in reducing our anxiety, we may well still find ourselves blocked, or sabotaged. Relax! You're not alone. It's a common story. Let's have a look at what might be going on.

Unconscious Needs Versus Conscious Wants

Essentially, a person has a "conscious" level of awareness which roughly speaking, can be thought of as the "known" part of thinking and feeling. You might say it's what you think you think, and what you feel you feel. Beyond this however, a person can also have an "unconscious" level of awareness which is not immediately apparent, but which nonetheless makes its influence felt in that person's life.

Psychological and emotional difficulties are often the result of there being a conflict between these two areas of awareness. Consciously, we may pursue one course of action, while unconsciously we may want or need something different. Since the unconscious is not by definition conscious (known), it doesn't have a voice in the same way that conscious awareness does. Unconscious drives lie beneath the surface of conscious awareness, and they make their agenda known by affecting the way that we think, feel, and behave, but often they do so unhelpfully, with little or no logical explanation. When serious internal conflict occurs, then mental and emotional disorder can follow.

Some typical but cliché fictional examples follow:-

Case One - Jane

Jane presents for therapy because she is overweight. She says she cannot stop eating junk food, no matter how hard she tries. She has tried every diet there is and is depressed and exhausted. She desperately wants to regain control of her eating habits. Upon investigation we discover that Jane is in a loveless marriage. She does not enjoy sex with her husband, but she is terrified to leave him. Here we see the unconscious mind conflicting with the conscious mind. Consciously, Jane wants to control her weight, but unconsciously, the agenda is to eat for pleasure to deal with the misery of her loveless marriage, and secondarily, to become increasingly unattractive so as to avoid having sex with her husband. Since Jane has already closed down any possibility of having her real need met (to leave or repair the marriage), her unconscious mind must use something less obvious as a strategy for surviving the situation.

Case Two – Mark

Mark loves motorbikes. He has ridden motorbikes since he was 17 years old, but recently, now aged 34, he has developed an "irrational" fear when traveling on the dual carriageway. Upon investigation under hypnosis we discover that although he has never had any serious accidents, Mark has behaved recklessly in the past, taking unnecessary risks and a "part" of him has become fearful of the consequences. At a deep level he has lost some trust in his own ability to apply proper care, and his ongoing experience has highlighted some of the dangers that he was not aware of as a younger man. Consciously he wishes to continue riding the bikes. Unconsciously, another "part" of him wants him to stop riding, or re-establish his now broken sense of inner trust, and lets him know this by providing fear each time he rides the bike at speed.

Case Three – Alan

Alan makes a lot of money. He was raised in a family that rewarded hard work. Alan's father is a top lawyer. He showed Alan affection when he achieved an academic award, but outside of that his father could be emotionally quite cold. Alan now works sixty plus hours per week, but presents with symptoms of depression. He cannot understand why he is depressed. He says that he has achieved everything he ever wanted, and has made a great success of his life.

Consciously, he has fulfilled the perceived agenda. He has made himself "loveable", but unconsciously he has unmet needs that are begging to be acknowledged. Upon investigation, we find that Alan is exhausted, but has failed to admit this to himself because he learned as a child that his "acceptance" in the World was dependent on being seen to be a hard worker. Being exhausted then is considered unacceptable because it threatens his "loveable" status, so it remains unacknowledged.

Consciously, he believes that he must continue to prove his prowess in the world of business in order to have self-worth. Unconsciously, he yearns deeply to be loved for who he is, not what he achieves. Though he yearns for it, he also cannot receive it, even when it is offered because it conflicts with his deeper belief system that affection is only to be accepted when it is earned through achievement. His need for rest, and his need to be loved for who he is, remains unfulfilled. His unconscious awareness communicates this to him with feelings of depression.

If you understand this basic principle, then you begin to see how deeper unseen thoughts and feelings will communicate with us in an "unconscious" way through symptoms.

In each of the above cases we can deduce fairly easily that what is really required is change in circumstances and/or belief system. The symptom is merely attempting to highlight this fact using the only voice it has – negative thoughts, feelings, and reactions. If we aim simply to remove the symptom, we are just inviting those parts of the psyche that are attempting to be heard, to step up the pressure.

Consider for a moment then that there is a constant dialogue between the conscious and unconscious parts of one-self. These "parts" of a person are constantly communicating their intention to one another. When we are intuitive enough to sense what's needed, and carry out the corrective action, we enjoy direct communication between these parts of the self at their best and most functional. Life requires ongoing maintenance of this delicate balance. Needs change, and adjustment is frequently required. Healthy individuals do this all the time. Put simply, when we are healthy, we have an awareness of our deeper needs, and take steps to ensure those needs are met. We are flexible, and we adjust as necessary. Then serious conflict rarely develops. Where there is serious emotional disorder however, we will often find that a breakdown in internal communication has occurred. Internal positions have become stubbornly entrenched, and often this has developed into a small or large scale war. The conscious and the unconscious agendas have become polarised and opposed. You consciously want one thing. Your unconscious wants another. You want the feelings to go away. Your unconscious wants you to hear what it has to say. Stalemate is the result. It's easily done. It doesn't make us bad people. It's just something that happens, and more often than not, it's due to a simple misunderstanding. The resulting internal conflict however will make itself felt in a variety of unpleasant ways. This conflict can create feelings of confusion, worthlessness, helplessness, hopelessness, anger, depression, anxiety, and desperation. The unconscious mind seeks to re-establish communication via these feelings in an effort to alert you to the need to "heal" the rift, and attend to the need. It does this not because it's angry at you, or because it hates you, or even because it wants to give you a hard time, but because we each are programmed right down to the core of our deepest being to seek wholeness and integration. Put more simply, your deeper being is asking you not to settle for a poor arrangement, whether that be in your circumstances, your belief systems, your behaviours, thinking styles, or expectations. From this perspective, anxiety, depression, anger, and its associated symptoms, can be seen not as some alien aberration that has imposed itself upon us to make us suffer, but instead as an important invitation from the deepest parts of our-selves to create a life with more balance. Indeed, in practice, we see it again and again, that when such imbalances are resolved, wellness returns.

SECONDARY GAIN – REASONS TO REMAIN UNWELL

It is true in my experience that most people who undertake a course of therapy have a conscious agenda to be well. There is no question at all that we consciously seek to be happy. How we go about that can be a little misguided sometimes, but basically we seek happiness. Nobody would consciously, wilfully sabotage their own healing process, would they?

Well, it does happen. There is in therapy a well-established concept known as "secondary gain". Secondary gain refers to an unconscious reason to remain ill. Let's take a look at Jane in case one. On the one hand Jane consciously wants to be slim. On the other hand she has something to gain by making herself unattractive. If she wants to avoid sex with her husband more than she wants to be thin, guess which drive wins? This unconsciously driven decision is known as secondary gain. We can experience secondary gain in all sorts of guises, and it can be an insidious force in our lives, thwarting our efforts at every turn. It can be subtle. If you have learned that every time you cry you get a hug from your otherwise seemingly uncaring husband, or wife, then overcoming depression will literally deprive you of your hugs, assuming you don't change your life in any other way. If your hugs are more important to you than overcoming your depression, then depression will remain until this conflict is resolved.

These are obvious examples. It can be subtler though. For some people a daily dose of adrenaline is as addictive as a daily shot of espresso. Negativity is easy, addictive, and seductive. Misery loves company, and if two moaners get together to set the world straight on a daily basis with a good old rant, there is no end to the negativity they can come up with to entertain themselves. If we believe it is "righteous" indignation, and that the world really deserves our judgment, then we can easily lock ourselves into justifying our negativity. As you should by now recognise, repetitive indulgence in negativity extracts a price in the form of emotional arousal. These two might be simply unwilling to give up their negativity addiction, but genuinely wonder why they feel so bad about life.

There are actually plenty of reasons to stay ill. Please be clear that I am not accusing, or blaming anyone of wanting to stay ill, even if some of these reasons could be applicable to your situation. This is in no way a blame game. It is a very small percentage of people who exhibit secondary gain, and most of the time they don't mean to. The process is usually completely unconscious. By definition then, we will not be immediately aware of the conflict of interest. It must be drawn out. It is therefore worth understanding what kind of reasons one could have to remain in illness because clearly they can hinder the healing process significantly. Painful as it may be to ask yourself such a frank question as "Do I actually, at some level, have good reason to remain ill?" it is certainly necessary, particularly if you're not making any progress, to do so. I'll list some of those reasons here and then we'll explore the concept further:

* Healing is hard work. It takes application, and is energetically costly. It's simply easier to remain unwell.

* We fear the demands of life. If we're ill, we can gain social approval to remain disengaged from the world, and responsibility.

* Financial benefits (either from the State in the form of incapacity benefit, or family financial support).

* Fear of taking ones power because you don't trust yourself to use it wisely.

* We fear the disappointment of trying to recover and failing.

* Pain tapes (replaying painful memories in your mind) and hysteria are a powerfully addictive form of entertainment. Giving them up can feel like losing part of your identity.

* Losing your identity. Who are you then if you're not your illness? You like to tell your "story", and are defined by it. Without your story, you would no longer feel special.

* You enjoy negativity. You are addicted to negativity. It gives you a buzz.

* Being ill is comfortable and familiar. Wellness looks scary.

* Being ill brings you attention/sympathy/special treatment.

* Being ill keeps people away, and you prefer it that way.

It is a well-recognised psychological fact that the unconscious mind will opt for the familiar but painful over the novel but potentially more comfortable.

This is simply because the emotional mind works largely on a "better the devil you know" basis. Familiar is considered safe, even if it's painful, hence we see people return to poor relationships, and repeatedly engage in painful behaviours. We again have to step in to make changes with the frontal lobe.

Caroline Myss wrote a book entitled "Why people don't heal and how they can". In this book she stresses that there is a price to healing. She reminds us over and over that healing is energetically costly. This is an important consideration. We need to ask ourselves

"Am I willing to pay the price to heal?"

What that really means is "Am I willing to make the changes I need to make?" If you smoke cannabis, drink too much alcohol, eat compulsively, indulge in damaging sexual promiscuity, snort cocaine, exercise to complete exhaustion, or engage in any other form of peace-destroying excess, you need to ask yourself honestly whether you are willing to let it go in order to heal your anxiety? If you work eighty hours a week and it makes you anxious, are you willing to downsize your life, and forego a new car every two years in order to fix your anxiety? Or is the lifestyle more important? Will you still be interesting and different if you don't have a dramatic story to define yourself by? Who are you without your suffering? What are you willing to let go of in order to be well?

Can you let go of your worry habit? Can you let go of your story? Can you forgive yourself or someone else? Can you give up your view of yourself in the world as a victim? Will you…?

These are challenging questions. Thankfully, there are alternatives. If any of these potential sabotage mechanisms hit a nerve with you, then do know that although it may be challenging, ultimately those behaviours are only trying to do you a favour. These are considered strategies for happiness by the unconscious mind. There are better ways of being comfortable. Let's begin with the understanding that "behaviours have positive intentions". So even though an action or a belief may not be productive with regards to our healing, it does at the very least mean well. Using the above examples, the cocaine user's behaviour is because he/she believes that being high will provide some form of benefit. Temporarily it may do, but in the long run, we are right back where we started, or lower still because the stimulation is only passing, and the "need" remains after the drug has worn off. So it's not a moral issue. It's simply a poor strategy for having that need met. In this case, the by-product of getting high is anxiety.

In summary, we exhibit secondary gain when one of our needs is perceived consciously, or unconsciously, as being more important than being well. We are looking to identify what the "need" is, and what that need is trying to achieve. We then aim to make sure that we meet that need in a healthy way, removing in the process any unconscious agendas which lock us into remaining unwell.

Let's look at some examples:-

One

Painful Behaviour - I always put the needs of others before my own. I feel like I'm constantly helping everyone else, and I get no thanks for it. People say I'm interfering. I'm exhausted and I don't seem to be able to stop myself from offering to help, even when I don't really want to, and have other things I need to do.

Need - To know that I am "loveable" by identifying myself as a "caring" person to others.

Effect – Depression, Anxiety, Hopelessness, Exhaustion.

Alternative Strategies To Meet Needs - Valuing myself for who I am and not ONLY what I can give. Recognising that if I "rescue" everyone from their problems, I am not serving them because I am not allowing them to learn, and find their own solutions. I can meet the need of feeling I am loveable by attending to my own needs which is an act of love towards myself, showing that I am therefore "loveable". Recognising that not attending to my own needs inadvertently sends the message that I am un-loveable. If I am not willing to be loving towards myself, then why would anyone else love me?

Two

Painful Behaviour - I keep doing drugs. I end up really disappointed the next day, and it takes me days to recover. I hate myself for doing it, but when I'm offered them I just can't say no. -

Need - To escape the boredom of mundanity. To be someone else for a while. For stimulation and excitement.

Effect - Highly anxious. Feeling out of control. Self-loathing. Guilt.

Alternative Strategies To Meet Needs - Build in some fun but healthy activities during the ordinary working week to "feed" the part of you that craves relief from mundanity. Recognise that it's okay to be "ordinary". Real friends will love you for who you are, and won't demand that you're the life and soul of the party all the time. Standing up for this position is an act of self-love. Explore alternative strategies for excitement – adrenaline sports, theme parks, travel. Trying novel pursuits.

Three

Painful Behaviour - I've been depressed for years. I have seen five different therapists and they've all given up on me. I know they are giving good advice but I just can't seem to make it work for me. -

Need - To be recognised as "special". For "identity".

Effect - Depressed. Lonely. Hopeless.

Alternative Strategies To Meet Needs - Find an alternative strategy to feel "special". Build a new identity to be proud of. Recognise that there is genuine pleasure in wellness, and that your specialness shines when we are well too! Give up the addiction to being "defined" by illness, and make a contract to stop talking about how unwell you are.

Four

Painful Behaviour – I keep losing my temper and upsetting people around me. I get a buzz when I'm doing it. It makes me feel powerful, but when I calm down I am filled with deep regret, and I hate myself.

Need - To be powerful. To be "heard". To have influence and control.

Effect – Self -loathing. Anxious. Hopeless.

Alternative Strategies To Meet Needs - Recognise the need to heal the wounds (disempowering belief systems) that have caused you to feel so disempowered in life that explosive anger appears as the only strategy for defence, and being heard. Understand that demonstrations of anger only make you feel angrier. Learn new practical strategies for non-violent communication and graceful assertiveness. Practice regular kindness.

Hopefully, these examples give some insight into the nature of need, and why it is so important to meet these needs if we are to create a space in ourselves where wellness can thrive. This is sometimes challenging stuff. If you look at the above solutions, some of them are uncomfortable. It's not difficult to see why some people would unconsciously choose to stay locked into their current anxiety-causing strategies rather than face what needs to happen in order for wellness and balance to return. You can see more clearly now why "quick fix" expectations are often unrealistic. In each of the above examples there is potentially quite a lot of work to do. Therapies which don't address the true root of a need are unlikely to be successful in achieving permanent resolution. This should now be self-evident, and it is a crucially important point for any anxiety sufferer to understand. Anxiety has a reason for being. It doesn't matter how many "techniques" you throw at it, none of them are likely to give you the lasting relief you seek unless the root cause of the anxiety is dealt with. To move past the conflict of secondary gain, we need to meet any identified needs with healthier means.

RECOGNISING "PARTS" OF YOUR PERSONALITY AND BALANCING THEIR NEEDS

In therapy, when we find conflict between what we think we want consciously, and what we actually need unconsciously, we look at it from a "parts" perspective. "Parts" here refers to the fact that different parts of the personality can seek different agendas. Jane, Mark, and Alan's earlier stories illustrate this dynamic in action. We also touched on parts when looking at the limbic system versus the frontal lobe, and how we could use compassion to soothe anxiety, or other emotional disturbance. I want to expand further here because to some degree we all experience these conflicts in some way on a day to day basis. Realistically, it's something that we expect in life. There are tiny, almost inconsequential conflicts, and then there are great big disastrous ones.

For example, I love food. As I walk past the bakers and smell the delicious waft of a hot cheese and onion savoury, my limbic system offers me a reward. It connects the smell with the potential pleasure of eating something tasty, and urges me to walk in and buy one. My frontal lobe counters that too many pies make me miserable because I don't like being overweight. This is a relatively easy conflict to resolve. Make no mistake about it though, if I give it a moment of consideration, there is definitely a conflict. I keep walking, with the resolve that I'll buy a low-fat sandwich for lunch somewhere else. I'm meeting the need to eat and have pleasure, but I'm doing it in a healthier way. This is part of the frontal lobe's ability to "plan" skilfully. That's the clinical perspective, but is that how I really experience things? Am I really thinking about this conflict in terms of what my brain is doing, or is my heart involved too? The clinical perspective is both true and helpful, but my direct experience is that there is one "part" of me that could just have five minutes of heaven with that cheese savoury, and there is another "part" of me that's simply raining on my parade! If I put faces to these characters, the cheese-savoury lover is about eight years old, overweight, loveable, and doesn't give two hoots about being fat. He just loves savouries! The guy that's raining on my parade is thirteen and afraid. He's afraid because he's realised that no one wants to go out with him because he's fat, and now has real weight loss work ahead of him if he is to have any hope of feeling attractive and finding a girlfriend. Also on his side is my forty four year old self who is now much more aware of mortality and illness, and has additional reasons for staying in shape. Does my eight year old self understand why I'm going for a boring low fat sandwich? In my case, yes because he and I have communicated plenty throughout the years, and he has accepted the situation (just about!), though he still on occasion kicks his toe into the ground when I say no to savouries. If the conflict is on a grand scale though, the answer is always definitely no, he does not understand.

Sometimes I treat him to what he wants, and I'm always proud of him when he helps me by not making a fuss when I have to make important decisions. I'm careful to make sure that treats aren't the norm because then they stop being treats. If treats became the norm they can quickly become problematic habits. Then I would be being unkind to my thirteen and forty four year old parts because it would result in out of control weight increase. My inner thirteen year old becomes genuinely unhappy when the pounds pile on, and I feel his presence strongly when I fail to acknowledge his needs. He is absolutely able to make me feel anxious, guilty, or even depressed if I don't listen to him. He can actually cause much more chaos emotionally than my eight year old because the stakes are ultimately much higher. While my eight year old may sulk, the thirteen year old can feel genuine alarm when things feel out of control. He will let me know about it too! So you can clearly see that it is truly a balancing act to meet the respective needs of all of the "parts" of the personality.

Parts can easily be pursuing different agendas, and those agendas can conflict, causing stress, tension, anxiety, anger, and depression. What we aim to do therapeutically is identify the common ground. You remember that we said that behaviours have a positive intention? Behaviours are driven by the needs of a given part. Using the example here, what do you think is the common intention of my conflicting parts? Answer: Pleasure. What I need to do is to get both "parts" to recognise that they are on the same side, and ultimately working towards the same outcome. At first glance they appear to be opposed. One wants health and a slim body. The other wants immediate gratification through comfort food. Can these two agendas co-exist peacefully? The answer is yes. But, there needs to be some communication, and a little give and take. So the first thing to recognise is that not eating pies every day also brings me pleasure. It just gives it later rather than immediately. By restraining my pie intake I get to enjoy feeling healthy, looking in the mirror and feeling okay with the way my body looks, and hopefully, enjoying the love of a good woman. I need therefore to communicate this fact to my eight year old. At eight he is completely unaware of such things, and he genuinely needs to have this explained before he will understand that we're not denying him pleasure for the sake of it. Having done that, we will usually find that he brightens up considerably, realising that I am a friend, not an enemy. Straight away, we've halved the tension, but we're not quite there yet. We still haven't addressed his "need" for immediate gratification. If the deal is to proceed, we need to offer him something in return for agreeing to meet our request for support. The best way to do this is simply to ask him. "If you agree to help me eat fewer pies, what would you like in return that will make you feel satisfied?" The answer to such a question is often astonishing. It's usual to get a reply like "I just want you to be nice to me", or "I just want to be loved". Often the "needs" that parts of our-selves are pursuing are misplaced efforts to a) get attention b) experience some pleasure in an internally hostile environment. In a therapeutic setting this can be a huge moment of breakthrough for a person as all the years of struggle and internal hostility simply melt into love. What heart wouldn't melt in the presence of such innocence? Then we come to see that there has simply been a terrible misunderstanding. Clients will often report grief at this point for the "wasted" years. Equally, we may receive a different answer from the eight year old. He may say "I love savouries! Are you saying I can never have another cheese pie?!" Then, we dialogue: "Not at all! How about once a month we treat ourselves to a cheese pie on the last Friday lunchtime of the month, and you help me out the rest of the time?" We keep dialoguing until we thrash out a deal that works for everyone, and then we handshake on it. Will my eight year old still give me an urge to walk into the shop and buy the savoury on occasion? Sometimes yes, but I will feel much less conflicted about making the skilful decision, and I certainly won't feel tortured about walking past the bakers. I will feel a simple love and understanding for his position. He is eight after all! Walking past the shop is actually an act of self-love from this perspective.

Maybe you can have a deep and meaningful conversation with the parts of yourself you've been at war with? Maybe you can team up and work together instead? You may be surprised by what you can achieve with a few minutes closing your eyes and speaking kindly with yourself.

The Victim Drama Entertainment Game

When we think of the word "power" it's easy to bring to mind an image of the strong wielding power over the weak. Those of us that value humility might conclude that power is to be avoided because under this definition it seems that power and humility cannot exist side by side. I would like to propose however that true power is full of humility, and humble to the point of being silent.

The word power derives from the Latin word "Poder". In French language we have the verb "Pouvoir" which translates as "To be able to", and conjugates to "Je peux", meaning "I can". This is a more useful definition of the word power. When we think of power in this way we can define it as a sense of quiet certainty. Power doesn't threaten or intimidate. It simply says "I can", without guilt, shame, or blame. Power is able to stand firm in the face of adversity, but aims to respect and support others at the same time. By extension, where there is a lack of power, the statement shifts from "I can" to "I can't", and that usually means that we're not going to have our needs met without help.

When we don't know how to have our needs met, or ask for help in a positive way, we will use whatever strategy happens to be available. The logic is that any attention is better than no attention at all. Within the context of the drama game, demanding attention can become highly manipulative, and that usually means becoming involved in a life drama which will bring the required attention. These strategies are very stressful for everyone involved because the drama games leave everyone depleted and disempowered. Even if you win, you still end up depleted!

Have you ever embellished a story to make it more interesting? The urge to want to tell a good story is a powerful one. Drama is very seductive for some people, and often needs no other reason to be than that it is entertaining. Some people seem to go from one crisis to another as a chosen lifestyle. Unfortunately, that entertainment comes at a price. Most people figure this out during their teenage years, decide that the price tag is too costly, and calm down. However, drama can continue in much more subtle and refined ways. Now, instead of us jumping up and down, swearing at our parents, and slamming doors, we find that we can get what we want with a simple pout, or even just a tonal insinuation - "No, really I'm fine!".

Eric Berne developed Transactional Analysis in the 1950's. Transactional Analysis talks about ego strokes. "Ego strokes" refers to how we receive attention. TA recognises that attention is currency. If we're not receiving our energy functionally by creating our own happiness and fulfilment in life, then we'll need to acquire it in some other way. Being unwell is a great way to court attention. Transactional Analysis analyses the transactions (interactions) between people. The currency in these transactions is power or attention (energy), and depending on the people involved in the transactions, it's not unusual for people to enter into manipulative ways of demanding attention. Berne called this "The games people play". Like all immediate gratification, this power satisfies temporarily, but we soon need more, and we have to "spin the wheel", or play the drama again to bring in our next fix. Ultimately, we remain disempowered because each of these positions is a position where we are not truly taking responsibility for ourselves, and from every position we can always blame somebody else, or something else, for our lack of happiness. When we're busy blaming someone else, we're not doing any work on ourselves because we don't see the problem as ours; we see it as someone/something else's fault. That makes it someone else's responsibility to fix. How can you heal it if you don't own it? So we remain ill, and we stay "needy", which means that we remain locked into a dysfunctional way of having our needs met. The drama game always sucks someone, or something else in too because you need more than one person for the drama to work in the external world. Put another way, children don't bother having a tantrum unless there's someone there to see it. So let's take a look at how the drama game works:-

Victims need rescuers to rescue them – Poor me. Blocks solutions. Perpetuates helplessness.

Persecutors need victims to persecute – Critical. Judgemental. Keeps "victim" oppressed.

Rescuers need victims to rescue – Keeps "victim" dependent and feels guilty if not rescuing.

Victims hold a great deal of power. It's easy for a victim to "guilt" someone into doing what they want them to do because a victim after all, is powerless. What kind of a monster would turn their back on the (seemingly) powerless? Victims create dramatic scenarios to entice rescuers, or to demonstrate to others that they are being persecuted in

194

some way so that they can remain helpless. Rescuers are usually pleased to come to their aid because they receive their power by solving victim's problems. Rescuers need to be needed. When a person refuses to play the role of rescuer in a victim's drama game, the victim will usually accuse that person of being a persecutor because this is the only other role left to extract energy. If the accused then refuses to take the role of persecutor by responding with anger or hostility (which would be stepping in to the role of persecutor), then there is no game. The victim is then forced to seek their own solution, or find another player.

The difference between a functional and a dysfunctional position is a mile and an inch. A "kind-hearted person" and a "rescuer" both do the same thing roughly in offering assistance, but where they are coming from intentionally differs quite radically. A rescuer rescues out of obligation, even when he or she doesn't want to because they feel awful if they don't. The rescuer needs to rescue in order to feel okay. A "kind hearted person" offers nurturing because they are kind hearted, but doesn't *need* to help in order to feel okay, nor will they feel dreadful if they don't, or can't help. They may well get a buzz out of having helped someone, but it matters not either way to them because they'll recognise that they are not ultimately responsible for that other person. A rescuer however, will feel that they are responsible for the other person, and of course the victim will want the rescuer to feel that way too, ensuring they are rescued. The difference between a victim and someone who's down on their luck is that a victim won't help themselves, and will rely on being rescued. An unlucky fellow will find a way through, with or without someone else, and though he could have been cast as victim, chooses instead to keep it functional, and seek solution for himself. The difference between a persecutor and someone with clear boundaries is subtle too. A persecutor will need to gain the upper hand to feel good about their selves, or get their own way. A persecutor makes others feel weak so they can feel strong. A person with clear boundaries will be assertive without wanting to hold power "over" the other person. The way to exit the drama triangle is through awareness of one's own part in the drama. With awareness, we can refuse to play the game. The healthy expression of these positions is:-

* To be able to be kind hearted, but not need to be needed to feel okay about yourself.

* To be able to accept help, but to also cultivate self-reliance.

* To be able to hold your ground without being a bully.

It's a tall order, and few of us get it right all the time, but awareness is a great resource, so just knowing about the dynamics that can occur here can be very helpful indeed.

We want, as always, to avoid analysis paralysis.

The variations on these dynamics are endless, potentially confusing, and without a fuller education, we run the risk of tying ourselves up in knots figuring out who's doing what to whom. I'm mentioning this model because a quick overview is worthy of consideration. Since we're thinking about how we might be holding ourselves back from wellness, we can use this model to identify unnecessary dramas in our lives, and the part we may be playing. There is value in this model, but take great care not to start seeing everyone as a persecutor, a rescuer, or a victim. That will only lead you towards irritation. Just do what you can to move towards healthy expressions of power, support, and need. It's okay to need help. Just ask for it in a healthy way.

PERSONAL BOUNDARIES

One of the most important ways in which we exercise our personal power in a healthy way is by letting other people know how we wish to be treated, and this is known as being assertive. Personal Boundaries are very important to our sense of wellbeing. In practice, boundary awareness is a skill that is learned and refined over years, maybe a lifetime. Let's understand why it's so important to cultivate good clear personal boundaries.

First of all, let's remember that anxiety results from an inner sense that we are in danger. In short, when we feel vulnerable, we are likely to experience anxiety. This is the body/brains way of letting us know we are being threatened, or are open to attack. Similarly, we experience depressed feelings when we feel that our lives are in some way out of control, and things feel hopeless and helpless. If vulnerability causes anxiety, then what is the antidote? Answer: A strong internal sense of protection. When we know that we can protect ourselves from external attack, should it be necessary, we cease to generate anxiety because our sense of vulnerability reduces. Without this sense of internal protection we can experience a constant sense of anxiety, as we go through life with a sense that we could be thrown at any moment into a situation that we can't handle, or worse still, we find that we are already involved in situations which regularly breach our personal boundary limits.

Life is complex. This means that a certain degree of conflict is inevitable as people try to meet their needs by the path of least resistance. Sometimes two people's needs conflict. Sometimes this can be easily resolved. Sometimes it cannot. Conflict, by definition, is not a very comfortable experience for most people. It is however a fact of life, and any attempt to avoid conflict at all costs will cause suffering, mainly to you. When you will do anything to avoid upsetting someone, it usually results in you saying yes to something that really is not actually okay with you. Setting personal boundaries can be thought of as setting limits. These are the limits of what is, and what is not, acceptable for you. This is not a matter of moral decree (i.e you should behave a certain way). It's about what feels right for you, and it's worth remembering that identifying what feels truly right for you involves first working out how much of what you feel is based purely on conditioning. You may have had parents who told you always to put other people first. It's normal to feel as a thirty year old then that putting yourself first for once must be a selfish and therefore despicable act. It's important to be able to recognise that what you are feeling is a conditioned response, rather than what's really right for you, and then to ask yourself whether that belief system is really working for you now? With a little bit of insight, you may be able to recognise that the demands that are being placed upon you aren't really fair. Again, we see the possibility of conflict between what you consciously want (for everyone to see how "nice" you are) and what you unconsciously need (autonomy and freedom). Different people have different limits. Michael Yapko, who really deserves the credit for clarifying this understanding, reminds us however: "When is it necessary to set limits? Answer: Whenever you are dealing with anything that breathes!"

Your limits are personal and subjective. More often than not, we fail to honour our personal limits of acceptability because we are sacrificing ours needs for someone else's. Whether we like it or not, we are wise to recognise that we are under the threat of constant manipulation. Manipulation is a strong word, and there are degrees of course, but in one way or another, living itself involves constant give and take. It is possible to give and take in a balanced way, but often, even if we ourselves understand how to do this well, others do not. That means that we will frequently encounter people and situations who demand more than we are actually able or willing to give. This will be willingly taken from us if we allow it. That doesn't make other people bad. It's just what happens when people are trying to get needs met easily. If we set limits, they just go elsewhere to get the need met. Sometimes the manipulative efforts of others are fairly harmless to us. At other times, we submit to requests or demands even when we know we will suffer as a result. In a way, this becomes a self-imposed sentence to endure a situation we know in our hearts we should not be involved in. It's here that we experience that strong sense of vulnerability and hopelessness. Our inability to set limits, and say "No", means that we find ourselves again and again sacrificing our own needs to please others. Anxiety and depression are also caused by not having our needs met, so failing to honour our own needs can create difficult feelings. So the saying goes, the road to hell is paved with good intentions.

Altruism is defined as the act of selfless concern for the wellbeing of others. While this is a noble concept we need to understand that in practice this is not as straightforward as it may appear from its definition. It is a recognised truth of psychology that we cannot be in a healthy relationship with another if we are "dependent" upon the "other". This means that healthy relationships are at best a two-way mutually beneficial arrangement. Ideally both parties are involved in this relationship because it is a pleasure to give, and a pleasure to receive. It is co-operative, as opposed to coercive. Exchange is mutual, willing, and largely unconditional. Everybody wins. Sometimes you experience the pleasure of giving, sometimes the pleasure of receiving. Either way, it is a pleasure, not a duty. Most importantly therefore, neither party is dependent on the other to supply anything in particular (except perhaps the general courtesy and respect two friends naturally extend to each other), and the relationship naturally flourishes in a healthy way.

Where dependency exists however, as in an unhealthy relationship, we see need. The relationship is unhealthily conditional. This type of relationship says "I will only remain in relationship with you for as long as you are able to fulfil my need/s". The often unspoken message in this type of relationship is "I will abandon you, or dislike you, or think badly of you, if you don't do as I wish". Remember that historically, one of our greatest fears is excommunication from our community. From an evolutionary perspective, for our hunter-gatherer ancestors, being ostracised from our group would have meant certain death. We have a deeply engrained fear of upsetting our community. Even so, consider that our ancestors would have had to set limits of reasonability to survive! Co-operation, rather than dependency, would have been the rule. In any case, we don't like people to think badly of us. Consider for a moment how often this affects your life? Some examples:-

* You don't take your new shirt back to the store when it doesn't fit properly because you are concerned that the store clerk will think you're an idiot for not trying it on first. You feel angry at yourself, but it's easier than dealing with the discomfort of returning it.

* You have arranged to meet friends on Friday, but your Mother wants to visit. You cancel your friends because your Mother scares you.

* The salesman has given you an hour of his time. Surely you now have to buy this vacuum cleaner, even though you're not sure it's the vacuum you need. (It would be rude not to now he's invested so much in you).

* You don't want to have sex, but your partner threw a tantrum last time you said no. You acquiesce even though you really are not in the mood.

* Your daughter is asking you to look after the children again. You wanted to go away this weekend. You cancel your plans because you feel obligated to help.

* Your husband/wife goes through your text messages, checking for infidelity. You let them because you're afraid they'll assume you're guilty if you don't. You wonder why your relationship is undergoing some trust issues.

* Your long standing customer is suddenly demanding a delivery on Saturday, even though you have already told them that you don't offer weekend delivery. You make an exception because you are afraid of losing their custom, and then resent it.

* Your friend is always telling you how awful their life is, but they never seem to take any of your (or anybody else's) good, practical advice. You listen endlessly!

We could go on. There are countless ways in which subtle manipulation occurs all the time. It is important to recognise that this is "normal" behaviour. People are busy, and to a degree, are seeking to have their needs met with as little bother as possible. Sometimes your sacrifice will mean their needs are easily met. If you are an easy target, or worse still, completely fail to communicate that their behaviour or demands are unacceptable to you in some way, then it's perfectly natural for that person to continue with the behaviour for as long as you allow them to do so. The fact is, when one avenue of having needs met is closed off, people find another way. This is a crucially important point. When you tell yourself you must do as you are asked, or accept a particular behaviour from someone, consider that this person will find another way to meet that need if you refuse to do so. The idea that you are the only way that person can have their need met is distorted. The truth is that you are the easiest way for that person to have a need met. If you stop doing it, they will find another way.

If they don't seek solution elsewhere then that is their problem, not yours!

An inability to set limits, and let others know what those limits are, is damaging to us. In psychology then, as a balance to the noble concept of altruism, we also include constructive-selfishness. It is called constructive selfishness for two reasons. Firstly, by setting personal limits, boundaries, we protect ourselves. Because we are protected, we are relaxed, and are less likely to suffer with anxiety and depression. At one level, when these difficulties do exist, they are a signal to others. They say "I am weak, please do not harm me!" This is all that's available as a protective strategy when we believe to our core that we are unable to defend ourselves. A failure to learn to set limits therefore, is a partial invitation to anxiety or depression to take up long-term residence in our lives. Conversely, if we are protected, and therefore emotionally healthy, we are actually in a position to help others. We are a beacon. We walk tall and strong, and show others how it can be done. We maintain our integrity, and have our needs met without damaging others. We then have spare capacity within ourselves to give of our time and energy freely to those who will not abuse our generosity. This then makes us constructively-selfish. In essence, by being selfish initially, we become ultimately more altruistic, or available, to others. We also help others in another way too. You will notice that I said that we are in a position to give to those "who will not abuse our generosity". Another way of saying this is that we can help those who are willing to help themselves. In "dependent" relationships, what you give will never be enough. In such relationships, the more you give, the less the other will seek their own solutions, which means they will remain in constant need. These are life's "victims". In such relationships you are seen as the solution (rescuer). Your attention, your sympathy, your time, your money, your thoughts, your wisdom - these are the currency keeping this relationship alive. In fact, the only person that can truly solve these problems is the owner. So all the while you are giving freely (and without limits), as well-intended as you may be, you are actually enabling this person to remain in their illusion that someone else can fix their lives for them. In the long run this is damaging to them. By setting limits, you are forcing this person to seek their own solutions, and accept responsibility for their own problems, instead of looking to you to "fix" it all for them. We must understand therefore, that there is a difference between helping a friend or loved one out of a tight spot, which is perfectly acceptable, providing we are willing, even if we sacrifice something in the process, and them being "dependent" upon us. There is no fixed rule for how to recognise the line between help and continued rescue, but generally speaking, if someone is always in crisis, that's a pretty good signal that

201

they have failed to accept personal responsibility. In such cases, your failure to set personal limits isn't only harming you. It's harming them as well. Every time you rescue them, you stop them from learning from their mistakes, or creating solutions. This then, is the second reason that selfishness can sometimes be considered "constructive".

ASSERTIVENESS

A fundamental mistake people make is assuming that other peoples' book of "rules" is the same as theirs. You should not assume that because certain behaviour is unacceptable to you, that this is necessarily understood by the other person. Often, we experience problems with other people because we have differing maps as far as the limits of acceptability are concerned. Maps need to be synchronized in order to know where we stand with people, and vice versa. This is not necessarily comfortable, but it is the only sensible way forwards. In healthy relationships, once the boundaries are mutually established, they rarely come into question again, providing they continue to be respected by both parties.

You will remember too, that sometimes, it may be silently understood by the other party that their behaviour or demand upon you is offensive, but because you fail to make your stand against it, the behaviour continues anyway. Either way, it is your job to let other people know how to treat you, and to let them know where your limits are. A failure to let other people know where your boundaries are sends the silent message that "It is okay for you to treat me however you want to". Letting people know what's okay with you, and what isn't okay, is called assertiveness.

ASSERTIVENESS SKILLS

In Transactional Analysis there is a model known as "Parent, Adult, Child". At its most basic it states that when a person behaves in a "parental" way towards another, it will throw that person into their "child" space. Conversely, when a person behaves like a child they will invariably throw the other person into a parental type response. Neither of these responses can be understood as being conducive to good clear heart to heart communication. Parental communication can be seen as overbearing and dictatorial, while child-like communication can be unreasonable, hysterical, and manipulative. The place to meet people if you want to clarify important issues is in the "adult" space. Assertiveness can be thought of as a communication that takes place in this adult mode. If the person you are communicating with flips into parent or child mode, pull them back into adult communication with you by using calm, reasoned, focussed communication, that brings the conversation back to the key points you are discussing.

Assertiveness is not aggression. It is possible to be assertive and remain graceful. The goal is not to get what you want at all costs. The goal is to let the other person know what your needs are, what your limits are, and why these needs and limits are important to you. You give the other person a chance to understand your perspective, and they are then much more likely to respond in a constructive manner. So the basic formula is as follows:-

When "X" event occurs, it makes me feel "Y" because "Z". Can you help me with a solution to this? Let's use an earlier example to show the formula in practice. For the sake of clarity let's assume that in this example the lady has never given any reason to suggest infidelity:-

* Your husband goes through your text messages checking for infidelity. You let him because you're afraid he'll "assume" you're guilty if you don't. You wonder why your relationship is undergoing some "trust issues".

Solution: "When you look through my text messages to check up on me (X), it makes me feel unloved, undervalued, disrespected, mistrusted, and lonely (Y) because the message you are sending to me is that you just don't trust me. I find it difficult to feel love in a relationship which is not built on mutual trust and respect. (Z) What I would like from you is that you will agree to stop going through my text messages, not because I have anything to hide, but because the lack of trust that you communicate to me when you do this makes it difficult for either of us to be close to each other, and I desperately want us to be closer. Can you help me with this?"

Notice that there is no "personal" attack in this statement. When using assertiveness skills it is very important that we seek to avoid using any language or insinuation that could be construed as a personal attack. Saying "When you act like a friggin' idiot by checking my messages it makes me feel really mad at you because it just proves what an insensitive jerk you are!" is not likely to elicit a very constructive response. Neither is it a very "adult" way of communicating. There are at least three personal attacks in that statement. Any assertive message that comes across as an attack upon that person's character, as opposed to a clear statement of fact, will be met with defence. When people go into defence, they stop listening, and communication has already broken down. In the first example above we have a clear statement of fact. The fact is he is looking through her text messages. She is simply stating what is actually happening. Then she explains how it makes her feel. Again this is about her, not him. He may still hear it as a personal attack. This can happen because the recognition of his bad behaviour begins to dawn on him, and it's a difficult pill to swallow. His pride is hurt so it feels like an attack. It is her responsibility to point out that it is simply a statement of how this behaviour makes **her** feel. It is not her intention to make him feel bad or guilty, but to initiate change. In our example above, she has actually offered an olive branch by saying "I desperately want us to be closer". This is not an attack. It's a plea for resolution. She then explains why it makes her feel these feelings (because), giving a sense of context and reasonability. Finally, she asks him to "help" her with solution. An interesting fact of psychology is that people generally find it very difficult to flat refuse a direct request for help. Her request for help is soft. It is not aggressive. It invites solution. The ball is now in his court.

Let's think about some of his possible responses:

Response One:-

"How dare you challenge me like this! I'll do what I want, when I want!"

What is being communicated in this response? Essentially, "I do not trust you, and I do not respect your feelings. I have no plans to change, and I may harm you if you challenge me again". There is only one sensible conclusion in this situation. This person will continue to disrespect you, and depression and anxiety are the likely result of living under such restrictive and threatening conditions. At least now you know for sure that this person is incapable of respecting your needs or your limits. Your silent agreement to these terms by remaining in relationship with this person is a lack of self-respect by proxy. Leave or suffer are your options.

Response Two:-

"I'm really hurt that you could think I don't trust you. I love you, but I just need to see sometimes, with my own eyes, that nothing is going on behind my back. It's not that I don't trust YOU, I just don't trust anyone!"

A grey area here! Whose problem is this? At least a channel of communication is now open, and further discussion can now take place. Whether it can be resolved remains to be seen. The outcome will be partly down to his willingness to recognise he has a problem and seek resolution, or on her willingness to overlook his paranoid behaviour, and trust that it doesn't really mean anything. Someone with a strong sense of self-worth would probably not settle for anything less than his agreement to cease the snooping and seek help for his lack of trust. Bear in mind that sometimes we earn our sense of self-worth simply by demonstrating to ourselves that we refuse to be the willing subjects of behaviour that devalues us. Even someone with low self-esteem therefore, could take this position, and benefit from it.

Response Three:-

"I'm really sorry I hurt your feelings. I hear what you're saying and I promise that I'll stop with the snooping. You're right. I should trust you, and we should work together on making things better. I've just been worried because we haven't been getting on too well lately, and I thought you might be leaving me. Are you with me? Can we try again?"

Reconciliation! Further open-hearted communication can now take place, and is likely to open into a much deeper mutual recognition and agreed honouring of needs and limits. With two "reasonable" people the above outcome is extremely likely. This is a true resolution to what might have appeared to be an insoluble problem. Her willingness to deal

205

with the discomfort of confronting her husband has actually paid off. Often it does. Even when it doesn't end in the solution you hope for, it does always let you know where you stand.

Obviously, every situation is different, and there are a number of complexities that mean that it's not always possible to follow the formula in quite such a structured way, but what's important here is at least the knowing that it is possible to communicate our needs in a direct but non-aggressive manner. I'm particularly fond of this model because the response received is very telling in be able to assess more clearly what this relationship is really about. Then at least we know where we stand, and we can decide whether we are willing to continue to stay in relationship with someone who is harmful to our sense of self, or whether to leave.

If you have been troubled with anxiety and/or depression, it's your continued job to reduce your stress levels. As uncomfortable as it may be to recognise it, those people who are not willing to respect your needs and limits will make you feel stressed and devalued. It's very simple. Keep people around you who care about you, and respect your feelings, and let those that don't, go!

Dealing With The Fallout

It should go without say that being assertive with someone who might explode and cause you physical harm is not advised or sensible. If your safety is under threat, you clearly do not want to antagonise the "sleeping dog". If things are that far gone already, you can assume that assertiveness skills are generally going to be pretty useless anyway. If you're in a physically abusive situation you really should seek specialised help that pertains to your particular circumstances. Nobody should be hitting anybody, ever! Outside of this, we are referring to the "emotional fallout" that can occur when we assert ourselves.

In Cognitive Behavioural Therapy (CBT) we have a term called "Low Frustration Tolerance". This refers to inability, or difficulty, in coping with uncomfortable feelings. In learning to set limits and practice assertiveness this is a big hurdle for many people. To some degree it is a difficulty for most of us because as we pointed out earlier, generally we don't like to hurt people's feelings, or refuse to help. In order to say "No" firmly, either to requests or particular behaviours, we need to be able to sit comfortably with the discomfort that doing so might throw up for us. These feelings could include (but are not limited to):-

Guilt, Uncertainty, Fear, Anger, Abandonment.

This requires a certain degree of strength, and skill, in terms of creating a perspective which allows us to stand firm in our resolution to protect ourselves. Here then are some tips on how we might go about learning to hold our ground despite having such feelings.

The first thing to recognise is that holding your ground is the priority. We have established that failing to set limits can be a fast road to depression and anxiety. Courage, remember, is not the absence of fear, but the decision that something else is more important. In this case we are talking about your wellbeing and self-worth. Do not therefore expect that being assertive and setting limits is necessarily comfortable. We can become more comfortable with it through practice because we learn that actually, mostly, people don't hate us for setting limits. Those that are worthy of your time and energy will come to respect you more as they see you respecting yourself more. Initially though, we can expect a certain amount of discomfort, and to a degree, a bit of disappointment from others as they are forced to look for other ways to have their needs met. Be willing to deal with this. Your willingness to tolerate discomfort in the name of self-protection sends a powerful message back to those vulnerable places within you. It says "You are protected. You can count on me to look after you. I won't fold because things get tough". Think about this for a moment. This may be the first time you've ever really done this for yourself? Take a moment to consider what the implications of taking this stance could mean for you? What you are really communicating back to yourself is "I've had a lifetime of being at the mercy of other peoples' desires, but from this point onwards that's going to change. From now on, I don't have to do anything I really don't want to do. I have control." This is a pivotal moment, and a powerful anxiety-busting message. You probably won't fully believe that message straight away, at least not at the deeper level of your being, but that's okay. The commitment and direction is there, and that in itself increases your feeling of safety. In time, the statement becomes something you believe more and more because every time you are assertive you learn that you actually **can** count on yourself when it matters. Then they are not just words. The belief is backed up with evidence. With this understood, tip one on holding your ground is simply to remember that you are committed to practicing assertiveness even if it is uncomfortable because it's too important not to do so. In practice, you will find that most people will respond quite positively to your new found ability to be assertive. They will respect you more, not less. If they are hostile because you're looking after yourself, they're probably not good people to have around you!

Secondly, we can benefit from a different perspective. I borrow here from Terence Watts' invaluable psychological model "Warriors, Settlers, Nomads". A full discussion of this is available inside Terence's book of the same title, but here's one basic therapeutic technique.

Think of a positive Warrior role model. Avoid anything that could be construed as dictatorial or evil. We are looking for a positive role model. Remember that there are plenty of Warriors who fight for good causes, or simply defend when necessary. Close your eyes, take a few moments to centre yourself, and then imagine stepping into the body of the Warrior. Imagine becoming the Warrior. Imagine that as you look down at your arms, you can see how strong they look. Feel the sense of strength that now runs through your being. Now turn your attention to your mind and emotions. Do you feel mentally strong? Do you feel that you could cope with conflict now? If you had to deal with conflict, would you be terribly worried about upsetting your opponent? You will notice that there is an okay-ness, a certain matter of fact quality to dealing with conflict when viewing the world through the Warrior's eyes. This is an important perspective change because it shows you that it is possible to deal with conflict in a matter of fact way. It's not the only perspective that exists on the matter, but it is a valid perspective, and it is the most useful perspective when conflict is unavoidable, as it is when a person breaches your boundaries. Can the Warrior deal with the discomfort of setting limits and saying No? Sure! He or she doesn't only deal with it, he hardly feels it! Connect with your Inner Warrior. When you need to draw on that strength, just step into that body, in your mind, and use that perspective. Review the situation through the eyes of the Warrior. Notice and remember how the Warrior perceives the situation. If it's working for you, then choose to use that perspective. With practice, you'll develop those strengths yourself, and again, you will feel better equipped to deal with not caving in to other peoples' demands. From the Warrior perspective, if they have a problem with you being unwilling to tolerate their disrespect, or acquiesce to their unreasonable demands, you're fine with that. That's their problem not yours! And if they decide they don't want to know you because you don't do as they wish, then that's fine too because real friends do respect your limits, and you don't have time for people who won't respect you, do you?

There are a number of other ways in which we can increase our tolerance of the presence of difficult feelings. From a CBT perspective we can learn to think logically and flexibly about our rights and the need to protect ourselves. In so doing we can begin to recognise logically that setting limits is a perfectly reasonable practice. Feeling guilt as a result is an irrational feeling, which does not accurately reflect the situation. In this way we can stop endorsing the perception that something is "wrong". We can further increase our tolerance by using the technique of sitting with discomfort as in "I hear and accept that you feel guilty". This was covered earlier, and if you've been practicing, you will now know how to do this. Positive affirmations will be useful here too, such as "I have a perfect right to let this person know that their demands are upsetting to me". So, with all these tools available, you really do have all you need to learn to be assertive, and set limits. For good measure though, let's just have a look at another tool we can use to great effect when we're working through difficult feelings.

CHAPTER SEVEN – PRACTICAL EMOTIONAL AROUSAL REDUCTION TOOLS

LEARNING TO LET GO

One of the really interesting things about anxiety disorders is their amazing ability to convince us that we need them. This isn't all that difficult to understand. If we look at it from the limbic system perspective, we can see that the limbic system actually believes that anxiety is necessary, and since the limbic system supplies our feelings, it's natural to assume that our feelings are telling us the truth. We then synthesize our future expectations using those feelings, and arrive at the conclusion that anxiety is a necessary strategy for dealing with life. Unconsciously, we actually invite anxiety to remain in residence. Anxious people are usually completely unaware of this because it is so intricately woven into the fabric of their perception, so their assumptions are absolute, when projecting into the future. An anxious person who is invited to a party will immediately factor their anxiety into their considerations about what to expect if they choose to attend. When they forward project their mind into that situation, a whole host of questions automatically arise.

Will I be well enough to attend? What happens if I start to feel too anxious to stay? What if people notice I'm anxious? What if I need to leave and can't get home? Will I make a fool of myself? I probably won't enjoy it because I'll be looking for the exit the whole night.

In fact, the event is considered almost entirely from the perspective of anxiety, and it simply doesn't occur to this person that it might be possible to enjoy an evening free of anxiety. Now this is not entirely unreasonable on the sufferer's part because they have found themselves to be anxious on most occasions recently, so why should this one be any different? What's not recognised though, is that they will have spent days leading up to an event running catastrophic mind-movies. This sets the whole event up as "threatening", and pretty much guarantees anxiety when the event arrives, thus reinforcing the belief that anxiety will always be present. With this belief firmly established, it's now the easiest thing in the world for anxiety to say "You need me. You need me to keep you on guard because this is going to be a tough night to handle". It becomes almost impossible to imagine a future where anxiety is not present, be it when thinking about a particular situation, or just the future in general.

We can easily assume then that we are at the mercy of our feelings. When we're overwhelmed emotionally, it can feel like we have no control whatsoever over these emotions, and that of course, leaves us feeling rather vulnerable, and thereby open to further anxiety. There is however an avenue which has not been properly explored here. What if it were true that we actually **do** have some control over these feelings? Then what? Would that change things? Consider that the expectation of fear being present (and the subsequent self-fulfilling experience of it) is based almost entirely on the fact that we've haven't dared to allow for the possibility that fear could not be present.

What we need is a strategy for experiencing the situation without fear, before it happens, in order to show that it might be possible to not have fear. Remember that the mind can act as a rehearsal room, and actors calm their nerves by perfecting their acts in rehearsals. When rehearsals go well, it's reasonable to expect that everything will be alright on the night. Rehearsing situations without fear is positive use of the imagination. We do understand however, that going from an anxious expectation to a relaxed one in a single jump is sometimes a bit too much of an adjustment for an anxious mind to process immediately. We have an elegant solution to this problem in the form of a simple exercise which can be used to help re-envision the event, and release fear, in advance.

We have already looked at learning to increase our tolerance to the presence of discomfort. This method does not conflict with that understanding; it compliments it.

The distinction here is that there are some feelings and emotions that need to be simply honoured and felt, and there are some feelings which are carried unnecessarily. So, for instance, if my Mother passed away two weeks ago, there is a very real need for me to experience my grief. I need to honour that feeling as a natural part of processing. To try to "release" my grief just two weeks after she died is simply unrealistic, and probably insulting to the parts of me which are grieving. If two years have passed since her death, and I'm depressed every day about her passing, then I might well benefit by choosing to let it go. I can still honour her, but being depressed every day, two years on, is not honouring her, or her memory. That is an unnecessary carrying of emotion. It's time to choose to let it go. With all difficult feelings we begin by honouring their presence with "I hear and accept that you feel X", but then we can ask a further question. It's not a contradictory question, it is a supplementary one. "I do accept that you currently feel X, but do we really need to continue to feel X? Is this feeling really serving me today? Could life be okay without it now? Did it once have a purpose, but now things are different?" How will we go about letting ourselves know that it's okay to let it go now? Can we give permission for the release? Does the limbic system need executive permission to release a negative feeling? Sometimes the answer is yes. Evidently, permission can be rather important. It signifies choice and movement.

The Buddha said "Carrying anger is like holding a hot rock that you intend to throw at someone else. In the end, the only person it burns is yourself". Often, we carry emotion and feelings unconsciously. We feel a feeling, and we feel that we are at the mercy of that feeling and have no choice about whether we carry it or not. Actually though, if we look deeper, we do have a choice. Consider for instance how some people grieve for things for years, and others move on quickly. What is it that pulls a person out of grieving? There comes a time, when a person says to themselves, "I can't go on grieving like this", and a conscious decision is made that it's time to stop grieving. Effectively, a person chooses to "let it go now" and a concerted effort begins to re-engage with life fully. We "choose" to start finding the brightness again. Similarly with anger, we often feel justified to feel anger. This is fine of course because often our anger is justified, but for some people that anger becomes a huge weight which is carried around long after its usefulness has ceased. We've all had the experience of recognising that we need to let go of something emotional because it's hurting us more than it's helping us. Remember that your unconscious emotional mind, being a non-deliberating, non-rational mind, responds to your conscious intent and conclusions about things. If you conclude for instance that "I will not rest until they know how much I suffered" (as purely an example) then that is one sure way of ensuring you stay angry. In fact it becomes a contract. Consider what other kind of contracts you make with yourself? How do these contracts, assumptions, and conclusions lock you into negative feelings? One method of "releasing" such blocked, held, or trapped feelings is simply by using your conscious intention to "release". It's important not to analyse how or why it works, but simply to do it (sincerely) and then return to the feeling and see how it has changed. The formula is simple:-

You sit quietly, close your eyes, and focus on the feeling by locating where the tension/feeling is in the body. It could be any feeling, from rage to grief, or anxiety to boredom. Notice what you are feeling. Where do you feel it? Is it in your stomach? Is it in your chest, or throat? If the feeling could speak, what would it say? I feel afraid? I feel angry? I feel threatened? Ask yourself whether experiencing that feeling is really helping you? Imagine for a moment how the situation would look and feel if you were calm. Is the outcome better? If so, then ask yourself, "Would it be okay to release this feeling?" If you can cultivate a full or partial "yes" to that question, you simply take a nice slow deep breath into the place where you are holding that feeling, and imagine the feeling dissolving into your breath as you inhale. Hold the breath for just a moment. Then, with the intention of releasing that feeling, you simply "choose" to exhale the stress in that single breath...nice and slow. Bring your attention back to where you were holding the stress. Let your breath return to its normal rhythm. Now how does it feel? Better? Less? Notice that the situation looks/feels better too doesn't it? Do it as many times as you want or need.

It may well be that the feeling is still there, but you will almost certainly be able to sense that it *is* different in some way. Sometimes it will be completely released in a single breath. Sometimes a percentage will remain. Sometimes it will feel different. For instance, we might release anger and discover that behind the anger is a layer of sadness. Be open to whatever remains. Now you can repeat the process with whatever remains. We begin the process with whatever remains as a new feeling in its own right. Even if the first feeling was "fear", and the second feeling is also "fear", we still approach the new feeling as a feeling in its own right. Emotional discomfort is often created by a number of different feelings all mixed together, and it is helpful to think of this releasing process as releasing "layers"...one by one. You may not always feel an immediate difference, but it may be that you are releasing only 1% of a layer at any one time, so stay with it. It does help. You can continue releasing for as long as it feels good to do so. As a practical guide, it's a good idea to do this little and often. Perhaps ten or fifteen minutes a day. Don't expect miraculous overnight transformations. You are working with feelings which may have been held for years, and they release in their own good time, but do consider that the releases that take place are real releases. You are literally releasing blocks from your psyche. Over time these small releases add up to shedding a whole bunch of emotional weight from your shoulders!

With the passing of time I have come to appreciate this method's value despite its simplicity, and I believe it is one of the most important anxiety busting techniques available. It actually serves many functions in one short easy to use technique. These include the following:-

* The act of asking whether we need to keep the feeling, alerts us to the possibility that it is a feeling, not a fact. It asks us to consider what the situation would look like if the feeling were not present. This is a re-viewing of the situation, and often helps us to realise that we have been labouring under the assumption that the feeling must remain present if we are to be safe. We can begin to see then that the presence of the feeling may not be as necessary as we have unconsciously assumed. This can give us our first real glimpse of what life would be like without anxiety. You won't understand what I mean by this without doing the exercise. Do the exercise, and then re-read this point.

* The act of sitting down for ten minutes with eyes closed, and giving undivided attention to our wellbeing is a meditation of sorts. This has a beneficial effect simply because we are using focussed attention in quiet time.

* The act of asking whether we are willing to be without a feeling helps us to identify what we might be choosing to hold on to. This is

214

empowering because we may have been telling ourselves that we were at the mercy of these feelings, when in fact some part of us may have been using them to serve a "need". You now recognise that the solution to this is to identify the need and find a healthier way of meeting that need. Then you may be willing to let the feeling go. My contention to you is that if there is no "need" served by a feeling, then there is no reason for it to be held on to, and that this is a truth which every human psyche can honour.

* This exercise sends a message to your feeling body of **permission and intent**. These are ancient principles of healing. "Physician, heal thyself" is an idea central to so many ancient disciplines of power. Personal power is summoned with intent. Mobilising your intention in this way is not to be underestimated. It is a direct communication within your own being that you intend to heal. Make no mistake about it. The moment of release is a symbolic, and literal, act of power.

* What is truly magic about this system is that each successful release literally shifts perception. Feelings that seemed completely stuck and inflexible can suddenly shift to reveal a surprising and enlightening truth. What was seen as absolute is revealed to be much more malleable and illusory than it had first appeared. This is quite difficult to English because the magic is in the experiencing of it. I have seen long held feelings of depression shift in just one breath. What we learn is that the states we believe are fixed and absolute, are in fact, simply states. When you release a negative state, you naturally move into a more positive one. We're just revealing a little more of that light we spoke about at the beginning of the book.

* This entire process is respectful to your sense of self, and to the limbic system. There is no forcing or coercion. It respects the fact that letting go of anxiety is sometimes scary. Though this makes little logical sense, it is in fact the way the psyche operates. Since anxiety is deemed as necessary for protection it is natural for an aroused limbic system to be a bit wary about becoming too relaxed. The limbic system sometimes views "relaxed" as "unguarded". The great beauty of this technique is that it allows the limbic system to release its "guardedness" at a very gentle pace. The net effect of doing this is that we can become

organically comfortable with the change, and see very clearly that an unguarded state is not necessarily threatening. We can begin to recognise that the biggest threat has always been anxiety itself, and then relax into being relaxed.

As with all of these understandings, placed in the context of what you've learned so far, this simple strategy can go a lot deeper than being just a technique. This is an act of kindness towards your-self. Being willing to engage with this process sends a really powerful message of goodwill to all parts of your being. It says "I care. I value you". No technique should ever be oversold. If we say, "This is the next big thing. Do this and you'll feel fantastic!", we're going to end up disappointed because the answer isn't in one thing. The answer is in all of these understandings working together like an oiled machine. So please don't approach any one aspect of this book as the one thing that will solve your anxiety. We need to appreciate the organic nature of change work, and in so doing, not throw something out because it doesn't fix it all immediately. The danger in doing that is that we can make the mistake of then underselling it by concluding it has no value at all. With these principles of sitting with what needs to be sat with, and then releasing what we no longer need to hold on to, we are talking about building a truly strong foundation for wellness. Please be patient. It takes time and practice, but the foundations you build will be really strong, and will last you a lifetime, with application. The process I've described here is a generic take on an age old psychological principle. Releasing emotion with intention and breathing is as old as the species. However, I would like to make mention of the Sedona Method. I have not quoted their method here because I don't want infringe any copyrights or trademarks, but the Sedona Method process is similar, involving more steps, and more specific mantras. I would definitely recommend the Sedona Method to your attention. It's simple, but it really works!

Relax-O-Therapy

One vital tool for reducing anxiety is learning to relax deeply. If you're not in the habit of relaxing, then you're not likely to relax until you **learn** to relax. We often think it's something we should just be able to do. It's actually a skill, and it can be learned.

The science behind relax-o-therapy is really very simple. If you've been anxious, then your emotional mind believes that you are in a war zone, and in a war zone you simply would not relax. So when you relax for half an hour a day, you send a message to your emotional mind that says "It's **safe** to relax". By repeating this relaxation every day the emotional mind begins to understand that your life is perhaps not quite the war zone it has been imagining. With this understood, the emotional mind begins to step down from red alert to orange...to yellow...to green to go. If we use our relaxation recording for a week, and then decide it hasn't "fixed" the problem, then we're missing the point. It's a cumulative effect. Buddhists "meditate" for years to quieten the mind. You may not be able to relax deeply at first. That's okay. With practice you'll get better at it.

Relaxation is simple, practical de-arousal of the emotional mind. It has the potential to completely change the way that you feel, in minutes. One of the great benefits of regular relaxation is the afterglow. When you cultivate stillness and deep relaxation, those feelings tend to remain with you long after you leave your relaxation session. Stilling the mind can be a genuinely profound tool in your anxiety-busting arsenal. The main obstacle is simply making the time to do it, and to be willing to sit through the urges you have to rush off and do something else. It's quite normal to experience a distracted mind at first. Many people experience busy thoughts whirling around as they begin. Be gentle with yourself. You'll find a disclaimer on the download page. Most people will find the recording pleasant and relaxing. If, for any reason that's not the case for you, then don't use it. Just concentrate on the rest of the learning here.

For everyone experiencing the deep pleasure of guided relaxation, keep using your recording. It will help. It's not everything. It's just one aspect of anxiety busting, but it's an important one. Half an hour a day, keeps the emotional ghoulies away!

Here's a link to download one of my relaxation recordings free of charge. It is on a private unindexed page on the website. You will need to use a password to access the page.

http://bit.ly/1pBjeMT

Access the link above using your internet browser, and you will be asked to enter the password. Enter it exactly as you see it here:-

relaxdeeply

There will be more recordings available from
www.youcanfixyouranxiety.com soon.

I am not covering the subject of meditation specifically in this book, but it should go almost without say that meditation is a brilliant alternative to guided relaxation. If that's your preferred method, go for it.

When you relax, your limbic system (emotional mind) hands control back to the frontal lobe (intellect). This means that for the 30 minutes or so that you're on the couch during hypnotherapy, you're in solution-creating mode. You can think clearly. You can consider possibilities which seemed impossible or unlikely when you were more emotionally aroused. This can happen with both hypnotherapy and relax-o-therapy. It's what we want.

Hypnotherapy is the positive mental rehearsal of a scenario in a relaxed controlled atmosphere. This could be a consulting room if you are seeing a hypnotherapist, or if you are using self-hypnosis, your own bedroom.

Having the said scenario occur (mentally) while you are very relaxed allows the brain to make a new more helpful assessment of the situation, and what can be expected. Thus, when we later enter the said scenario in real time, the limbic system already knows that it can be approached without anxiety, and duly obliges with a positive feeling. At one level hypno-therapy is therefore a form of positive associative conditioning. Remember Pavlov's dogs? In other words, we associate a relaxed feeling with a given scenario, and condition this to become an automatic response. Professional hypnotherapists will find out what your needs are, and tailor sessions with appropriate content, suggestions, and metaphors, which will help you to feel more peaceful about something which is troubling you. Recording the session and replaying it later can be a good idea. If you don't fancy visiting a hypnotherapist, then the principles transfer very well to self-help too.

SELF-HYPNOSIS

The term Self-Hypnosis sounds rather mysterious, so let's simplify. My preferred definition of Hypnosis is "Deep Imaginative Involvement". The state necessary to achieve this is one of concentrated focussed attention. Technically it is not necessary to have relaxation in order to use hypnosis. Being in shock for example is a state of "trance". Likewise, anxious and depressed states can be said to be powerful "trance" states too. Put simply, it means having a fixed focus. Consider that these negative states are also hypnotic states, and you begin to understand what hypnosis really is. If you fear hypnosis, you really shouldn't. It's just another word for what happens all the time. Sales people knowingly or unknowingly use hypnosis regularly. The TV and media are constantly hypnotising us with attention grabbing headlines. Sales people, in all their forms, direct buyers' attention to the benefits of owning a product, and ultimately they are guiding a buyer's attention towards imagining just how good those benefits will "feel", thus enticing the buyer to purchase.

Hypnosis used for therapy does have a specific focus however. We do aim to use hypnosis to create relaxation. When you have focussed attention, imaginative involvement, and relaxation together, you have the optimum conditions for learning. In many ways that's what hypnotherapy is...re-learning. We are ultimately teaching the unconscious mind that life and specific events can be approached without anxiety, and that the organism (you) remains safe in the absence of anxiety. The language that the limbic system uses is primarily that of the imagination. We constantly run mini-movies in the background of our awareness, which anticipate outcomes of forthcoming events. The limbic system responds very literally to our forecasted expectation. It's worth remembering then that the brain itself tends towards a negative bias as it has evolved to err on the side of caution as a protective strategy. Therefore, we need to remember that it will automatically lean towards a pessimistic version of mini-movie expectation unless we train it to do otherwise.

The first thing to do is to figure out exactly what scenario you wish to positively rehearse. If you are socially anxious for example, you may wish to rehearse going to a pub with friends for the evening. Think about how you would like things to be and how it would happen *if it went well*.

Before you engage with your self-hypnosis, imagine the sequence of events as they will happen when they are unfolding calmly and pleasantly. Think of the movie as an A to B scenario with a beginning, middle, and end. It doesn't need to take a long time. You might spend five or ten minutes only, imagining your movie unfolding. You can see yourself smiling, speaking to people, maybe laughing, forgetting to be self-conscious, noticing instead that you're engaged in conversation etc. In addition to this visualisation, you can make "suggestions" to yourself such as "I am feeling calm and relaxed". Use present tense.

You can adapt your suggestions to any attribute you wish. The golden rule is to keep suggestions positive and definite. Never talk about what you *don't* want to be. Talk about what you *do* want to be. Don't say therefore "I am not feeling anxious". Instead say "I am feeling relaxed". When you have visualised your movie from start to finish with a positive outcome, you simply give yourself the instruction to come back to normal awareness, and gently surface, opening your eyes when you feel ready. Remember that repetition is the key here. Hypnosis is not a magic bullet that will fix all our ills in one go. It is a brain re-training process, and like all process, it is repetition that builds new neural pathways. This isn't a theory, it's a fact. All learning uses this format of see first, and then do.

Here's a quick format for self-hypnosis:-

* Make sure you're in a comfortable environment where you won't be disturbed. You may wish to use soothing music in the background but silence is fine if you prefer it. Seat yourself comfortably. Allow 10-20 minutes.

* Close your eyes and begin by focussing on your breath. Notice the feeling of the breath as your chest rises and falls with each inhale and exhale. Give yourself permission to settle but don't try. We want to dispense with urgency. We're not trying to become enlightened here. It's simply ten minutes of quiet time. If distractions occur such as thoughts, or urges to do something else, just notice them and then let them go, like leaves in the wind. Use your breath as an anchor which you can come back to if your mind is distracted or drifts. This is to be expected.

* After a couple of minutes of this, all the time not trying, but just settling gently, then engage your imagination by imagining a colour that represents feelings of peacefulness for you. Imagine being surrounded by a wonderful comforting layer of this colour, and then imagine that you can breathe it in too. As you breathe it in, imagine it filling your whole body and relaxing every muscle with its soothing qualities. When your body wants to relax, allow it.

* When you start to feel relaxed you will notice that your thoughts will slow down and your feelings will become more peaceful. Then imagine that you are descending ten broad steps down into a beautiful garden. Think to yourself that each step that you take is a step down into deeper levels of relaxation, and count them down from ten to zero.

* As you reach zero imagine stepping into the garden and being filled with a wonderful sense of peace. Imagine seeing beautiful flowers and scenery. Engage all of your imaginary senses. How does it smell? Can you feel the warmth of the sun? Is there a nice breeze? What do you hear? Birdsong? Trickling water? Use what feels good for you.

222

* Spend some time absorbing the peace and when you are ready, find somewhere to rest in the garden. Imagine settling down in your chosen spot. Then, closing your eyes (within the garden) and letting your mind drift off to your chosen positive rehearsal scenario.

* Play through your positive movie seeing the event or situation going well. All the time you can be using statements like "I am feeling calm and relaxed", "I'm noticing how nice everyone is being to me", "I'm actually doing really well as I relax into..." If, for any reason you feel uncomfortable, you can simply imagine opening your eyes and returning to your peaceful spot in the garden. If you're relaxed when you begin your rehearsal though, you should find that it's quite easy to remain relaxed as you run your rehearsal.

* When you've rehearsed your scenario positively, all the way to the end, give yourself the suggestion that you can come back to ordinary waking awareness, feeling good, wide awake, and refreshed, and bringing with you those peaceful feelings which can stay with you after the session.

* Gently surface, and when you are ready open your eyes, feeling good!

You have in the past literally hypnotised yourself into believing bad things. Now you know how to hypnotise yourself positively. Keep it simple. You'll notice the difference! If you use this tool, do keep a record of how much better your experience of an event is when you positively rehearse it first. Then you'll know for sure that you have a powerful tool available to you any time you need it. I do this every time I go to the dentist!

ANALYTICAL HYPNOTHERAPY

Analytical Hypnotherapy is a different discipline. It can't be practiced alone. You need an Analytical Hypnotherapist to facilitate and guide the process. I still want to say a few words about it though because it's been the most powerful tool in my therapeutic toolbox throughout my career, and it may be highly relevant for some readers who may resonate with the purpose of this therapy.

Some areas of the therapeutic community are divided in their opinions about analytical hypnotherapy, and I can understand why. What it boils down to for me is this. Analytical Hypnotherapy practiced poorly has the potential to create more problems than it solves, but that doesn't mean that it's not also a very powerful therapeutic tool for the good when practiced properly. It really depends then on who is facilitating the process, how they are using the tools, and for what reason? If your therapist just drags up loads of unprocessed emotion and leaves you to sit with it without instruction, or any effort to heal it, to me, that's potentially more harmful than helpful. If you have a sensitive, switched-on therapist who understands the process of healing, who guides you to resolution, and works skilfully to create a powerful new perspective on old wounds and beliefs, then it will probably be a positively life-changing event.

Analytical Hypnotherapy is taught, and practiced, differently around the World. The Freudian style of "free association" is basically a process whereby the patient is guided into hypnosis, and then encouraged to follow a free train of thoughts and memories which are relayed to the therapist in real time. As the client remembers, and relays these memories, the therapist may ask questions designed to elicit further information. These questions may guide, but should never lead. The therapist remains "invisible" in the process, other than encouraging further engagement. Much of the client's recall will be banal and irrelevant, but at some point in the flow of memory, something significant may emerge. When this happens, the client may spontaneously, or with guidance from the therapist, make a powerful emotional connection with a hitherto unrecognised significant event from their life. This can sometimes result in what is called an "abreaction". Abreaction can range from the slightest rise in breathing rate and blood pressure, to full-blown sobbing or howling.

The theory is that the abreaction fulfils two purposes. The first is that the mental connection between a long held pain and an unrecognised causal event is finally made in the mind, bringing deep understanding and resolution to the client. The second is that the "repressed" pain is literally released from the psyche, sometimes explosively, in the form of tears or shaking that were never expressed at the time of the event. A

224

course of analytical hypnotherapy may last ten or fifteen sessions, and this process of allowing the mind to wander and release long-held tensions continues until there is no more significant new recall.

The second method commonly used is called "regression to cause". The process is similar, but instead of the mind wandering from one memory to the next, the focus is placed on a particular problem or feeling, and the client is encouraged to travel mentally back to the root of that specific difficulty.

There are a number of potential problems with the model of analytical hypnotherapy. The process itself has the potential to stir up limbic system arousal. The act of repeatedly remembering painful memories can be distressing, and it can be argued that there is no value in doing so. Another potential problem is that of "false memory syndrome", where a person makes erroneous connections, or has memories which never really happened. Memory is fluid, and can be inaccurate. Dreams or imaginings for instance, particularly those long since passed, may be confused with reality. A person could be so desperate to find a "reason" for their ills, that their mind could construct a fantasy based "memory" to fit the bill. This is a very real possibility and could have potentially far-reaching consequences if a client becomes convinced that they have been abused for instance, when they have not. An inexperienced therapist can also potentially "lead" a client to construct memories in this way with suggestive language or questions, such as "Were you ever touched inappropriately?" This would be **bad** practice, since although it's a question, it could also be a "leading" suggestion around which a false memory could be constructed. Instead, the invisible therapist should simply ask "What happened next?" It sounds like a minefield doesn't it? I wouldn't blame you for thinking you might give this one a miss! There are potential pitfalls, but there is another side to the story.

Here's a section from my practice website explaining the process:-

"We use hypnosis to locate the root cause of problems, release the carried emotional burden, re-frame the event accurately, and reconfigure the limiting beliefs that were taken on at that time. Often, in life, we will have had experiences which will have proven too much to cope with at the time

when they occurred, particularly as children when we didn't have the necessary resources or understanding to emotionally process the event or situation. Though we may feel we have dealt with those issues intellectually, it is commonly the case that the emotional impact of those experiences remains unresolved. Unresolved emotion can be held in the psyche, manifesting as ongoing tension, fear, or defensiveness. It can have a powerful effect on our present day lives.

When we successfully locate a repressed emotion under hypnosis, we often make contact with that emotion in a very real way, and it is literally "released". This release can be profound...a real weight off the shoulders. With the repressed emotion now freed from the psyche, it is possible to re-frame the situation with the understanding we possess as an adult. If we are lacking that understanding, then it's the role of the therapist to help to clarify an accurate picture. Re-framing forms a substantial part of the analytical process. It's not always a trauma that creates a problem though. Sometimes it can be something very innocent which was simply misunderstood or taken too literally. Often it's a case of righting wrongs (which we do by re-viewing and re-framing the situation at its creation point) at the mental and emotional level, thus creating a new root from which a stronger today can feed. We cannot change the past, but we can change our perception of what the past means to us, and how it affects what we do, think, feel, and say today."

I've used analytical methods, albeit in my own very controlled way, for my entire career. My approach has been simple. The goal of analytical therapy for me has always been to amend unhelpful belief systems at their root. Wherever possible I have avoided encouraging big abreactions, and my therapeutic methods have used techniques which distance my client from a re-experiencing of the causal event. Pure hypnoanalysts may disagree with this method, but I have always wanted to strike the right balance in getting the job done, with the minimum of discomfort for my client. If an abreaction has happened, that's been okay with me, but my primary goal has been to amend the belief system. In essence I want to help my client to experience for themselves that some part of their history contains an erroneous assumption which has left them wounded ever since, and have them correct that assumption there and then, so that their new understanding becomes **felt** experience. If you change what the believer believes then you change what the prover proves. When this happens, it can change how you feel at a very deep level.

I've never done anyone any harm. I've never had a complaint about my work, and I've never had a situation that I couldn't handle. I have seen many powerful healings take place using these methods. I've had people come in the door unable to breathe because their chest was so tight with tension, who have floated out of the consulting room an hour later breathing deeply and smiling again. I've had people express to me that they massively regretted the lost years they had spent living under the assumption that they were worthless, after just a one hour session, saying that they wish they'd done this work years ago. I've seen severe depression and anxiety lift significantly in just one session. With my hand on my heart, I have seen these things happen. On occasion, I have been astonished.

Some people still believe that it's an outdated therapy with no value, or worse still, the potential to do harm. My take on it is that it depends on who's giving it, who's receiving it, how the session is facilitated, and what for? Properly handled, amazing breakthroughs can happen. Poorly wielded, it definitely has the potential to make a mess.

So, that's the information. I cannot speak for other therapists, but what I can say is that properly trained analytical hypnotherapists will be aware of the potential for problems and will have tools for making sure they avoid them. I understand why the community is divided. I'm just reporting the facts as I know them. If you feel strongly that your wounds are rooted in past events which remain unresolved, then it may be something you're interested in investigating. If it's not for you, that's fine. I believe I've given a balanced and honest explanation. I'll leave it with you to consider!

FORGIVENESS

"Carrying anger is like holding a hot rock that you intend to throw at someone else….in the end the only person it burns is you".

Yes, I know that's the second time you read that statement. That's because forgiving, and letting go, are in many ways the same thing. When we feel that we have been wronged, we often assume that to "forgive" that wrong would be to condone it. That's not really what forgiveness is about. Forgiveness is for you, not for the other. Forgiveness is about giving yourself permission to let it go. Like a hot rock, it is burning you. It may be yourself, another person, a situation, a loss, the World, or life itself that has wronged you. Indeed, morally, you may be perfectly entitled to feel furious at what has befallen you. No-one would disagree that it has been an awful ride for you. The question is though, are you going to continue to punish yourself by carrying the weight of a past that can't be undone? It's just more suffering on top of what has already happened. That's letting "them" win! It is our belief that we have been wronged by life that holds us in chains. To give up the belief that you are chained by that event or wrongdoing to an immutable fate is to give up your chains. But why should you?

The quick answer to this is that staying locked in your story of the past stops you from moving into a brighter future. Now of course, the logic goes that we have been so badly hurt by what happened that any chance of a bright future has been forever decimated. It is this feeling that holds us in our story. By remaining in that story we rule out the possibility that this belief may not be 100% true. It is a catch 22. You won't actually know that there's a future for you until you let it go, but you won't let it go because the story argues there's no point. What do you do?

Forgiveness is letting go of all hopes for a better past – A course in miracles.

Forgiveness is challenging. No one is saying you **must** forgive. It's entirely your decision. Neither is anyone suggesting that you simply choose to do it and then it's done. It is a process, and like all processes it takes time. However, there is very definitely a decision to be taken, and that decision is the decision to heal, or not to heal. Once the decision to heal has been taken, then the process can begin. That doesn't mean it's done. It just means that you initiate the process. The process of forgiveness is not something you do once and then it's done. It's easy to forgive the fact that your buddy still owes you a fiver from 1995, but bigger stuff is more challenging. It's something you continue to re-affirm over however long it takes, possibly a lifetime.

We also know that when an emotional mind becomes aroused, it becomes much more past-focussed. That's why part of the plan for solution involves dealing with the stresses in your life today. In essence then, it becomes easier to forgive when you're more relaxed generally. This is common sense. We all know it's impossible to let go of anger when we're in the middle of being angry! We have to take some time to calm down and gain perspective. Then something softens. Keep this in mind. It is important.

Why did this happen to me? The book "The Forgiveness Formula" by Kathleen Griffin addresses this question beautifully, and in essence, answers that there are many possible reasons including "accidentally" and "for no good reason at all". I am touching only briefly here on the subject of forgiveness because a lack of forgiveness can be a source of stress and anxiety, particularly if we have the feeling that we can't forgive ourselves for something. Unfortunately if we're really upset with ourselves, we can assume we're unforgivable. If forgiveness is standing between you and wellbeing try finding other peoples' stories of forgiveness. They may inspire you. Otherwise, again, a therapist could be enormously helpful. Punishing yourself with anxiety and depression is a powerful subconscious agenda, and the very nature of the bind will make it difficult to self-resolve. Though you may feel that no amount of punishment could ever be enough, life really wants you to learn from a mistake, and make your reparations to the World by doing something helpful with your lesson. You simply can't do that if you're too busy beating yourself up. Hopefully, what you've learned in this book will lead you to be able to soften your position. If you need more help, then please go and get some, and make yourself useful again! Life is really too short for endless self-punishment.

He who has not yet forgiven an enemy has never yet tasted one of the most sublime enjoyments of life – Lauter

CONTRACTS

Contracts we make with ourselves under duress can later become a lead weight. Consider this scenario. Sarah has been married for eight years. She discovers her husband Dave is having an affair. Drama ensues. Dave leaves, Sarah is devastated. Sarah makes a solemn promise to herself that she will never allow anyone to hurt her like that again. Ten years later, Sarah is finding that all her romantic relationships are failing, and she feels that she's to blame. Every time a new partner begins to get close, she does something to sabotage the relationship. She says she doesn't want to do this, but it just keeps happening. Before she knows it, she's said the wrong thing and ruined everything again.

Contracts live within us in much the same way that beliefs do. Consider Sarah's contract. It seems harmless enough on the face of it, but what it really says is "I'll never let anyone get close enough to hurt me again", which by extension means "I'll never let anyone get close". Love is being vulnerable.

When you share your heart with someone, you also "open" your heart to them. The only other option is to "close" your heart to the World around you. Closed hearts make for bitter lives. Open hearts are vulnerable. It's a dilemma for sure. Few, if any people go through life without having their heart broken in some way. It plugs directly into the issue of living courageously. Broken hearts do take time to mend, and every heart-break leaves a scar. We can't force letting go. Neither should we be complacent about the narrative we explain our lives by. At some point we need to stop defining ourselves as the heartbroken and start living fully again. Of course, we all need to be discerning about whom we let in to our heart space, but Sarah's contract is set out as an absolute. Her subconscious mind remembers the promise she made to herself, and now any time anyone gets close enough to hurt her, the subconscious programme is activated, and she find herself behaving in a way that ensures that the person in question is actively rejected. This ensures that her "rule" that she must never be hurt is not violated.

I recently worked with a young lady who discovered that she had a contract running with her-self that promised that she would never be well. When we explored this further we discovered that having suffered with anxiety from a very early age, her attempts to feel better during early life had been so disheartening that it had been easier to just create a contract that ensured she didn't have to feel that disappointment again. She said to me that until we had undertaken this work, she'd had no idea how matter-of-factly this contract had lived within her. She said that she could now see very clearly that it had been held as an "unquestionable fact within her being". She just "knew" that she could not get better. When a fact like that is kicking around in your psyche, it's no small wonder that attempts to heal are thwarted. Do you see how that contract acts like a belief within the unconscious mind? Beliefs are facts as far as the unconscious mind is concerned, and it actions them accordingly.

Contracts are often made under duress. We make faulty contracts when things feel so bad that we feel we have no other choice than to make a promise to ourselves which will protect us at that time. In Sarah's case, she really felt that she couldn't take another rejection at that time, so she promised herself never to be vulnerable again. Our young lady above decided at that time that she couldn't handle the deflation of further failed attempts to fix her anxiety. The problem is that contracts live on long after they have ceased to be useful, and unless we let the unconscious mind know that the programme is no longer required, it will keep faithfully executing the according behaviours and beliefs without question. Perhaps you can have a think about the contracts and promises you have made to yourself along the way? Are they still serving you?

CONTRACT RE-NEGOTIATION

If you've identified one or more unhelpful contracts in your being, you can consider a re-negotiation. It's a matter of internal communication and mediation. If you've been following the exercises so far, you will by now have some sense of how to communicate deeply with yourself. Re-negotiation of contracts uses this self to self, or part to part communication. The part of you that feels fear about something is the part that's committed to the contract never to do X again. So the renegotiation involves dialogue between that frightened part of your-self and the part of you committed to wellness. The idea is quite simple. You put time aside where you can be undisturbed. You sit quietly and begin to turn your attention and focus inward, and you connect with your old contract. A good way to do this is to speak out loud whatever the contract says. Using our example above we could have Sarah speak out loud "I'll never allow myself to love fully again". What will happen when Sarah speaks this is that she will feel the truth of that statement (for her) intuitively. This is usually quite subtle. Don't expect it to be anything else. It will just be a subtle sense that some part of you endorses the statement. If this is any way confusing then just try speaking some different statements first to see how your body responds. Try some statements that you know to be completely true, like "my name is...Sarah", and then some statements that are completely false like "I am a Zebra, and I live on the African plains". This should help you to "tune in" to the subtleties of how statements make you feel. Having connected with that subtle sense of endorsement you are now in a position to open a meaningful communication with that "part" of your-self that carries the contract. You begin with an unconditional acknowledgment. You say "I get that you learned to fear (in Sarah's example) opening your heart to people". Just take a moment to let that sit. As always, sincerity is everything in acknowledgment. Let yourself feel the sincerity of the statement. It is a witnessing of sorts. When an event is witnessed deeply we are then in a better position to move forwards. Often, narratives are held on to because we feel that no one has known our pain, or acknowledged our suffering. Next you say "I also get that you made a commitment to never allow that to happen again, and I champion that...in principle. The problem is, that promise was made under duress at a time when things were really difficult, and since then time has moved on. Things are different now, and that promise has become a great hindrance rather than a help. I would like to try to love again. Can you help me with this?"

Then, you dialogue. Your job is now to communicate to this fearful part of yourself that you are in a better position to try again. You give valid reassurances where necessary, and if there are reasonable terms requested to trying again, you do all you can to honour these. If you can't get complete acceptance, then see if you can negotiate a trial, temporarily, which implements "some" change, with a view to reviewing

232

the agreement at a later date. You renegotiate the terms with yourself and when you have the new terms negotiated, you shake hands and call it a deal. If, for any reason, you find it difficult to find closure or resolution, don't force it. Just be kind to yourself. Say "I understand that you need more time to heal", and close with a sense of self-support. Remember everything you have learned here about reducing stress and anxiety. Keep applying these measures. Eventually you will arrive at a place where it feels safe enough to re-negotiate your contracts with yourself.

This all sounds rather formal, so do remember that it really is a symbolic gesture for the mobilisation of your intent. As with all these things, don't oversell it. It's not meant to be an epiphany (though great if it is!) It's a small happening that grants permission for change, and sets the wheels in motion. With the new contract in place, you now act in accordance with your new agreement. Again, therapy can help here if you can't, or don't wish to do this alone.

DON'T SWEEP IT UNDER THE CARPET!

"Tough guys don't cry...they just have heart attacks"

Repressed tension and conflict within the psyche will inevitably manifest itself in some way. Where there is conflict, there must also be discharge. The difficulty is that sometimes the problem area is perceived as taboo. Since we are not allowed to think the unthinkable, the mind is forced to redirect the tension into a more acceptable form. This is why Freud believed in the beginning of the last century that many problems were of a sexual origin. It might have been very valid in Freud's day. In the Victorian era, people were putting pantaloons over chair and table legs because chair legs were considered too sexual to be on open display. Cultural repression of the sexual theme was common, and sometimes extreme, and Freud concluded that hysteria was one of the possible results of this repression. Sexual energy is a powerful natural force that will not be suppressed. To be anti-sex is to be anti-life, and life has a way of letting us know when we're off track. That energy will find a way out. If you suppress all that natural energy, it's going to cause a problem somewhere. It demands expression. If hysteria is more acceptable than sexual expression, then hysteria will have to do.

Emotions are equally powerful natural forces that demand acknowledgement and expression. If a feeling is considered unacceptable, then it is likely to be suppressed, and if it can't come out "here" then it's going to come out over "there" because one way or another, that force is going to make itself felt. We're back again to our earlier techniques of "acknowledging and accepting" our feelings without judgement. This means allowing an unacceptable feeling such as (purely as an example) "I hate my Father" to be felt. You may have been hurt, and you need to acknowledge and process that feeling fully before it can be released. We have a problem if we feel that said emotion is such a taboo that we are not allowed to feel it, right? So now we have a problem with anger because that anger is playing itself out in inappropriate ways as it tries to find expression. Sweeping it under the carpet doesn't work!

What makes dealing with anxiety (or emotional arousal) a little tricky sometimes is that for some people there is a natural avoidance mechanism when it comes to the real problem. This is of course an "unconscious" process, and it rarely happens in quite such a black and white way, as in the above example. It's often more subtle than this, and frequently many small anxieties add up to a great big one. Unless we deal with the underlying anxiety (the real problems), the false focus will continue. Sublimation can take all kinds of forms. It can be the person who's working eighty hours a week and kidding themselves that they are just fine with it while battling depression. In fact, some part of them is not okay with it at all because it means they are not seeing their kids grow up, and they're exhausted all the time. Here there's conflict, but working less hours has been chalked up rationally to be a non-option, so the conflict remains. It's an existing feeling which is considered unacceptable to feel, and pressure builds in the background. It's going to come out somewhere. This person has a panic attack because that conflict will make itself known. He might panic in a business meeting and develop a fear of public presentations, but the real cause is not a room full of people. It's the unrecognised stress in his life.

234

Now this is good news for us. You'll remember I said "anxiety doesn't drop out of the sky on us", but that it feels like it does sometimes? Well that's because of this process of sublimation. Now you can stop telling yourself your anxiety is for no reason at all. It isn't. It's just about identifying what is calling for your attention, and then working on those needs.

Earlier, when exploring some of the naturally occurring loveliness of a healthy open-hearted human being, I mentioned that we would return to explore the integration of the dark side of the human being. The subject of sublimation leads us beautifully to that point. If feelings can be considered unacceptable, then we can see that the same conclusion can be reached when it comes to different "parts" of ourselves.

THE SHADOW SIDE OF HUMAN BEINGS

This is a vast subject. It is deep and thoroughly fascinating for those who choose to delve. In practice, it's not really necessary to start digging into shadow work for basic anxiety resolution. It is worth covering here though because there are two aspects of this understanding that may be very important to many anxiety sufferers, particularly those who are troubled with anxiety about dark thoughts. OCD sufferers will know this well. Such material often presents as part of the anxiety or depression symptom pattern, and it's all too easy to conclude that we must be bad people if we find negative material in the psyche. In this respect, the following understanding may be very helpful. If we can normalise the presence of negative material, we can stop thinking that there must be something terribly wrong with us for having dark thoughts! I felt it was important to include this section because there needed to be a balance to the opening sections of the book where we focussed simply on humanity's naturally occurring positive qualities. One way of thinking about shadow material is as follows:-

I spent twenty years putting stuff in the box, and the rest of my life trying to get it all out again!

The "shadow" is a Jungian (Carl G Jung) term alluding to all of the parts of ourselves that live outside of our awareness, usually because they've

235

been discarded, repressed, disowned, or lie undiscovered. Thus, they lie in the "shadow" that we cast behind us as we walk forwards into the light. Metaphorically, everything that we can see in front of us, that is, all that is allowed to remain consciously beheld by ourselves and others, is considered acceptable. That which is deemed socially or personally unacceptable is tossed over our shoulder into the shadow we cast behind us, out of sight, and supposedly at least, out of mind. The trouble is, in this context, out of sight isn't out of mind because these disowned aspects of our-selves don't really like to be disowned. They seek integration as part of the whole, and in the same way that feelings have a way of letting us know they want to be accepted into consciousness, so also do these parts of ourselves alert us to their presence. When they are not welcomed willingly they tend to force their way into our lives in inappropriate ways.

From the moment we're born, we are shaped. We are told what is, and what is not, acceptable about ourselves. Our environment has a massive influence in this regard, and we then extrapolate what we think is acceptable, and we continue to censor ourselves too. Human nature doesn't like to be too rigidly defined. We are in nature more "wild" than many of us care to admit. We're just extremely good at keeping a lid on it! Here, wild does not imply evil or out of control. It simply means that Victorian sensibilities are a long way from the hunter-gatherer culture we inhabited less than twenty thousand years ago. So while we aim to own only all the "nice" or "acceptable" bits of ourselves, we live in terror that we might discover, or that someone else may discover, the "unacceptable" parts of ourselves. In practice, we start to fear our own being. So the theory goes each part of ourselves that we disown, repress, ignore, or deny, causes us to have a loss of essential energy because we can no longer access the energy that part of ourselves holds for us. We can only access it if we also own it. The more censored we are therefore, the more we are missing access to parts of our essential energy. This makes people uptight.

Censoring is, of course, a good thing, and necessary to a point. We have come to a collective consensus that for order to reign, there are aspects of our humanity that need to be tamed and kept under control. Take violence for instance. Many biologists agree that we are, as a species, hardwired for violence, but we have learned to suppress our violent impulses, and most of us agree that the World is a better place for it. If everyone responded with violence to every angry urge, we'd have chaos in the streets twenty four hours a day. So ownership of our violent capacity, with the intention and mastery of control over it, is the correct position. But what if you come to fear that you could, under some circumstances, be violent? What if the very idea of violence under any circumstances caused you to feel terribly disturbed? Indeed, this is the case for many OCD sufferers who worry that they cannot be around knives etc. When this happens, we try to disown that aspect of ourselves. But we cannot because it is part of our nature. All that happens is that a great tension and conflict develops because we are trying to get rid of something which is completely part of our wholeness. From a shadow perspective, completely disowning your capacity for violence also leaves you unable to protect yourself, should you be attacked, and the psyche recognises this as a loss.

Your "wholeness" will sense that the disowning of this part of yourself is bad for you, and will seek to let you know by bringing this aspect into your consciousness against your will.

So we find ourselves in situations where the very thing we are trying to deny about ourselves is, again and again, brought to our attention in different ways. What is happening is that the wholeness of our being is asking us to reclaim our discarded self. Though there are certainly parts of our shadow that are unavoidably ugly, the principle is that we can use vast amounts of energy trying to suppress or deny their existence. So goes Shakespeare's quote "The lady doth protest too much, methinks", often used to highlight a situation where someone emphatically denies some facet of their personality, and in their protestations actually reveals that it's much more a part of them than they are willing to become aware of. The problem with shadow material is that much of it really is culturally and personally unacceptable.

So, some examples of shadow material might include but are certainly not limited to:-

Sexual Deviancy. Greed. Hedonism. Hostility. Power. Racism. Envy. Anarchy. Avarice. Hatred. Violence.

These are all qualities we like to think that we, as decent people, don't own. If we search ourselves honestly though, we can see that we all have the potential to exhibit any of these qualities. They are, whether we like it or not, part of our makeup. How do we come to terms with this? The key is to be able to acknowledge the existence of these parts of ourselves, and integrate them into our being, without choosing to cultivate them or place them at the front and centre of our personality. What that means in practical terms is not being afraid of the fact that we find these qualities in the psyche. On the face of it, we find the issue a moot point because if we're not exhibiting these qualities to any great degree then why should it matter whether they exist potentially or not? The answer depends on what the quality is, and to what degree it is denied or feared.

The stronger our aversion to any particular "shadow" quality, the more we are likely to fear it.

When we consider the recent public disdain for banks being bailed-out while bankers continue to bask in fat champagne-soaked bonuses, we are right to be outraged. What it helps us to look at however, is our own greed. Greed is a part of human nature. It's fuelled partly by the fear of scarcity. What we aim to do is to own the fact that we have the capacity for greed, recognise it within ourselves, and then with it firmly in the light of consciousness, ensure that we do not allow it to control us. We see the impulse, but we choose not to act upon it mindlessly. This is a healthy position. But, what happens if we are horrified by the notion that we could be perceived as greedy by others? Then, we must do away with that part of ourselves. We go to extraordinary lengths to ensure that nothing we ever do exhibits a tendency towards greed. This is noble in ambition, but in practice, it delivers a lot of stress. Now, we are afraid to ask for a well-deserved pay rise. We give attention to everyone but ourselves. We constantly worry that people won't like us if we say no. In short, we go too far, and undervalue ourselves. In addition to this, our level of disgust in others may increase. We "project" our insecurities onto others. That creates stress and tension because it gives us a sense of moral superiority, which creates an "us and them" feeling, encouraging anger and hatred, right and wrong. Then we find that we are losing energy because we are constantly angry, and trying to "kill" greed wherever we see it. We resent others for their success, and secretly because we would never admit to ourselves, we are envious of their success. We wish we had the front to ask for more.

This, in fact, is the root of much of the conflict in the World. Anarchists hate Governments and Governments hate Anarchists. Both actually have a valid position, neither of which is right. Conservatives hate Socialists and Socialists hate Conservatives. Democracy and Communism don't fare much better. Both sides actually want a bit of what the other has got. But neither would ever admit it! War ensues. There is no easy antidote to this pain. Shadow work is uncomfortable. It involves climbing down from your high position and admitting that you're flawed too.

We can assume that where we find strong resistance to personality traits in others, it is a signpost pointing us back to where we ourselves have work to do. A disowned part of yourself is asking to be brought home. The quality we detest in others is firmly in our shadow, asking for our acknowledgment. What we are doing in shadow working is bringing these qualities in to the light of consciousness. Then, they are no longer able to exert powerful influence from a "hidden" position. Many cultures have woven into their mythologies the profound understanding that demons (defined as "that which hinders") exert their power by remaining un-named and hidden. By "naming the demon" you gain some degree of mastery over it. In some strange sense, our shadow material represents a part of our personal power. When we reclaim parts of self which were previously disowned, or considered unacceptable, we gain some measure of control over that part. Ultimately it's about embracing these qualities in a safe and integrated way. It is the denying of these qualities that give them power over us.

So if you're troubled with dark or negative thoughts, you should know that they exist as part of the make-up of nature and the World, and by extension, the archetypal human being. You are not bad or wrong for being unfortunate enough to be troubled by them. The trick is to recognise that they've been part of the World forever, and they say nothing at all about whether you're a good person or not. This material should not be feared. Acceptance of its presence without the cultivation of the negative is the wisest stance. The correct response is "My brain is presenting dark stuff. So what!?"

We may find that acknowledging this is uncomfortable or tinged with grief, but there is another way of integrating the shadow material. We also can choose to be playful with it, to hold it with lightness, humour and even empathy. While much of it is no laughing matter, it remains a reality, so we minimise our suffering by minimising our resistance and repulsion. This is historically how we have worked with shadow material. This is why the irreverent amongst us enjoy politically incorrect satire and comedy. In many cultures it has been a long established part of tradition that these forces within the psyche are given life through drama and ritual. Every religion does the same. Sometimes these take the forms of dances that play out the battle between good and evil. Puppetry, theatre, cinema, storytelling, and literature, are other ways in which these universal themes are addressed. Though the Tarot cards are often considered an "occult" tool associated with magic and dark arts, they are actually cards representing the hidden archetypal potential of the World psyche, both positive and negative, and another tool for acknowledgement of the contents of the World. In Western culture we have the sport of boxing and horror/slasher movies that serve as a kind of homage to the violence in our beings. As distasteful as these things are, we can recognise that there is a certain collective appetite for them, and this is no accident. These are "safe" outlets for the collective shadow.

However we approach our shadow material the idea is that the unwanted (shadow) force is given space to manifest in a harmless way, thus allowing it to be acknowledged, so that it doesn't manifest in an overwhelming or damaging way in our lives. Our dreams and fantasies too, are from a Jungian perspective, considered a natural mechanism for the presentation and integration of shadow material. Though naturally we should be incredibly careful about what kind of fantasies we entertain and to what degree, we can see the role that such fantasies may play in maintaining equilibrium within the psyche.

There is a famous Native American fable called "The Two Wolves" which sums up the correct position beautifully.

A Cherokee elder was teaching his grandchildren about life. He said to them, "A fight is going on inside me...it is a terrible fight between two wolves. One wolf represents fear, anger, envy, sorrow, regret, greed, arrogance, hatefulness, and lies. The other stands for joy, peace, love, hope, humility, kindness, friendship, generosity, faith, and truth. This same fight is going on inside of you and every other person too." The children thought about it for a minute. Then one child asked his grandfather, "Which wolf will win?" The Cherokee elder replied..."The one you feed."

Therapeutic work in this area should be approached very carefully. While not inherently dangerous, a certain amount of respect should be brought to the process of integrating the shadow material so as not to be overwhelmed by more than we can digest at any given time. For now, it's enough to simply understand that negative material is a natural part of the human psyche. We all have it, and we're simply aiming to repress as little as possible while integrating safely that which calls for our attention. So now you know there's no need to freak out if you have dark thoughts. It comes with the brain.

ALCHEMY, ARCHETYPES, AND THE HEALING POWER OF STORIES

Carl Jung trained with Sigmund Freud. They were good friends for some time. Jung was a reluctant visionary however, and lived a life full of profundity and visions. As a result, he developed a psychology which was built on a much grander framework than Freud's, and they eventually fell out over their disagreeing Worldviews. Jung devoted his life to the study of the unconscious mind, and worked tirelessly as a true scholar of our time. He was extremely well versed in all forms of mysticism, and as a reluctant visionary was frequently perplexed by powerful dreams and visions which he recorded and studied. Over time he came to realise that there was great meaning in many of his dreams, and he decided that the language of the unconscious mind must be symbolic. He saw that throughout human history this fact had long been recognised and utilised by those who had successfully harnessed the power of the unconscious mind. He then set about studying these historical disciplines in an effort to decipher their meanings and workings. Central to Jung's obsession was his fascination with Alchemy. Alchemy was the ancient art and study of seeking to transmute Lead (the basest of all metals) to Gold (symbolically the finest of metals). Although this was originally a physical discipline practiced by chemists, and derided by most as a waste of time at the physical level, the process itself became a metaphor for spiritual transformation. The idea was that one could move from the base state of physicality to the pure gold of the Actualised Soul. The goal of alchemy was self-actualisation; to create from ones base self a being made whole by both the negative and positive aspects of life and being; the successful integration of opposites (polarities). The continued repetition of performing the chemical steps of dissolution and reconstitution into a new form became a meditation on the nature of personal transformation. Alchemy was essentially a form of Magick and its followers sought the ever elusive Elixir of Life-The Soul-Immortality-The Philosopher's Stone. Jung saw this as an important model and metaphor for self-improvement and change, and studied it extensively before compiling his own thoughts on the relevance of the model to contemporary psychology. Jung's conclusion was that ultimately, human beings are inherently programmed to seek a state of self-actualisation, that is, to become complete. He called it Individuation. Jung says:-

Individuation is the natural process of human maturation. It is an innate tendency of the psyche to achieve total integration. We have no choice about whether we individuate, any more than we had a choice about going through puberty. What we can choose to do is to co-operate with the underlying inevitable tendency, and thus save ourselves a great deal of pain, anguish, embarrassment, and a variety of psychological disorders, often manifested as physical symptoms.

It is often described as having two phases:

* Adaptation to the world in first half of life.

* Reappraisals of relation of ego to unconscious in the second half.

We see again here this idea of spending twenty years filling the box (adaptation to the world) and the rest of our lives recovering (reappraising) the box's contents. What the above says in plain English is that we spend the first part of life fitting in, and the rest of life working through the emotional and psychological mess that "fitting in" has caused us at the unconscious level!

Carl Jung didn't find that his life experience was a good fit with the models he had been given to work with. During his work, with both himself and his patients, he repeatedly encountered hugely important symbolic contents emerging from the unconscious mind which simply would not fit into Freud's highly personal models. Although he acknowledged the existence of the individual unconscious, he also started to think about the universality of certain experiences across cultures, and posited a much larger World view. He decided that there must be a repository of human experience which all people could access, but which remained essentially unconscious. So normally, one could not consciously dip into this repository, but under certain circumstances such as during the dreaming period, and in other unusual states of consciousness, forces and forms could burst forwards from this mysterious continuum, erupting into conscious awareness with primal force. He called this continuum "The Collective Unconscious". He based his theory on the fact that certain symbolic forms crossed cultures. So regardless of whether one lived in Tahiti or London, one could still dream about something being birthed, and the symbolic impact of that dream could be interpreted in a similar way regardless of culture. Even stranger still, he noted that some of the archetypal forms his clients encountered were alien to the culture the client had grown up in, but known to cultures elsewhere. Apparently, even with no conscious knowledge of a certain myth it is still possible to experience an archetype which derives from any myth, some of which are obscure to say the least. I experienced this personally some years ago when I had a dream in which I was trapped in a very foreboding landscape. In a moment of crisis I found myself shouting with enormous power "Hermes!" at which point I was lifted from the ground at about a hundred miles an hour. Although at the time I had heard the word Hermes I had no conscious knowledge of what Hermes represented. Upon later research I learned that Hermes is "The Winged Messenger of the Gods" who can rescue souls from the underworld, and in fact is central to ancient alchemical practices. The dream involved a rescue from the underworld just as the myth would depict, and since I was right in the middle of a deeply transformational process at the time, the theme was spookily apt!

Essentially Jung was pointing out that we all share a common nature. The forms and forces which inhabit this normally invisible mental world he called "archetypes". If a stereotype is defined as "solid impression", then archetype is "original impression". In Jung's terms - 'Archetype' is defined as the first original model of which all other similar persons, objects, or concepts are merely derivative, copied, patterned, or emulated. He explained that these archetypal forms and forces are immensely powerful, and could manifest within a person's psyche in a multitude of forms. Jesus, for instance, can be considered to be an archetypal force. It was for this reason that Jung placed so much importance on "myth" as a means of understanding the forces which have shaped our World and our lives, both individually and culturally.

Jung said: *If we bear in mind that the unconscious contains everything that is lacking to consciousness, that the unconscious therefore has a compensatory tendency then we can begin to draw conclusions - provided, of course, that the dream does not come from too deep a psychic level. If it is a dream of this kind, it will, as a rule, contain mythological motifs, combinations of ideas or images, which can be found in the myths of one's own folk or in those of other races. The dream will then have a collective meaning, a meaning which is the common property of mankind.*

When we look back through history we find that the oldest traditions of healing are myth based. From the very first campfires of our ancestors, stories have been passed from generation to generation. The healing power of the archetype is in some ways very similar to the healing power of the metaphor. Both are stories, and in some way these stories invite us to awaken and embody those archetypes in our own beings. Archetypal myths allow us to engage on a direct basis with these archetypal forces and draw strength from them. Actually, this is not nearly as strange as it sounds. Whatever you engage with, mythically speaking may be considered to be archetypal. If you are religious for example, you engage with the archetypes of your faith and you draw strength from them. From this perspective, Jesus, Buddha, Allah, Yahweh, are all very real. If you have an interest in shamanism then you may draw strength and guidance from your connection with the ancestors, or power animals. If you are interested in nature, and believe Nature to be alive and minded, then it's possible to gain strength from mountains, trees, and rivers. Today, we have modern myths which function in much the same way. By George Lucas' own admission the "Star Wars" series is an obvious re-drawing of ancient myth for modern day folk. It has it all - shamans, ritual, rites of passage, survival of death, love, loss, heroism, mysticism, the force, and of course the ultimate triumph of love over hate and goodness over evil. It's not as comical as it may sound that a surprisingly high percentage of people wrote "Jedi" on their Census forms recently when asked what their religion was. Mythologically, it's totally viable. Consider the Wizard of Oz, perhaps the most well-loved and enduring movie in history. Why such endurance? Well, simply, even if we don't consciously give it much thought, it speaks to us at a very deep level. The scarecrow, the lion, and the tin-man are all representations of parts of our-selves which believe themselves lacking, but find ultimately, that the very qualities they sought had been with them all along. Perhaps more importantly still though it was the journey they took to seek those qualities which brought them to the understanding of this truth. It was the journey itself that was the making of them. It's a powerful story because it is one that we are all engaged in, and it's one that's more than relevant to our own journey through anxiety. These myths remind us of the hero within each and every one of us. Indeed "The Hero" is an archetype itself, and when you engage with the story of the hero in any form, then that archetype can be activated in your own being. With archetypes, it is much less about whether a story is "true" or not and much more about what the story means and inspires within us.

Joseph Campbell said: Myth is the secret opening through which the inexhaustible energies of the cosmos pour into human cultural manifestation.

Such a statement may look like gobbledygook, but when you look more deeply, you realise that myth has actually been shaping our reality since the beginning of human history. Our cultural morality is based on myth. Our strengths and our weaknesses are based on myth. Myths have always told the stories of life, and in so doing, have shaped it. What is particularly interesting about many myths is that they usually contain a heroic protagonist, and a villain or archenemy. No hero is complete until he or she has first been challenged! Who can admire a hero who simply breezes through the story without being tested? And what is a challenge if it does not involve a precarious situation? A challenge that is easily solved is not a challenge at all. The whole point of a challenge is that there is a genuine possibility of failure. In religious literature we see this theme surface again and again. Jesus' final challenge involves a direct confrontation with the force representing his polar opposite, Satan himself. He is tempted by Satan, but ultimately overcomes this force with unswerving faith and heroic humility. Buddha too meets with his "demons" in confrontation before gaining liberation. Greek myths speak plentifully of dangerous journeys into the "Underworld", and great battles with powerful mythical creatures. Here, the underworld is a symbolic representation of the unconscious realm, where the hero is tested many times before earning freedom, victory or some other power. Christian myths tell the tale of the quest for the Holy Grail or Chalice, filled with many losses and failures before success is earned. Our beloved children's fairy-tales are also heavily loaded with powerful messages that have shaped each and every one of us much more profoundly than we may be consciously aware of. Again and again we see these themes of challenge, failure, learning, earning, and eventual victory. Unconsciously, these tales have shaped our lives and expectations, teaching us what to aspire to, what to love, and how to live heroically.

There is a lovely story from Monsters and Magical Sticks (a hypnosis book). Here I paraphrase. Mum and Dad sit down with their sleepless young child and spend an hour explaining that there are no monsters in

246

the corner of the room at night. After an hour of logical explanation, believing that everything is now understood, the young boy says "...what shall I do when the monsters come though?" Logic was having no effect at all in this case. So they decided a different approach might be more suited. They made him a magic wand out of a nice stick with some coloured thread and a small crystal and presented it to him in an ornate box explaining that they had obtained it especially from a magician and that it could vaporise all monsters. The boy was thrilled. He came back three days later with the box and the wand and said that he wouldn't need it now because all the monsters were gone for good. Often the unconscious mind really can show us how certain aspects of our life are understood symbolically, and as with monsters and magical sticks above, sometimes, symbol is the superior healer because we can engage with the aspect at the level at which it exists, as a story. Change the story, change the way the story lives within you, and you change your reality, perhaps not only figuratively, but quite literally.

With some understanding now in place of just how important and powerful mythology is in our lives it's important to understand too that not all myths have an empowering effect upon us. Alan Watts, a famous theologian, wrote a wonderful book called "Beyond Theology – The Art of Godmanship". This book literally changed my life. In this book he looks historically at the religions of the World and concludes that although there are quite definitely destructive forces in the World, we have made a fundamental mistake in our categorisation of these forces. Western Christian mythology places much emphasis on good and evil, and tells us that there is an important battle taking place between God and Satan who are apparently enemies to the end. Alan Watts points out that there has always been a place for destructive forces in some of the World's most ancient religions, but that many Eastern religions deified and worshipped these forces as a natural part of the cycle of creation. They believe that there can be no progress without destruction of the old to make way for the new. So, even though destruction is painful and difficult as it is occurring, it can be viewed ultimately as a positive force, bringing change and renewal. These deities are recognised as having equal importance, and are not categorised as good or bad but simply as part of the whole. Chaos is also opportunity. When we look at Nature and consider that Nature is perhaps the most evident face of reality, this

247

cycle is easy to see as life and death, summer and winter, seedling to fruition to compost.

Watts goes on then to suggest that off-stage, in the green room of creation, mythologically speaking, Satan is in fact God's right hand man! When they go on stage, in the visible arena of life, it's all drama. It appears that there is a great battle, the outcome of which is edge of your seat stuff, gritty, unbearable, terrifying, and sometimes awful. It's hard not to get caught up in it all. The trick though, Watts suggests, is to know that creation looks after itself in a way which is not visible to the audience. For me this is a much more helpful mythology than the one I inherited as part of my upbringing. We can find existential peace in this understanding because we can learn by extension not to fear the destructive archetypal forces within ourselves. Taking the view that these difficulties are archetypal themes of drama and growth as opposed to out of control forces can be extremely reassuring. Archetypal forces are undeniably powerful, and certainly real enough, but there is solace in understanding that your personal reality is ultimately created by the myths you engage with. To a degree, you have choice.

So is this purely academic or does it actually mean something within the context of anxiety busting? At one level your life is a story. "All the World's a stage and all the men and women merely players" said Shakespeare's Jaques. Who is in your play? What or who is around you that inspires you to embody your heroic spirit? What or who is in your mind space? Do you spend your days trawling the internet reading horror stories about how this person or that person was sectioned, or couldn't cope, or has been depressed for fifty years? Do you have people around you that constantly tell you about Uncle Jim who got anxious and never recovered? Are your family and friends positive heroic role models? Or, do they simply convince you that you're destined to lose? What myths do you use to explain life to yourself? Do you spend your free time watching tragedy or comedy? Are you obsessed with The News, World Corruption, and Politics? Do you follow a religion? What does your religion tell you about yourself and the World? It's all a story, and it all colours our overall atmosphere of being. Do you have awareness of what a powerful effect those myths can have upon your own explanatory style? All stories have their place, but when you're

248

fragile with anxiety or depression it's time to out the stories of tragedy and loss and hit the comedy section of your bookshelf or DVD collection. The world won't collapse if you take some time out from the seriousness of your story, or your obsessive focus on the dark side. There's a lot to be said for understanding that the World isn't actually filled with darkness and light. What it's filled with is the story of darkness and light. When you can view it this way, it's much easier to take that step back and relax a little. The story will play itself out regardless of how much mental energy you use on it. One client once said to me "I know it's crazy, but when I fly, I am convinced that the only reason that the plane doesn't crash is because I'm holding it up with my mind...If I relax, then I'm sure it will crash". There's a parallel here with anxiety generally that's something along the lines of "If I don't stay focussed on the negative, everything will unravel". This view is, upon inspection, no less irrational than a plane that must be buoyed by concentration.

Listen. Here's a true story. People recover from anxiety and depression all the time. Many people not only recover, they flourish. These are the stories you want to surround yourself with. We each need to understand individually that the players and story-tellers in our lives are having a profound effect on us, for better or worse. If you are receiving negative stories, be that from books, the internet, other people, religion, media, whatever, then you need to seriously reconsider what stories you are giving your attention to. The internet in particular is flooded with negative stories. One thing to remember is that most people who frequent forums about illness are the people who haven't yet recovered. They probably haven't recovered (yet) because they haven't yet approached their difficulty in a way that can bring about solution. We looked earlier at reasons that people can stay ill. We have to acknowledge that a percentage of those that say they've "tried everything and nothing works" will have one or more of these reasons unresolved. Equally, many will be simply in the process of recovery, but not there yet. It takes time. Few emotional difficulties are truly intractable. What you see much less of on the internet are the stories of success. If you must search for stories look for them using the words anxiety resolved, or successful treatment. Those people are busy getting on with life, and gave up frequenting the forums long ago. In this respect support groups are a double edged sword. On the one hand it can be of great value to meet others who are going through what you're going through. It validates and normalises your experience, as well as provides obvious moral and practical support. One potential problem with support groups though is that they, in themselves, can exert pressure in subtle ways to remain unwell. If the group itself meets a need for community and attention, then recovery implies the loss of the same. If we have no other way of having that need met, a subconscious agenda to remain unwell can easily establish itself. Equally, we need to be aware that the ratio of positive to negative stories in such a group will be weighted towards the negative since by definition the regular participants are at low points in their lives. Be aware of the power of the story and the people around you. Seek out the stories and the people that feed you emotionally with positive perspectives, and keep them handy at all times!

Chapter Eight - Depression

So far we've focussed on an overview with the majority of emphasis being upon anti-anxiety understanding. Since both anxiety and depression are the result of stress overload, it's fair to say that everything you've learned here so far can be reasonably applied to anxiety and depression equally. However, there is a difference in our experience of these states, and there's an important distinction to understand here. Anxiety tends to be more immediate. I find that anxious clients are generally much quicker to follow the programme than those who are depressed, and by extension, tend to recover more quickly. The highly motivated, recently anxious client might just need a few sessions before they are well on their way back to being on their feet. This is not surprising. Anxiety is a highly motivated state, so it's usual for people to spring into action to do whatever they need to do to get back on track. With the right understanding and guidance they can make short work of recovery from a minor anxiety illness. Part of the symptom pattern of depression however is lethargy, lack of hope, a feeling of pointlessness, and helplessness. With this in mind, it's important to understand what we're up against in the presence of depression because these symptoms can be a serious hindrance if we don't know how to handle them skilfully.

Overcoming Depression - Positive Action

Depression does not **usually** exist without reason. I highlight the word usually here because sometimes, it does. I acknowledge this. When depression is present with no reason, it's wise to visit the doctor. There could be a medical problem which requires medical treatment.

For the most part however, depression is the result of prolonged stress, catastrophic events, poor nutrition, alienation from self or others, and circumstances involving loss of control. The key words which characterize depression are "hopelessness" and "helplessness", so any recovery plan should therefore include a practical strategy for tackling the causes of such feelings.

251

One of the difficulties we face when approaching a solution to depression is the fact that a major part of the symptom pattern of depression, namely hopelessness and helplessness, disables the very thing we need to create solution – action. You should by now understand that depression is at the most basic level an ancestral response to famine, drought, disease, or inescapable crisis. The evolutionary logic is that if the environment has become uninhabitable then the best strategy is to retreat, conserve energy, and await better conditions. This is a hibernation-like response, so the apathy and disinterest we feel when in this "withdrawal" time is part of how depression is "supposed" to feel. If we can recognise the truth of this, we can understand that we are in the grip of an emotional mind (limbic system) response pattern, as opposed to a truly desperate or hopeless situation. Depression would have saved our lives when we were living a hunter-gatherer existence, but most depression today is unnecessary and unhelpful. Depression argues that since there's (apparently) no hope, it's really not worth trying to make things better. Depression argues that nothing can or will help. Depression can be very persuasive here. It is quite usual therefore for a person experiencing a depressed response to find little pleasure or motivation in re-engaging with the world, and as a consequence it is quite usual for this person to remain disengaged from the world. This manifests as a belief or feeling for the sufferer that they are somehow different from everyone else, that they are no longer a part of the World. This feeling sets-up behavioural patterns of withdrawal that ultimately reinforce this perception, as explained in our CBT section earlier, making it a self-fulfilling prophecy. In other words, the more we behave in a depressed manner, sleeping in late, not showering or dressing, not leaving the house, not dealing with our responsibilities, avoiding social interaction, feeling sorry for ourselves, insisting that everything remains hopeless, the more we encourage our limbic system to respond with further depressive feelings.

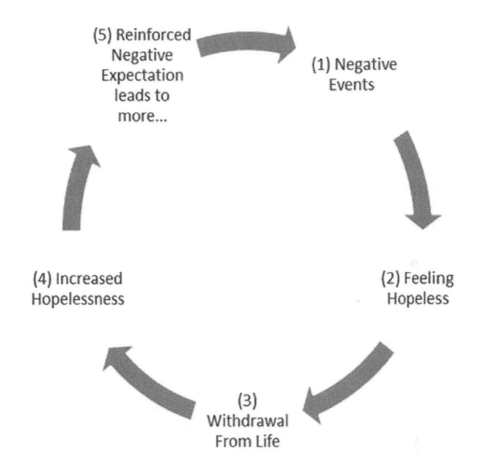

It is very important that we understand this cycle. If we are to escape this cycle we need to step off the circle. In practice recovery requires (amongst other things) the following action:

* Learning to tolerate negative events and feelings.

* Creating opportunities for fun and fulfilment.

* Creating hope.

* Re-engagement with life.

* Meeting unmet needs.

* Reappraisal of expectations, and interpretational style (how we explain events to ourselves).

Our job is to convince our limbic system that the crisis which caused us to become depressed has now passed. If we continue to behave as if our depression is an inescapable problem with no possibility of change, or indeed that things are as bad, or worse, than they were when our depression began, then our limbic system will be forced to continue supplying us with a depressed response. One of the ways then that we will convince our limbic system that a depressed response is no longer required is by behaving as though the crisis has passed. So what does this mean in practice? This means **normalising** life. It means behaving **as if** things were normal even if they don't feel normal.

The central obstacle to achieving this normalisation is "feelings". Ninety per cent of what we do or don't do is driven by feelings. When we are in the grip of a depressed response, it's all too easy to fall into the trap of "buying into" what our feelings are telling us. If we are to escape the cycle of depression then what we need to do is stop listening exclusively to our feelings, and start taking action that leads to normalisation. So we're back to CBT here. Remember the following.

* *Feelings are not facts. Learning to distinguish between facts and feelings is a vital skill to master. (Michael Yapko)*

* *Depression says "I'll do it when I feel better". Try instead "I'll feel better when I do it".*

At first, we are likely to feel a sense of futility in doing this. It is usual to take positive steps and feel initially that it doesn't seem to make any difference to how we feel. However, this is temporary, and it's a mistake to give up too soon. If we give up too soon we will simply reinforce our sense of hopelessness because we will have "proven" (inaccurately) that there's no hope. It's not that there is no hope. It's just that we haven't stuck at it for long enough to enjoy the results. We need to be persistent. We need to dig deep and be unwilling to settle for depression's explanation of what our lives are about. We need to go about taking the action that we know will improve things even if we currently feel that it won't, and we need to be patient. It takes time. What we don't want to do is try one anti-depression exercise and then base our whole conclusion on whether "it's working" or not on the outcome of that one thing. It might take two weeks of doing that thing every day before our mood lifts. Be persistent! The limbic system needs to see that things are changing before it will lift its depressed response. Do not expect overnight success. It doesn't work that way. It's about changing the landscape of your life, and we have to do that despite our continued negative feelings. If we are persistent, eventually the limbic system will lift the response pattern as we prove it is no longer appropriate by behaving as though it doesn't exist. One of the best ways to lift depression fast is to build something you can be proud of. Finding something you have a passion for, and working with that, is super anti-depression medicine.

Another cognitive mistake to be on the lookout for is the one where we say "I could go for a walk today, but it didn't clear my depression yesterday, so what's the point?" There are two mistakes here. The first is that we are expecting that going for a walk will either work or not work as a remedy. This is very black and white. The reality is that simply going for a walk is not likely to clear depression, but it might make some difference. If it clears it by ten percent, then it's worth doing. Going for a walk is preferable to staying in day after day looking at the four walls and ruminating. The second mistake here is assuming that something is only worth doing if it pays an immediate dividend. You didn't feel that way about going out for walk before you were anxious or depressed did you? You'd just go for a walk because it's good to go for a walk! We don't see results until we have been consistent with our efforts. We want to normalise experience, so you just do what you do without any massive expectations. The goal isn't to create immediate radiant illumination. It's to convince your limbic system that you are part of the world. So within reason, it's sensible to build the plan, and then stick to it regardless of immediate results, and regardless of how we might feel on any given day. We need to build a little flexibility into any plan so that we have options if we're really not up to it on a given day, but we should not allow our feelings to fully dictate our actions.

With this understood then, we want to create a plan of action for you. Since different people have different unmet needs there is no one-size-fits-all plan. You can build a plan specifically for yourself based on a very simple question:-

HOW WOULD YOU LIKE THINGS TO BE IN YOUR LIFE?

I'd like you to consider this question in detail and then come up with three definite solid goals that you know will make your life feel more normal. These don't have to be huge goals. They can be small, but they do need to improve the landscape of your life. Here are some suggestions:-

* Have more fun (Define it. Arrange it.)

* Clear up, and organise a room in your house.

* Deal with all outstanding paperwork.

* Buy some new clothes.

* Recycle your old clothes and tidy your drawers.

* Improve your diet.

* Take regular exercise.

* Reduce food/alcohol consumption.

* Go for a daily walk.

* Visit old friends.

* Learn a new skill/language.

* Grow a plant. Nurture it.

* Do something nice for someone else.

* Work towards changing your job.

* Take up a hobby.

* Quit smoking.

* Start a "gratitude journal".

* Commit to notice what's good in life.

* Volunteer to help others.

* Repair a relationship.

* Finish a project.

* Join a club.

* Engage more socially.

* Out of bed by 8am - washed and dressed.

GOAL SETTING – SMART GOALS

A time-honoured method for approaching goals is known as "S.M.A.R.T" (yes, another one!) which is:

* Specific – The goal is clearly defined. For a person with agoraphobia (fear of stepping outside) - Instead of saying "I'd like to be better soon", we might set the goal as "To be able to visit the local shops by myself within two months"

* Measurable - Can the outcome be measured? Is it possible to say whether the goal was achieved or not?

* Achievable – Are there any practical obstacles to achieving the goal that may make it impossible to achieve the goal?

* Realistic – If you decide that you are going to be head of a multi-billion pound empire within eighteen months, your aspirations are probably unrealistic. Instead, you might set a more realistic goal of attending a

college course that will teach you some business skills with which to begin your new venture.

* Time-limited - This means that when setting a goal, we should give a date by which we aim to achieve completion. Goals which are not time-limited tend not really to be goals but "hopes". The difference between getting something done and wishing something was different is often a completion date!

In summary then, if you have great things in mind, or even goals that just look impossible, consider whether you can do "something" towards that goal, and then re-assess the situation once that smaller goal has been achieved. There is value in this on at least two counts. You have successfully moved a step nearer to solving your problem or achieving your ultimate goal, and you have also shown yourself that little steps are both possible and fruitful. This can build your confidence to move on to the next step or next goal.

When this principle is applied to anxiety-busting it can be just as useful. If the goal of being well looks like an impossible one, then just focus on small bite size chunks, one at a time. We can easily make the mistake of framing recovery in black and white terms. Instead, we just keep improving what we can while being patient that over time these small improvements in relaxation levels, circumstances, and understanding, will accumulate to create a big change through time. In practice this is what actually happens. The best change is the change that happens gently and organically. Then it is fully accepted as the norm by the subconscious mind. Such change rests on firm foundations. The structure will not then be blown over like a house of cards when times are tough.

Now, using the S.M.A.R.T goal-setting format above, is it possible we could now take some positive action? While it is true that no one thing here is going to lift your depression in isolation, as far as is possible, you want to be thinking about all of these things. It doesn't matter if you can't meet all these suggestions right way. Just choose the ones you can meet, or better still choose your own, and just make a commitment to start moving. It may appear like a lot to be thinking about, but the truth is, once you're back on your feet these are just the things that a healthy life consists of, and you'll naturally start to do these things again. Our goal is to normalise life and to show your limbic system that depressed feelings are unnecessary and unhelpful.

ANTI-DEPRESSANT LIVING

Now it's not entirely unusual for depressed people to disregard everything written above and decide that they are some kind of exception. If you've forced yourself out once or twice and felt worse, not better, it's understandable that one could conclude hopelessness. Well, let's not be too hasty. I'm sorry to labour the point but it's an important one. Recovery takes time. If we throw in the towel on the first, second, or even third round, we're not going to get very far. We have to initially contrive happiness. I know you don't want to hear that. You just want to be happy again. First there's the decision to be well, then the determination that you'll break out of the depression. Then you start behaving as though you are well. Essentially, you fake it to make it. Eventually, your brain will agree. We know that being around happy people can brighten us up. Inspiring people who say the right things can remind us of our strength and resilience. Laughter is infectious. Misery however loves company. If you seek out other people who are anxious, depressed, negative, or otherwise miserable, and spend all your time with them, that's all your brain will have to "mirror". No positive input equals zero positive output. If the four walls of your house remind you of your misery too, then that will have the same effect. Mirror-neurons are neurons which respond in sympathy to the incoming signals. They respond to our environment. When you see someone smile, it reminds you of happiness, and you might feel more inclined to smile yourself. Certainly those mirror-neurons kick in when we're watching the football and we're ready to show those players how to kick a ball properly! What you surround yourself with will get under your skin if you stay in it long enough. That's why simple things like cleaning the house or throwing out your old junk can contribute towards lifting depression. If you've got time on your hands, then volunteering is a well-trodden path out of depression for obvious reasons. So, we can't give up just because we don't feel great straight away. First of all we have to create a backdrop to our lives which is bright and positive. Think of it as preparation for when you *are* feeling better.

Here's a tale from my own life which illustrates this principle. After moving away from London I found myself working in the accounts department of an insurance company, as a junior. I was putting on a very brave face, as I had done for the last few years, but internally I was tortured with daily anxiety and depression. I was just surviving.

An opportunity arose for me to undertake some professional qualifications which would be funded by my employers. It would be a two-year study course which would lead to a mid-level qualification in credit management. I seriously doubted whether I would have the energy to do it. I was already deeply fatigued and depleted having just clawed my way back from serious mental illness. I was certainly not well yet; but I reasoned well. My thinking was this: "I'm pretty useless right now. I'm recovering, but I've been deeply unwell, and it's obvious at this point that this is a process which is going to take time. Since there's little light on the horizon immediately, I may as well use this time to do something practical and progressive. Then, when I am well again, I'll have something to build on."

The course was structured in four units of six-monthly study with an exam at the end of each unit. I was waking early every day anyway because of my terrible sleep pattern, so I studied sixty to ninety minutes a day, every morning before leaving for work. I had to dig deep. The studies were challenging, but two and a half years later (I had to re-sit one exam) I emerged with my qualification.

This did wonders for my self-esteem. Now I was somebody employable. But, there was another completely unanticipated benefit to taking this path. It had actually been deeply healing as a process. I had approached these studies as a project to make good use of the time I had written-off to illness, but they turned out to be an intrinsic part of my successful recovery. The continued sense of hope coupled with intense focus on a meaningful goal, as well as the boost to self-esteem from doing something valuable, created the perfect conditions for wellness to flourish again. Ironically, I never used the qualification. Less than a year later I began my training as a therapist! It never mattered to me though. I got far more than a qualification from those two and a half years.

I always say that if we've been depressed, we have to make things better than okay for ourselves because we've got to show that emotional mind that things can be good, despite those bad feelings. It really doesn't believe it at first. It's expecting us to fall back into negativity because we always have. We need to dig deeper than we've ever dug before. We have to make this time different. We have to make changes that really send a message of determination and commitment to wellness, and then we will start to feel better. What the believer believes the prover proves remember? Then the subconscious mind will start to believe that we are serious about recovery, and will start responding with a bit of enthusiasm. Sitting around saying we can't be helped, and that we've heard it all before is not going to fix the problem. We also need patience and perseverance. It won't happen overnight. It will happen over weeks and months, possibly many months. We need to be consistent and persistent. You really can't afford the luxury of negativity indulgence. Someone non-depressed/non-anxious can to a point, but if you're anxious or depressed, you can't. Think of it this way. Depression thrives on the dull and hopeless. The way out is to build the life you want, despite anxiety or depression's best efforts to convince you otherwise. You need to fight for it. This quote from Confucius is my favourite all-time quote. It sums up for me everything you need to live life successfully.

"He who says it cannot be done should not interrupt the person who is doing it." Confucius

When your life is truly a bright place to be filled with things which are pleasant and pleasing, it is very difficult for depression to thrive in such a place. Some professionals argue that remaining depressed is a choice. I'm not sure I agree, but I do believe that if we want to find a way out, we can, when we know how. Sometimes though, we have to think the unthinkable and do the undoable to achieve it.

You say "I'll do it when I feel better." Try instead "I'll feel better when I do it...."

Brain Chemistry -Cause or Effect?

Faulty brain chemistry is often cited as a cause of depression, and is therefore obviously also an important area to understand. Physiology varies from person to person, and in the same way that some people are blessed with very strong constitutions physically, the same is also true with regards to mental and emotional constitution. Persons with poor physical constitution may have to work harder than others to maintain wellbeing, but they can often still lead a good life.

We also have to make some distinction with regards to the type of depression experienced. Most depressions are what we might call in plain English "ordinary" or mild to moderate depression. Anyone can experience ordinary depression, and it usually follows a roughly predictable (albeit unpleasant) pattern, commonly triggered by a difficult time of prolonged stress or loss. Ordinary depression can come and go. The Royal College of Psychiatrists tell us that standard depressions will usually resolve themselves within four to six months. Then we have Bi-polar Disorder which was formerly known as Manic Depression. Bi-polar is really a lifelong medical condition with no known cure, though it is manageable, and sufferers can lead satisfying lives once they have the right support. This condition is characterised by severe emotional swings between extreme lows, and manic highs. During the "mania" phase a sufferer can become dangerously carefree, and will often behave in a manner which they later regret, such as spending money recklessly, indulging in drugs, gambling, or promiscuity. This is then followed by the "depressed" phase. There are other depressive disorders which need different handling. These disorders occur much less frequently than common depression and require specialist medical treatment, usually with medication. For the purposes of this book, please assume that we are discussing in this section the brain chemistry issues noted in "ordinary" depression.

It is a widely held medical belief that Serotonin levels in depressed people are generally, but not always, low. Serotonin is a chemical neuro-transmitter within the brain which is responsible for carrying signals between one brain cell (neuron) and another. We have approximately three trillion brain cells firing signals from one to the other at any given time. The brains computing power is vast indeed! There are many different neuro-transmitters active in a brain, but Serotonin is believed to be the most important in regulating our overall level of well-being. So Serotonin is often referred to as the "feel-good" neurotransmitter.

Serotonin is released by chemical factories within the brain, used to transmit signals, and then re-absorbed. Then, more Serotonin is manufactured by the brain and released into new circulation, and so on. Selective Serotonin Re-uptake Inhibitors (SSRI's) are medicines which inhibit (block) the re-absorption of Serotonin into the brain. So by slowing down the rate of re-absorption it is possible to make the Serotonin go further by having it stay in the brain for longer. The net effect of this should be that you feel happier, since more Serotonin in play equals more feel-good factor. SSRI's are the most common types of anti-depressant medication in use today, though there are other types of anti-depressants available too (MAO inhibitors/Tricyclics). Most people have heard of Prozac. Prozac is the brand name for Fluoxetine. This is still in very common use today, and there are many other different anti-depressant drugs available from your GP which have a similar action to Fluoxetine. Some of these drugs have courted widespread controversy. Seroxat (Paroxetine) for instance has been in the news because of its alleged addictive qualities, side effects such as increased suicidal tendency, and uncontrollable aggression in some people, particularly younger people. Panorama (BBC investigation team) investigated over a two year period and found evidence of a medical cover-up of such information. Users were not informed of the risks despite the fact that the pharmaceutical companies were aware of potential problems.

I have worked with many clients who were using anti-depressants successfully. Many people do not suffer noticeable long-term side effects, and for many there is clearly a marked improvement in their overall state of well-being. The picture therefore is complicated. It is clear that in some cases medication helps. This is for you to decide and for you to discuss with your healthcare professional.

Balanced serotonin levels appear to be necessary to good mental health. It appears that when Serotonin is depleted within the brain that this must be the cause of depression, and that depression must therefore be a chemical problem to be rectified at the chemical level. This is all reasonable enough except for one missing fact.

Serotonin is a mood regulator, but it is also regulated by mood.

The production of serotonin in the brain is increased and stimulated by positive living. Every positive thing that happens in your life can lift your mood. Knowing you have something fun to look forward to can lift your mood. Knowing that you will get better soon (or any light at the end of the tunnel) will lift your mood. Deciding you are going to beat your depression will lift your mood. Remembering your sense of humour, going to the theatre, having dinner with friends, making something, helping someone, volunteering perhaps, finding a part time job, studying, or just learning! It all **potentially** lifts mood, and it all stimulates Serotonin production. If it doesn't help one day, it might do on another. Stay with the programme!

With this established there is one final important consideration here. My contention is that most people can help themselves. With the correct mix of understanding and application you really do stand a very strong chance of fixing your anxiety and/or depression without medication. That doesn't mean that you shouldn't use it, only that some people prefer not to. With that said, there are exceptions. There are folks in the World who have done all the right things for extended periods of time, who have continued to be troubled, despite their best efforts. I encourage you not to jump to the conclusion that you will be one of them, especially if you are at the beginning of your journey of recovery. That's typically what an anxious or depressed mind would do, so be aware not to endorse such negative thinking with un-evidenced assumption! However, for those who have struggled on, seeing endless therapists, reading countless books, applying daily CBT, drinking herbal potions, and seeking strange solutions without relief, it might be time to consider some chemical assistance. Don't write it off. In the same way that people's bodies can fall out of balance and require medicinal treatment, so too can the brain.

There is emerging evidence that prolonged stress, anxiety, and depression can cause atrophy in the brain. In particular, studies are finding shrinkage (up to 20%) in the hippocampus region which regulates memory, including emotional memory, and is absolutely integral to the emotional brain. Interestingly, further studies on SSRI's have noted that they may have a regenerative effect on brain cell population, and promote re-growth of the hippocampus:-

http://www.ncbi.nlm.nih.gov/pmc/articles/PMC60045/

There remain some question marks over the serotonin based explanation of why anti-depressants work. It has been proposed that although SSRI's boost serotonin availability, it may be that this secondary action (which may turn out to be primary) explains a) why antidepressants typically take four to eight weeks to work fully and b) why recovery can continue once medical treatment is discontinued.

The need for medication is more likely to be indicated if you have been struggling with long-term anxiety and/or depression, but that is not an absolute rule, only a probability in most cases. If this interests you, the internet is a wealth of information, so do your research. For now, let's just say that if you feel that you've really done everything within your power to help yourself without satisfactory result, then there may be new reasons to consider medication as more than an absolute last resort.

EXERCISE, NUTRITION, AND DRUGS. THE NATURAL WAY TO BOOST YOUR BRAIN CHEMISTRY

Stress places additional demands on your body. Think about it. A body that is constantly primed for survival is running at a much more demanding pace than a body which is relaxed. In addition to this, the body will draw more heavily on certain nutrients during times of stress, meaning we're more prone to depletion during these periods. With all this considered it is sensible then to pay even more attention than usual to diet and nutrition during stressful periods.

I am not a nutritionist, and I'm therefore steering clear of offering any specific dietary advice. A quick internet search should turn up plenty for you to read immediately though be warned that nutrition and pill popping is big business, and there are still people selling snake oil on every corner. Do your homework before you sign up for the next big wonder-pill! The best nutritionists will guide you simply towards a healthy balance of nutritious foods, with maybe a few suggested supplements.

What we will say then is that your brain needs certain amino acids and vitamins to manufacture a plentiful supply of neurotransmitters and feel-good chemicals. We know that drinking and drug taking will deplete serotonin production levels in the brain. We don't need science to tell us this. Any standard hangover is evidence enough! When our serotonin levels are balanced, we feel happy and contented. When serotonin is depleted or unbalanced, we will tend towards depressed or anxious states of mind.

Smoking, drinking, drug-taking, poor nutrition, stress, and over-exertion generally speaking will deplete production of the bodies feel good chemicals, while good nutrition and healthy living will increase it.

Pay attention to your diet. These are things perhaps easily overlooked or disregarded when we are treating anxiety or depression, but you can take it as an absolute given that if you're eating high quality foods (plenty of whole grains, quality proteins, fruits and vegetables) and enjoying an appropriate level of exercise, then you are going to be giving your body and brain the support it needs to re-balance. If you eat only chips and pizzas, drink fizzy sugar, and do no exercise at all, then you're clearly not giving your brain what it needs to function well. It hardly needs repeating, but reduce your refined sugar intake as much as possible. It's the poison of our time.

There are some nutrients that many people are deficient in even when eating a healthy balanced diet. For instance, we obtain most of our Vitamin D from sunlight. If you live in a country where there is little light in the winter, or have a vocation which involves being out of sunlight most of the time, then you may well have a vitamin D deficiency, since obtaining the proper amount of vitamin D from an ordinary diet is hit and miss. Though the science is yet to be proven absolutely, a link has been suggested between winter-time blues known as Seasonal Affective

266

Disorder (SAD) and Vitamin D deficiency. Some of the other important nutrients to consider for healthy mood are the B vitamin group, the omega oils, and zinc and magnesium which many of us are deficient in. I am deliberately avoiding going any deeper into detail than this. I am bringing the matter to your attention and I urge you to investigate further. I think we are wise to stop short of becoming obsessed by what goes into our bodies, and wiser still to remember that it is unlikely that *all* of our emotional distress is down to some nutritional deficiency. I also think that we are very unwise to completely disregard nutrition as a significant factor in our overall wellbeing. The mind affects the body and the body affects the mind. Balance, as always, is the key. I'm sure most people will agree.

A survey by the mental health charity MIND found that 82% of people with mental health difficulties looked to exercise to lift mood and relieve stress. Two-thirds said it helped relieve symptoms of depression, and over half said it helped with stress. Put simply then, exercise gets your energy moving and counteracts feelings of apathy. Exercise improves serotonin production and releases endorphins. Endorphins create euphoric feelings. Blood levels of beta-endorphins have been found to increase to as much as five times their resting levels during a prolonged bout of aerobic exercise (over 30 minutes). Providing you don't have any physical problems that might mean that you are unsuitable for exercise, then you might consider bringing more exercise into your life as part of your strategy for anxiety and depression busting? Remember, especially where there is depression, the subconscious mind is a lazy mind, and if your energy is low, you'll be able to easily convince yourself that you don't have the energy, or that it's not worth it. That's the time to be lacing up your trainers and stepping outside. We tend to have more energy when we use energy. Exercise is energising. So don't fall into the trap of believing those feelings that say you don't have the energy. You probably have more than you think, and you'll surprise yourself by finding that you return from your exercise with more energy and a better mood than when you left. Have you been saying you'll do it when you feel better? What could you say instead?

Okay, so if you've been following this closely, you will have figured out that you need to get a new job, have a heart to heart with your spouse, love yourself daily, have perfect children, quit the smokes, stop drinking, ditch the coffee, ensure that you are in bed asleep by ten pm every night, take up jogging, get a great hobby, drink at least 6-8 glasses of water a day, eat five fruit and veg every day, think positively, stay in control.....in a perfect world, maybe!

Here's the real point. We need to use common sense. Everyone has their own unique limitations. What's good for one can be bad for another. A certain amount of stress is good for you. It keeps you motivated and on your toes. A little bit of what you fancy can do you good. My great Grandma Emmie really was 102 years old when she died. She had a large Guinness and a shot (or three) of whisky every day. She had nine children, and lived through two world wars. She survived asbestos, smog, and worked her fingers to the bone. She was delightfully cantankerous. No one's telling you how to live your life. We're just taking a look at the obvious causes of anxiety and reminding you to be mindful. Anxiety is often caused because something is calling for our attention and not being heard. Emmie may not have had the luxury of attending to all of her wounds. You may. Sometimes that calling is a practical matter, like we're drinking more than some "part" of us is comfortable with. Or, we actually will never be satisfied in this particular job, no matter how positive we are about it. Then we need to change things, right? It's no good bending over backwards to de-arouse your brain and create powerful positive metaphors if you're drinking espresso at 10pm, not sleeping because you're amped on caffeine, and then asking why you're still anxious. You just need you to be honest with yourself about what really needs changing.

On the other hand we don't want to become anxious about needing to have everything "just so". These are only guidelines. I want to hand over to you and let you figure out what needs changing. The whole idea of this book is to give you some circular understanding which is to hand which will remind you of the many areas you could focus on to improve things instead of thinking everything is hopeless because you're having an anxious day. This again, is a powerful antidote to hopelessness. Improving things in any area equals solutions as far as the emotional mind is concerned, and solutions are soothing remember? So even though deciding to improve something today might not make you feel better today, it will make you feel better to know that something you decide to change today may make you feel better tomorrow!

Here's a checklist for depression to summarise what you will be aiming to keep in firm focus:-

DEPRESSION – CHECK LIST FOR RECOVERY

* Find ways to have your emotional needs adequately met.

* Avoid excess drink, drugs, and smoking, which upset brain chemistry balance.

* Eliminate or reduce caffeine intake – it's a powerful stimulant followed by inevitable "crashes". Switch to decaf and remember it's also in soft drinks like coca-cola.

* Think and focus positively.

* Stay physically active - exercise is an important key to regaining positive mental health.

* Reduce negative introspection – Stop the internal monologue about how terrible things are, have been, and will continue to be. Your limbic system needs to hear something positive if it is to start feeling better!

* Challenge negative assumptions about yourself, the world, and other people.

* Create positive goals – ensure these are realistic.

* Take action.

* Change unbearable circumstances. If they cannot be changed immediately, then change what can be changed immediately, and start taking steps towards meeting your eventual goals to leave the situation. This alone will make a big difference to the way that you feel.

* Learn to sit more comfortably with the discomforts of life (increasing frustration tolerance).

* Amend expectations to ensure they are realistic and don't cause distress when/if not met.

* Tackle mind menace talk (Should, have-to, ought-to and must).

* Eat a nutritious diet – in particular ensuring you have all your needed vitamins and amino acids.

* Make sure you have adequate rest.

* Learn to relax deeply.

* Recognise and assess more clearly what you do and do not have a great deal of control over. Being able to accurately assess your level of control will stop you from telling yourself you "should" have been able to do more, or that you are powerless when you are not.

* Learn to make good decisions that do not lead you into depressing events or let downs.

* Identify those situations that increase depressed feelings, and if appropriate, stop entering them. If the things that make you feel depressed feelings are things that you would like to be able to like (being sociable for instance), then look at the aspects of your thinking which are making you feel depressed, and make some changes. If you get depressed because you keep saying yes when you mean no (purely as a for instance) then learn to say no.

* Social Enjoyment – Getting out, seeing people, being sociable.

* Ensure you do not mix solely with depressed or unwell people. Mirror neurons (brain cells) mirror environment and make us feel accordingly. Misery loves company.

* Recognise that improvement won't happen overnight. Sustained changes are necessary.

* Remember that your limbic system (emotional brain) hears everything you tell it. If you tell yourself everything will remain awful then it will have no choice but to respond emotionally as though that is a true statement, which can only lead to more depressed feelings.

* Cultivate determination to not be a "victim" in life. Cultivate determination to recover.

* Stop telling your "depressed" story to people. You are not your depression. Refuse to be defined by your "depression". Consider who you are when you're not depressed. Focus on being that person.

* Do not "avoid" your problems or things that need doing. Focus on solutions instead. Do not run negative mental simulations of future events. Imagine how things will look when they go well, not how they will look if they go badly. Your limbic system can only respond to what you show it.

* Recognise that feeling "depressed" involves having feelings of apathy and negativity. In order to beat depression we need to dig deep. Digging deeper does not mean using more energy (that we might feel we don't have), but it does mean being unwilling to settle for depressions explanation of how things are. Remember, depression will argue "You can do it when you feel better". We say "You'll feel better when you do it!"

* Stop/decrease unnecessary thinking. Make a stand and refuse to spend hours and hours a day just going over and over things. Get a hobby. Take a walk. DO something. Do not just sit around thinking. It literally does your head in!

* Do something nice for someone else.

* Clean your house! Throw out your clutter. Clean out your drawers. Tidy up those piles of paper. Get going on all those little jobs that have been bugging the hell out of you for the last two years. You will be surprised how therapeutic this is!

* Go to bed at a reasonable hour and get up every day before 9am at the very latest, preferably seven or eight. Stay in step with the rest of the World. This "normalises" your existence. Get washed and dressed when you get up. Be disciplined about this. Getting up at midday and staying in your dressing gown all day just reinforces the notion that there's something wrong with you. That's what "ill" people do!

* Get out of the house every day even if just for a short walk.

* Stop incessantly surfing the internet for a solution to your problems. The answer is not there. The answer is in your life, and in taking appropriate action.

* Stop feeling so urgent that you "must" have this fixed immediately. That just creates tension that makes you feel more depressed. Accept your feelings today while making provision for a better day tomorrow...

Chapter Nine – Anxiety As Opportunity

Going To The Next Level

Albert Einstein reminds us:

"You cannot solve a problem on the same level that it was created. You must rise above it to the next level."

To solve a problem you are required to grow, transcend, acquire new tools, create new perspectives, change the circumstances, engage new ways of thinking, do something differently. The whole of human evolution has been a problem solving enterprise. When we are faced with a difficulty, we are asked to search "outside the box". What we have been doing has not been working, so we have to become more than we were to create a solution. This is growth. This is evolution. Essentially you acquire more tools on an as-needed basis, and those new tools don't only help you to fix the immediate problem, they also re-define who you know yourself to be. Now that you are skilled in the art of cooking, you will always be able to make yourself a tasty meal even with limited ingredients. So from this perspective a problem or difficulty helps you to become more than you were. Put formally, you will, in solving a difficulty, have undertaken some personal development. Now of course, the more skills you have, the more confident you feel in life because skills equal self-reliance, and being self-reliant means you don't have the vulnerability of having to rely on someone else. If you're less vulnerable, you're less anxious. So when we welcome difficulty as the messenger, and go about seeking solution, then we're in the positive flow.

Someone once asked a Zen Master "Master....why is there evil in the World?" The Master replied "To thicken the plot".

When we're anxious or depressed, it's frankly horrible. However, when you are on the other side of this difficulty you'll be thinking very differently about it indeed. I guarantee you that one thing recovering from anxiety and depression brings you is a lot more empathy for the suffering of others, for a start. You will also have acquired a huge body of felt experience which will stay with you for the rest of your life. What

273

you are learning here will form a part of that, but you will gather knowledge, understanding, and tools from many different areas. If you had never been unwell, you would never have needed these tools, and you would never have sought them out. Without these tools, in the long term, you can be sure your life would have been a poorer place because the tools that anxiety or depression have brought to your attention are tools which focus on living well.

We can think of it this way. If we've become chronically anxious, it's because something is out of balance. We are it seems owners of a conscious mind, and an unconscious mind. If we fail to register something which is out of balance consciously, then our unconscious mind will make sure we start listening. So, anxiety from this perspective is not some hideous demon which has come to make our lives unbearable, but instead a call for us to wake up to the patterns which we can no longer live with. You might ask "Why now?" Why then did I suddenly become anxious or depressed? The answer to that is often that you've been living at the edge of what's acceptable for you for a long time. Eventually, your unconscious mind lets you know there's a problem. Or maybe, some part of you just wants a better quality of life *now*. Perhaps it's time for you to break out of your negativity? Maybe you're exhausted from always doing too much? Maybe you're utterly bored because you've been doing too little? Maybe you're angry all the time, and your unconscious mind is letting you know that it's ruining your life? Often, anxiety and depression is a call to start listening. It's hard to see this perhaps in the short term when it just feels awful, but then of course we are in those moments seeking immediate relief. On a grander scale though, the question that we are all being asked existentially is whether we're willing to continue feeling like crap, or whether we're going to do something about it?

Perhaps it needs to feel that bad to get you to do something?

We can handle a lot of negativity before we're mobilised to act. Some people never act. I know I had to get pretty much to rock bottom personally before I started seriously doing something. This is a very important point. Often we just want the problem to go away so that we can go back to doing what we've always done. We fail to recognise the greater significance of this opportunity for healing, and regard our symptom instead as a proverbial pain in the butt, robbing us of our right to lead a wonderful, happy, *dysfunctional* life. Please know that I am not making a judgement here. The emphasis on the word dysfunctional here is the emphasis your unconscious mind will place on the behaviours, thoughts, and beliefs which have become unacceptable for you. This is where the conflict lies. You're happy with your pattern of drinking six pints of beer a day, while another part of you is not. It might have been okay when you were nineteen but now you're thirty two, you're starting to feel it, and your unconscious mind wants you to know that something needs changing. You're happy to work eighty hours a week, but another part of you is not. You're happy to believe that your body must be perfect before you can love yourself. Guess what? So, as miserable as anxiety and depression can be, we can bring something valuable out of the experience. No, you won't be the same person that you were. It probably will change you forever, but that's not always a bad thing. Sure, some parts of you won't be all that relevant any more, but you will also discover aspects of yourself that have been dormant and waiting for maturity before they flower. You'll almost certainly have more empathy and understanding. You may find that you have less time for things that don't really matter. You will appreciate health and simplicity more. When you've spent time wishing for nothing more than just to feel okay, it tends to make okay seem pretty good!

When you're through your anxiety and depression you'll be richer for it. Keep this in focus.

MY RECOVERY STORY

By 1993 I was extremely ill. I had an explosion of anxiety in my life that was off the scale. I had severe physical symptoms and became very weak. My gums were bleeding. I had continual mouth ulcers. I had painful eczema all over my hands that felt like paper cuts every time I touched something. I couldn't sleep properly. I had night terrors when I did sleep. I couldn't breathe properly because my solar plexus was clamped tight with anxiety. I had a dangerously palpitating heart. My hands were constantly soaked in sweat and overheated. I felt phantom cobwebs brushing my skin all the time, and permanent pins and needles

275

in my fingers. My immune system was shot. I contracted flu three times in that first year, and one bout of stomach flu was so bad that I was passing blood. Though never diagnosed, I suspect that I also had glandular fever. I couldn't cry because I was in shock. I had constant panic attacks. I was absolutely desperate. I had dark rings around my eyes. I looked exhausted, and I was just incredibly scared all the time. This was accompanied by the complete conviction that I was sensitive to supernatural forces and under constant psychic attack from unseen realms. Two healers I saw told me that I was dangerously close to dying. Everyone was very worried for me, and frustratingly, absolutely unable to help. The circumstances that led to this will remain private, but suffice to say that it was an extreme state of anxiety equalling at least the worst state of anyone I have ever helped since.

I suppose I had my fair share of anxieties in my youth, but I wasn't always an "anxious" person. Prior to illness I'd been quite strong, particularly in my late teenage years, which were the best years of my life. I had a lot of wonderful times. But like I said, I broke myself. I was only 22 years old. The first year was a complete crisis. I was unable to work or function, so I moved to the countryside and shook with terror most days. Over the next couple of years I pretty much tried every therapy under the sun without success. Though I had been helped in small ways with these therapies, I remained essentially very unwell. Really slowly, I was recovering, but I was going nowhere fast despite what I felt were my best efforts to be well. Years of being very unwell can grind you down. I really wanted to be well, but I just didn't know how to do it. In hindsight, I can look back and see that my attempts to be well were sincere, but still a little misguided. I couldn't be blamed in hindsight. I was trying, but I didn't know at that point what was needed to be truly well. Things had been awful, but I was still hoping, or expecting, that I'd experience a dramatic overnight healing. Outside of this naive hope, I still believed that I was otherwise helpless and going nowhere. I genuinely believed that no one or no-thing could help. I didn't give up exactly, but there was a good deal of resignation in my heart. My efforts to heal were by now well-intended but completely unfocussed, and certainly lacking any measure of true commitment. I was forever reading books on healing and psychology, and it was all very nice, but I didn't think anything would help, and so it didn't. One mistake I made was thinking that if I read the book, then I'd done the work. I never really followed the advice I was absorbing because I didn't believe it was appropriate to me. I placed my own illness as so severe that these nice authors' suggestions were simply inapplicable to my situation. It's an easy bind to fall into. So I continued with a session of Reiki here, some acupuncture there, Kombucha brew, supplements, books, homeopathy, spiritual life, shamanism, hands on healing, essential oils etc. You name it, I tried it. I was always looking for the quick fix; a sonic boom to clear all the pain away. So, when nothing delivered on this wish, I labelled it a failure. This was my mistake. I hadn't really taken on board that it was *me* that had to change, not what I "knew" or what was done to me. I was thinking "Reiki" was an answer, or "Shiatsu" was an answer. I looked to each of these disciplines as the answer. Looking back, it seems strange that I should have been so short-sighted. As I said, anxiety blocks access to our usual intelligence! I was also young, and in some ways, immature. I couldn't account for that at the time. I can now see that quick fix thinking is far from productive because it just reinforces helplessness every time something doesn't "work". The fact is, everything helps, and nothing works because when you're expecting to go from deaths door to super-health in a single course of miracle treatment, you end up constantly disappointed. I was looking outside of myself for something to "fix" me. It was of course ultimately fruitless. I lived a lot of misery, and I wasted a lot of time.

It was six years before my moment of illumination happened. I was utterly exhausted. I had been fighting for years, and losing. I had hoped that this holiday camping in Cornwall, in what turned out to be the wettest week of the summer, would provide some relief from the unbearable torment of my everyday existence. It was of course, wishful thinking. The anxiety was worse than ever from the moment I boarded the train, and no amount of green hills or stunning scenery made the slightest difference. In fact the apparently beautiful environment just amplified how awful life had become. I couldn't enjoy anything. There was not an ounce of pleasure left in me. I was a complete loser, literally. I had played the game of life, and I realised I had lost miserably. There had been years of suffering, and with the best will in the world, there was, I now realised, absolutely no hope. It was really the lowest moment of my life, where I truly gave up. I was completely crushed. I felt like my insides had been scooped out. Where my guts should have been was just this terrible disgusting aching sick feeling. I raged against my illness. I hated life for dealing me such a desperate hand. I hated myself for being so hopeless and helpless. I hated myself for the mistakes I'd made which had led me to this point. But, the worst part of it was the agony I felt for being so useless to my poor fun-loving wife. My illness had put such a terrible strain on her when we should have been having the best years of our life. There was just deep despair, and absolutely nowhere for it to go, except deeper into my bones, deeper into the gaping aching black hole where my guts used to be. Previously, I had feared the consequences of suicide too much to consider actually doing it. At this point I was moving beyond that and looking longingly at the cliff edge. I wasn't just feeling sorry for myself. I was utterly spent.

Providence decided however that I should be reading "The Road Less Travelled" while on this most miserable holiday of my life. This particular book opens with the theme "Life is Hard". Oh? I'd never thought of it that way. I always thought it was meant to be easy and lovely, and I was therefore getting a raw deal. M Scott Peck, the author, a psychologist himself (now departed), went on to describe how the raging against this "life is hard" fact is responsible for so much of our suffering. He went on to discuss his therapeutic experiences, and how we can toughen up to meet the fact that life is hard more gracefully, while accepting responsibility for ourselves. For the first time in years I had a moment of utter clarity. I suddenly knew what I must do. Somehow that book cemented for me the fact that I was going to have to **own** the problem to fix it. I'd always been looking for someone or something else to fix me. Something just shifted in me. It seems obvious now, but I was very lost at the time. I somehow knew that one way or another I was going to be well again. This simply could not go on. Amongst other half-believed rationalisations, I had cited lack of finances as a reason for not seriously seeking the help I so desperately needed. Money was genuinely tight. In fact, we had next to nothing. At this point though, money became an irrelevance. I broke through these "reasons", with reason. There was, I reasoned, no joy in living at all at that time. In fact, suicide had been on my mind for some time. If life had ceased to hold any joy at all, then I had nothing left to lose. If I was prepared to consider suicide, then I reasoned money couldn't be the obstacle I was chalking it up to be. Finding money would be far less of an imposition than killing myself right?! Having nothing left to lose is a powerful healer. Hell, I could rob a bank! (I'm not advocating this!) So, I decided that I would make my therapy an absolute priority. This time it wouldn't be half-hearted, or the wrong type of therapy. This time I'd find someone who could help me own my problem fully, and fix it properly. I would find the money. God, if I had nothing left to lose, surely I could get a loan if I really needed it? Actually, I never needed a loan because of course that was just depressed thinking. My therapy was expensive, but I just needed to be willing to re-prioritise.

I decided I would do "whatever it takes" to get well.

When you let yourself know this and you **really** mean it, something has to shift. I don't say this lightly. Remember this was the culmination of six years of intense suffering. When I say really, I mean really! Think about what a statement like that says to your unconscious mind. Fear, anger, depression, and anxiety don't stand a chance in the long run against a commitment like this. This was commitment with a capital C. At this point it was my last chance. It was either going to happen or it wasn't. I owed myself one last super push to recover.

I didn't find the therapist I really needed immediately. I found a good hearted therapist who helped me a little, but it was through his referral after a period of months, that I found my way to meet a therapist, Clare, who became without doubt one of the most important people in my life. To put "therapy" into some kind of context, this particular therapy went on for about three years. Not every week, though at first it was, but later, with periodic support. This therapist brought about in me an utterly profound transformation. At the beginning, I was convinced that I was un-helpable, a lost cause, but she showed me some things about myself which I might have had to work a very long time to understand had she not been there to show me. For the first time ever I felt completely unconditionally accepted. I was a mess. She didn't judge me. I'd brought it on myself. She didn't judge me. She reminded me, and demonstrated to me through the use of brilliantly revealing therapy, that from a larger perspective, I was innocent. From a larger perspective, most of us are. She helped me to find out experientially how deep the hurt and anger ran in me, and showed me how to clear it. She helped me to understand the areas in which I had conflicting parts of myself pursuing different agendas, and how to bring balance and reconciliation. She helped me see how harshly I had judged myself, and how hopeless that had made me feel. She helped me to check back into my body after spending so much time alienated from myself. She helped me to accept my imperfections, my confusions, my uncertainties, my mistakes. She helped me to forgive myself. She also helped with much else, and in time I got better. I'm really glad that I saw it through. I've had some great times over recent years. I am alive again, and I am more grateful than I can say. A great deal of the understanding found in this book is down to her. Thank you Clare x

The understanding that I have poured into the book is also my own, and it is hard-earned. It is born of first-hand experience. I've been to the bottom of the anxiety, depression and despair pit. With help, and a whole truck load of courage and determination I also found my way out. My message to you is, "You can too". I am not completely scar-free. I have to manage my stress levels carefully to this day, but in most ways, life is better now than it has ever been. I am grateful to just be okay. When there's true joy, and there's quite a bit these days, it's a bonus. I work on making the space for that to happen as often as possible!

CHAPTER TEN – EMOTIONAL RESCUE

In a way, chapter nine is the end of the book. There are still a few fresh items to share, but chapter ten, here, is for reference as well. Emotional rescue is a large part of a therapist's job. Of all the content in this book perhaps this chapter on "Emotional Rescue" is the chapter I invite you to read, and then keep to hand for a refresher, should you need it. I frequently saw people tie themselves up in knots when the emotional weather got a little bumpy. So here's what you need to remember:-

ESCAPE IS A STATE, NOT A THOUGHT!

Ok. The first thing to ask yourself is "Have I become frantic?" If you're revisiting this chapter for some relief from a negative emotional state then the answer is almost certainly yes. Stop. Think. What have you learned from this book? Remember? Acceptance, comfort with discomfort. Sit with what is. Stop wishing it was something else. The number one cause of your current immediate sense of crisis is your lack of acceptance of how you're feeling right now. What you are feeling right now has little to do with real problems, and everything to do with how stirred-up you've become because you're so frantic that you must not feel this way. Deal with this frantic urgency to not be feeling what you are feeling and you will calm down.

You can't "think" your way out of an anxious feeling!

Of course we concede the point here that application of CBT skills will help, but in many ways those skills are preventative more than they are emergency rescue tools. By all means, use what you know, but the fact is, emotional arousal takes time to calm down once it's unleashed. What I'm referring to here is not thinking that you can solve your current feeling of anxiety with an epiphany of thought. There may be exceptions to this, but generally it's not the case. I've placed this super-crucial point in the emergency rescue part of this book because it's the number one cause of crisis, and the most likely place you'll slip.

So, you've been making good progress, and one day for no apparent reason, you've found yourself feeling rotten. You make the mistake of freaking out! Don't worry. It happens to the best of us. It takes a few rounds before you become practiced at the art of extricating yourself from such stickiness. You'll get there. You are getting there. You'll learn something important from this. I'll get to what you'll learn in a minute.

So now you're telling yourself that you have read the book, you've heeded the points, and it "worked" for a while! But now it's all come unstuck. It was all worthless! Your brain kicks into overdrive. Doubts arrive. Questions start to flood your mind at a mile a minute.

"What if nothing works? What if it's something I've done wrong? What if I've just been kidding myself that I could get better? What if...? There must be a reason I'm feeling like this?! The book said anxiety doesn't fall out of the sky so that means something must be wrong! Maybe it was that glass of wine I had last night? Or maybe I'm working too hard? I have been worrying about my Mum lately. What if I've stressed myself out? Oh no! That would mean that I'm worrying too much...but I can't worry any less than I do...I've been trying my best...I must really be broken...worse than everyone else!"

And so, on it goes! For a moment your anguish is deeper than ever because hope is once again dashed. If it wasn't bad enough last time you felt anxious, now it's worse because you've been feeling better and by now you're supposedly an expert on how not to be anxious, and your expertise suddenly isn't working, right? The implication is that "it hasn't worked" and therefore we're back to step one. Anxiety will say that. It doesn't mean it's true.

What's happening in fact is that you are having a human experience! That's all. You're learning that some anxiety is a fact of life. This in itself is not a problem. The problem right now is that you've had a strong reaction to this fact, and that's caused you to stir up a bunch of anxiety dust. You've been hoping of course that you'd never have another anxious day in your life. After a time of feeling so much better, it's quite natural to default to despair and disappointment when those feelings make themselves felt again. However, this is the most important moment of your journey. In some ways your journey cannot complete without successfully navigating this moment. The ultimate escape from anxiety is not to never experience anxiety again. That's unrealistic.

The ultimate escape from anxiety is to be able to feel it without it being or becoming a crisis.

When you successfully navigate what I call a "blip", you learn many things. First of all you learn that the extremity of your anxiety in the past was a direct result of your own failure to successfully deal with an anxious period. You previously made the mistake of becoming anxious about your anxiety. This may sound harsh, but if you're honest with yourself, you'll concede the point, and that's actually a good thing for you. It means that you got in a mess before because you didn't know how to navigate the territory. Now you do! So, it's time to prove that you are not in fact helpless. Just one experience of successfully creating calm from a potential crisis will change your life forever because now you will know that there's always a way forward. All your past despair has been born from the belief that you were powerless. Perhaps you were once, but that's not true today is it?

Anxious days aren't pleasant, but they don't need to become a crisis either. You didn't know this in the past. You were caught up in the drama and panic of your feelings, and the anxiety snowballed to become an avalanche. This meant that the anxiety could go on for weeks, or months. What you will learn now is that if you take the right action you will be back on track in hours or days. Don't **expect** immediate relief. That will simply make you feel frantic if you aren't feeling better in five minutes. This is about learning to tolerate the immediate discomfort with the knowledge that it will pass, and it will pass much more quickly if you can cultivate stillness. Think about all of the tools that have been provided for you in this book to do this. Use them, **without urgency.**

"WHY?" CAN STRESS YOU OUT

Okay. So here's the solution. It's very simple. What you're feeling right now is not the result of a major crash in your anxiety reduction skills. It does not mean that you are back to square one. It's not a complete failure in your ability to lead a balanced life. In fact it's probably not anything to do with anything you have, or haven't been doing. Your current crisis is a direct result of your limbic system being overloaded in this particular moment, on this particular day, for reasons which may be obvious or perhaps that you may never know. At least twice a year guaranteed, and often more, I have a day or two where I feel rotten with depressed or anxious feelings. Often I can figure out what needs work. Sometimes I don't really know. I suspect that a bad night's sleep may often be to blame. These just happen sometimes. What I do know though, is that if I follow the rules, it will pass! I still have to remind myself what the correct procedure is, so let me be that reminder for you right now.

The first thing to do right now is to stop asking "why?!"

Your brain is temporarily stupefied with fear, and you've become utterly convinced that if you can just work out what's making you feel anxious, you'll be able to somehow "solve it". Your frantic quest for the answer to that question has turned you into a Whirling Dervish in a dustbowl. The more urgent you become for an immediate answer, the more dust you throw up, and the less clearly you will see the solution. It's like having your fingers in a Chinese finger trap. The harder you pull, the tighter the trap becomes. To escape the trap you stop pulling. You push your fingers closer together and the weave loosens, allowing you to remove your fingers easily. The way out of this crisis right now is to relax. Your mind has been caught in the Chinese finger trap. It appears to you that the obvious thing to do is to think harder, deeper, and faster, in order to solve the problem, but the more you do this, the more ensnared you become in discomfort. Your distress is literally being caused by your speeding urgent mind.

The repetition of the question "Why am I feeling bad?" and your subsequent urgency for an immediate answer is the primary cause of your current distress. You can't "think" your way out of anxiety. Stop trying. The second thing you need to do is some "acceptance" exercises. You know the format. "I hear and accept that you feel…" This is part one of how you stop trying. The literal antidote to the urgency you're feeling is to slow those thoughts down. This means reducing the intensity of your feelings by entering a state of being that contains a feeling of

284

(some) peace. This is found in the state of relaxation, or put another way, stillness. It's not enough to know that relaxation is what's needed. You actually need to enter the state. Knowing and being is not the same thing. It's completely understood that relaxation may appear to be impossible to you right now. Know that it is not. The main obstacles to achieving a relaxed state right now include a lack of belief it's possible, laziness in application, distraction, and impatience. These are exactly the qualities which have hindered you in the past.

It is true that you will need to "practice". Ideally you will take this seriously enough to find at least ten to twenty minutes to devote to relaxation practice daily. This is a preventative medicine, but it's also so that you know how to make use of these skills when you really need them. Now is no time to be lazy. It does take a certain amount of discipline to sit yourself down quietly and engage with the relaxation process, but you will save yourself a huge amount of energy by doing so. You have my relaxation recording to use, but any form of relaxation practice or meditation which helps you to enter a state of stillness will deliver what you need.

STOP TALKING ABOUT IT

This probably sounds like strange advice coming from a therapist, but it's actually a really important point. Take note! This is one of those areas that would appear to be of no consequence, but can actually be a defining strategy in any recovery plan. What should it matter if you talk about your anxiety or depression, or not? Well, it matters loads! Here's why. First of all, you are sick of talking about it aren't you? Has talking about it ever helped you to feel better in the long run? Ok. You may have had a moment or two where it felt good to unload, or talk it over with a friend, especially if that friend gave you some snippet of wisdom or advice that illuminated you for a while, but these are special moments that don't repeat too often. Ninety nine per cent of your talking about it has resulted in you feeling less hopeful because by and large, talking about it doesn't fix it. Still, there may be a constant urge to talk about it at any given opportunity because we continue to hope that someone can fix it, or that sharing the burden will halve it. This is a strong drive. Many of my clients would be on the phone to a friend or family member the moment they started struggling. It's actually an avoidance compulsion, and I would seek to ensure that they ceased the behaviour as quickly as possible.

Anxiety tends to be all consuming. When we're in an anxious space it's pretty difficult to think about anything else. In the same way that we can mistakenly believe that we can think our way out of anxiety, we can also make the mistake of believing that we can talk our way out of it. Though it may not be obvious, constantly talking about your problem actually reinforces it. This is quite a subtle point to communicate. There is power in making a contract with yourself to stop talking about it. Talking about it feeds it. It keeps you focussed on your problem. It acknowledges the presence of something that you feel that you can't deal with alone. This is not just some trite snippet being repeated to you because it's in the solution-focussed methodology handbook. It is actually a really important part of your empowerment. There is something quite profoundly empowering about making a personal commitment to stopping talking to anyone who will listen about your problem. It sends a message back to yourself which says that you will fully "own" the problem. By extension, this says that you will also solve it. You will not look to others to fix it. You will own it, and you will by your own efforts take care of it. More profoundly, you are also making a stand that you will stop being defined by your problem. When you are talking about it, you are being defined by it. You are saying "It's me….the anxious person…I need special treatment". You don't want to be that. To all intents and purposes you will be just like everyone else. If you are ever to believe that you are normal, like everyone else, then your behaviour first needs to reflect that. Is everyone you know constantly telling you how bad they feel? No. They are getting on with life, and that's exactly what you want to be doing.

Now, I know this is harsh advice. If you really need to have a chat with someone, by all means do so! Just don't make a habit of it. This will initially be hard work. The desire to keep talking about it is a strong compulsion. It is also a habit. Recognise that this will need work, but that it is work worth doing. Every time you successfully "own" the problem by not talking about it, you add a little bit of power to your being, and send yourself a signal of strength and determination. It might take time, but stay with it. Over time you'll appreciate just how much of a difference this will make.

Therapy time is an obvious exception to this point, as is genuine discussion of some other aspect of your difficulty with a view to resolving a specific matter. The point is, stop talking about it for the sake of talking about it as a habitual means to try to make yourself feel better in the moment. Once in a while it may help, but it won't work as a long term default strategy. It will have the opposite effect. Ask yourself whether you can just "own" the problem today, and if you can, using what you've learned, you'll probably find a way to fix it. That's confidence building!

COURAGE, PERSEVERANCE, PATIENCE, & COMMITMENT

Recovering from any emotional or mental health difficulty requires courage, perseverance, patience, and commitment.

* *Courage* – To be willing to meet your difficult feelings and get on with life anyway.

* *Perseverance* – It's a marathon, not a sprint.

* *Patience* – It takes time, and there will be some failures along the way.

* *Commitment* – This is nothing less than your life that you are working to heal.

During my recovery period I undertook a grand project - again in search of the miraculous healing formula! I went on a shamanic self-development class which involved fasting for twenty four hours, going into an incredibly hot indigenous sauna (known as a sweat-lodge) for a further three hours, and then standing out all night on a hill in deepest Devon in the pouring rain, in October, to examine my motivations and patterns in life. I was supposed to be there until sunrise. I survived until about 2am after hours of hanging in there with the second hand ticking, and then I quit. It was a difficult decision. But, I was hallucinating ghostly figures coming over the hill, and feeling about as weird as I ever had! I desperately wanted to prove to myself that I could do this. I was the only one in the group who didn't make it until sunrise. Naturally I felt that I had failed myself, but I was smart enough to know that given the choice I would make the same decision again. I really had given it everything I had. On this occasion, my best was insufficient. Everyone else arrived drenched and freezing the next morning, congratulating each other on their shamanic prowess, which initially I envied a little. Later, when they had left, I stayed at the site for an extra day and got to talking with a gentleman (the land owner) who was uninvolved with our group, but who had been watching our antics over the last couple of days. He also ran similar groups. I told him my story. He just laughed. "These practices were designed for Arizona...not Devon in October. If you'd been one of my students I'd have had you stay in one of our shelters. I'm surprised one of you didn't die of hypothermia!"

One of my friends told me that William Blake, a famous poet, cracked open a bottle of Champagne to every failure and celebrated it. I felt much better. I realised that actually my "failure" had been a complete success. I'd dared to let myself fail, and in that regard I'd been perhaps as brave as everyone else at least. The reason I knew this was true was because I had given it everything I had short of being a reckless fool. That was good enough for me. I remember myself with great fondness for failing that night. I'd been brave enough to try, and brave enough to fail. It was a wonderful relief when I realised that I didn't have to expect more than I could give at that time, and as was pointed out, more than perhaps should have been asked of us. I learned a lot from that experience.

Overcoming anxiety, depression, anger, OCD, panic, and similar difficulties takes time. Think of it as many small races. Some you win. Some you lose. Overall, as long as we win more small races than we lose, then we're still getting somewhere. It's definitely a marathon and not a sprint. We need to be okay with the idea that we'll need to persevere. If we expect to go from A-Z obstacle free, then we're lining ourselves up for disappointment. Failure can often teach you much more than success. Expect that you will fall down sometimes. You're allowed to. Learn from it and move on.

* *Our greatest glory is not in never falling, but in rising every time we fall.* *~ Confucius*

288

To expect defeat is nine-tenths of defeat itself. ~ Francis Crawford

There is no failure except in no longer trying. There is no defeat except from within, no insurmountable barrier, except our own inherent weakness of purpose. ~ Elbert Hubbard

Everyone should fail in a big way at least once before reaching forty. ~ Al Neuharth

Do not look where you fell, but where you slipped. ~ African Proverb

Many men fail because they quit too soon. They lose faith when the signs are against them. They do not have the courage to hold on, to keep fighting in spite of that which seems insurmountable. If more of us would strike out and attempt the "impossible", we very soon would find the truth of that old saying that nothing is impossible...abolish fear and you can accomplish anything you wish. ~ Dr. C. E. Welch

I've come to believe that all my past failures and frustrations were actually laying the foundation for the understandings that have created the new level of living I now enjoy. ~ Anthony Robbins

There is something good in all seeming failures. You are not to see that now. Time will reveal it. Be patient ~ Sri Swami Sivananda.

Commitment

How can I even begin to say enough about commitment? We simply cannot have courage, patience, and perseverance, without it.

Milton Garland

My advice is to go into something and stay with it until you like it. You can't like it until you obtain expertise in that work. And once you are an expert, it's a pleasure.

Eddie Robinson

The will to win, the desire to succeed, the urge to reach your full potential. These are the keys that will unlock the door to personal excellence.

* Alexander Graham Bell

What this power is I cannot say; all I know is that it exists, and it becomes available only when a man is in that state of mind in which he knows exactly what he wants, and is fully determined not to quit until he finds it.

* Thomas Paine

It is necessary to the happiness of man that he be mentally faithful to himself.

* Margaret Meade

What people say, what people do, and what they say they do, are entirely different things.

Choosing to change is deep stuff. It's really about your contract with life itself. Some people might even say it's a huge part of what you are here to do, if you think philosophically. Life is asking each of us individually, "Are you going to make a success of this or not?" To answer this question positively we need to cultivate a bit of fighting spirit. Note the word "cultivate". It doesn't necessarily arrive neatly boxed and wrapped with a coloured bow and a gift tag. We need to grow it. It's gutsy stuff. In so many ways, this is what makes life worth living. It isn't neat and tidy. It doesn't come with an instruction manual. Things don't work out how we want them to all the time. We don't always get our own way. We do have to work for what we want. Conflict is inevitable. Loss is inevitable. Some degree of failure is inevitable. Failure is an integral part of success. But then there are moments of breakthrough, victory, illumination, brilliance, and joy! These are the moments that we live for, and they come packaged as part of a deal. The deal is a handshake with life itself, and life says "This will cost you". When we're healthy we say "Sure...where do I pay?" Sometimes we're in credit. Sometimes we're not. When we're not in credit, we need to recognise that we're working with a deficit, and still be determined to get back on track. That's challenging. Our willingness to put work into life ultimately determines what we receive back. It is true that some people have bigger energetic bank accounts than others, but what use is it to sit around and bemoan our fate without any effort to change it?

So fighting spirit is important. As we've said again and again, the question is not "Can I be well?" The question is "Am I willing to do what it takes to be well?" If you don't know how to do that, then it's your job to seek out the resources that will help you to acquire the necessary skills, as we discussed earlier. If you've forgotten what life is like when it's good, spend a few moments remembering, or imagining. Ask your friends and family to remind you of better times.

It is true that some people, sadly, have had a very unfair ride in life. I'm not meaning to negate that. My aim is simply to point out that we all need to dig deep sometimes. That is between life itself and each of us individually, no-one else. My contention to you though is that fortune really does favour the brave. Life rewards effort and courage...eventually! Remember this. It is important.

Commitment is essentially a stand that you take. That's not to say it won't be tested sometimes. It will be. It's not to say you'll feel 100% committed every day. You won't. But, you know when you're really committed to healing because you'll find that you really are not willing, in the longer term, to accept your own excuses for why you can't heal. It is true that part of the healing process is really trying, and then really failing. It's so easy to see this as an indication that it's not possible, when in fact, a committed person simply rests, re-groups, relaxes, thinks, learns, and tries again doing something a little differently perhaps. Remember ......

Effort only fully releases its reward after a person refuses to quit - Napoleon Hill.

DOUBTS...

You're welcome to have them but I'd recommend you think of them as a big stinking pile of ...

By now, you should know that what you tell yourself about yourself is pretty much what you'll get. Are you still telling yourself that you are different from everyone else, and exist in some kind of special circumstance? Let me tell you something. Everyone who is anxious or depressed thinks that. People who suffer with anxiety also suffer the following symptoms, and recover:-

Dizziness, feelings of unreality, palpitations, feeling faint, light-headedness, sweating, exhaustion, dry/metallic mouth, feeling nauseous/sick/weak, trembling, nerves, knot in the stomach, dread, dissociation, loss of confidence, constant worry, inability to think clearly, freezing, difficulty talking/communicating, poor memory/concentration, disconnection...the list really does go on and on.

The point is, they are symptoms, and they will clear when your anxiety reduces. If you're in any doubt, get checked out with your doctor, but just know that these **are** standard anxiety symptoms. Believing you exist in a special circumstance and that your anxiety or depression is so much different or worse than everyone else's (and therefore incurable) is part of the symptomology of being anxious or depressed. Everyone who recovers from an anxiety or depression disorder experiences that feeling throughout their difficulty. Thinking that way can waste time. The quicker you extricate yourself from that way of thinking, the better because hope heals, and when you buy into the "I'm different" belief you are denying yourself hope and solutions. Instead, when you're thinking SMART you can remember that feeling helpless and hopeless is just another one of anxieties little tricks. You might feel it, but what have we learned about feelings? "Not Always So".

DIGGING DEEPER

Digging deeper isn't really about working harder. It's about being unwilling to settle for an unproductive explanation. If I had a penny for every time I've heard someone say "I've tried…" Or "I can't…" I'd have forty seven pounds and fifty two pence. Some clients have contributed as much as fifty pence each. It's my job to remind you that your thought patterns limit you. Now, there are certain limitations which need to be respected. If we're scaling our anxiety at a nine out of ten, then sky diving probably isn't for you right now. Outside of these obvious limitations, we pretty much need to remember that within reason, while not being reckless, we want to challenge anxiety based limitations wherever we find them. Giving in to anxiety and depression merely reinforces the need for it to be there.

When you avoid a situation, or get snagged on a problem which you decide you "can't" solve, then you just told anxiety you agree with the feeling that everything is dangerous and useless, which is the same as saying "Do more of that in future please". If you then say "I've tried to solve it and failed", you also remind yourself that it can't be solved in the future. Instant-hopelessness! You have successfully depressed yourself. This means that months pass without you ever questioning the assumption that it can't be done, while you're wondering why you're not improving, which is a big stinking pile…

It's short sighted and uncommitted to say "I've tried and failed" and then give up, and decide it's hopeless. That's a good way of staying right where you are. We need to be really honest with ourselves and say,

"Have I really done everything I can, or have I only done as much as I am willing to do right now?" If what you've been doing is all you're willing to do, then fine, but at least be honest enough with yourself to say right now, "I'm not willing to change my lifestyle. I know therefore I'm not doing everything I could to improve the situation". Then at least you can stop saying that you've tried everything and nothing works, which creates hopelessness. If we are into feeling sorry for ourselves and in "victim" mode we'll often say that we've done everything we can and we're defeated, then believe it, feel sorry for ourselves a bit more, act powerless and feel more depressed. If that belief were really tested it probably wouldn't stand up to scrutiny. Some people wait for others to scrutinise their limiting beliefs. The committed get on with doing it themselves.

Important note: Scrutinising your limiting beliefs is not an invitation to berate oneself. It just means that when you say "I can't, I've tried, I will fail, I'm different", then you have an opportunity to dig deeper to challenge that assumption, to test it, to see if that limitation which creates a feeling of hopelessness is really true? Life is like music. You have an octave of notes, and you have an infinite number of potential tunes you can create with those notes. Some of those tunes can feel dark and menacing, and some can be uplifting and soothing. To say that the tune you hear is the tune you're stuck with has got to be limiting, yes? You can test your beliefs and still be kind to yourself. Essentially you're asking:-

* ***Is that explanation I'm currently buying into helping me be where I really want to be?***

* ***Is it truly absolute? Is there any other (more constructive) way I might view this?***

If we can honestly say that we've done everything we can, or that we genuinely don't have the energy to do any more right now, or even that our belief appears right now to be absolute and doesn't fall down when tested, then we go to work on cultivating some peace around that. So we go back to sitting with what is for now, getting comfortable with the discomfort, and being patient. It's okay to have days off. Tomorrow is another day, and the emotional weather might be different. Perhaps we'll work something out in our sleep that night? Perhaps we'll learn something that helps us to see things differently from a book or a TV programme? Perhaps our therapist can help with a solution? Then we live to fight again. Remember you can have rest days too. Sometimes, today is not the right day to push. Perhaps you need a rest. If you need a rest, have one. Just don't make every day a day off. Digging deep is important because it creates hope from hopelessness, but it doesn't mean you have to exhaust yourself. It just means not being willing to settle for the dis-empowered explanation.

RECOVERY EXPECTATION

Quantifying a "one-size-fits-all" approach to how long it takes to recover from emotional difficulty is not an easy task. I remember once being on the receiving end of some questionable therapy with an expensive, well respected, but lacking social skills therapist. I was having a really hard time. I had raw fear coursing through my veins after a session with this person. I telephoned him to ask what he thought might be going on, and for some reassurance. He was off. I felt like I was imposing on his precious time (not all therapists are like this I promise!) "It takes as long as it takes" was his reply. "How long is that?" I asked. "Could be weeks, it could be years" was his reply. Well thanks very much for that. That really makes me feel better! All I needed was a little reassurance, and a reminder that I was going to be okay because I'd gone temporarily stupid with fear. In actual fact, within about two to three weeks the intense fear subsided...no thanks to him.

I think what he was trying to say was that recovery does happen in its own sweet time, and to some degree we have to accept this. I've stressed repeatedly throughout this book that recovering from anxiety and depression sometimes takes time. That much should be really clear by now. So let's have a look at what constitutes a reasonable expectation.

The Royal College of Psychiatrists tell us:

The good news is that 4 out of 5 people with depression will get completely better without any help. This will probably take 4-6 months (or sometimes

295

more). Someone who is depressed will find it hard to believe that they can ever get better. You can reassure them that they will get better, but you may have to repeat this over and over again.

Here's my experience. About fifty per cent of my clientele averaged around three to seven sessions. That's one to two months. This group comprised people with "simple" difficulties like fear of the dentist, fear of flying, some anger difficulties, mild anxiety or depression, stress reduction etc. We expect to be able to take care of these kinds of difficulties with relative ease. Then a further percentage will be up around the eight to twelve sessions mark. These would be moderate anxiety and depression difficulties. Then there is a very small percentage who would be with me for thirteen to twenty sessions, often over longer periods of time. I had longer term clients who worked with me over periods of eighteen months or more but they would mostly be pretty well recovered long before that. They simply wished to have ongoing support. If it's taking time, don't freak out! You are where you are. People heal at different paces.

Serious chronic anxiety, depression, and OCD, is likely to be a longer-term recovery. Almost certainly we are talking months, not days or weeks. We do sometimes perform the seemingly miraculous. I've seen people who have been quite unwell improve astonishingly quickly. These are usually motivated individuals with the right temperament who are really hungry for wellness, and whose life circumstances and history make such a quick recovery feasible. They literally lap up every bit of information they receive, process it accurately, and apply it eagerly. This is not the norm though. It can happen, but we don't expect it to happen necessarily. For most of us, recovery is a gradual organic process, and thank goodness it is. Why? Well, consider this. If someone really could wave the magic wand for you tonight, and tomorrow you wake up and all your problems are solved, would you believe it? What would happen next time you were faced with a crisis? Would you know what to do? So when you consider these questions, you can begin to see that real change is built on that solid foundation of gradual incremental movement from one state to another. Anything else is a house of cards. You need to know **why** you're solid. You need to know that anxiety is rising, and then take the correct action. If you went from ill to well overnight, you'd probably have serious doubts about your ability to stand firm. That's why we need to travel through process for permanent results.

So now you know the territory, you know how to deal with it. Ultimately, overcoming anxiety and depression is really about having a rock solid faith that your house is built on such a firm foundation that you won't be blown over when the wind picks up. When you earn this through gradual change, it is established as true fact within your being. Now what the believer believes becomes true strength. You effectively prove to yourself that you can weather the storms, and part of learning that, involves having to weather a few storms. In practice that means that recovery is rarely a straight line process. In fact, we should expect to have "blips" during our recovery.

Recovering from anxiety and depression is not usually a straight line process.

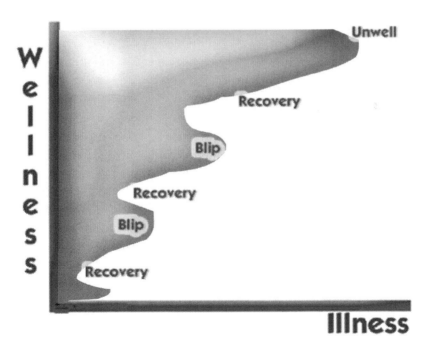

A useful way of thinking about recovery blips is that when our anxiety or depression hits initially, it's analogous to an earthquake. There is an almighty disturbance, and then there are shockwaves. The shockwaves are our blips.

Another useful model is that if you picture a pool of water and you imagine that you drop a huge weight into the middle of that pool, you will find that ripples race out from where the weight breaks the water surface. Each one of these ripples carries the "signature" of the original disturbance. Note that even though each individual ripple carries information about the original disturbance, as the ripples get further away from the epicentre they also become more widely spaced and less intense. Anxiety works in a very similar way. So in our diagram here, we can see that as we move further away from the epicentre (forwards in time), we get distance from the original disturbance, and the intensity of the shockwaves reduce over time. They also spread further apart meaning that they come less often.

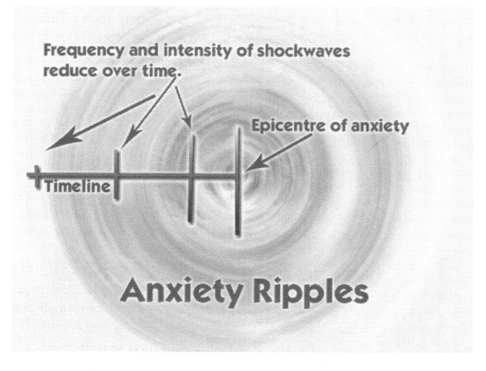

In practice then, this means that when we feel the anxiety shockwaves they carry the same signature. This can feel as though we've gotten nowhere because the quality of the anxiety feels so similar. In fact, the intensity and duration of the anxiety episode is less intense. Note this. The quality of the anxiety remains similar, but the intensity and duration is reducing. We must keep sight of this. It's only when we look at where we have been, and how bad it used to be, that we can see that in fact, it is better. It's usual for our worst day next month to be equivalent to our best day looking back. The blips are a normal part of recovery because we learn that we do bounce back more quickly and more completely each time we blip, and this increases confidence in our ability to cope long-term.

Recovery therefore is at one level a matter of time...

SPEEDY RECOVERY

Now I am going to completely contradict myself. Sometimes we get lucky. This is more likely to happen if you're working with a skilled therapist, but it could conceivably occur just by working on yourself. Sometimes we have a breakthrough where we make a major shift. There are many scenarios where this might happen, so I won't list them here. Suffice to say that we seemingly are graced from time to time with a moment that really has been waiting a lifetime to happen. When these occur in the consulting room, they are moments which transcend me doing my job, and leave me feeling profoundly honoured and humbled. We mustn't expect it. They are moments where many conditions meet to make the breakthrough possible. These changes happen when they are ready to. Good therapeutic work can definitely be the catalyst. It just won't be forced. Not everybody has these experiences, even when they meet with a therapist. I'm just highlighting that it can happen.

An example of speedy recovery might be when undertaking some parts work, or analytical work, where everything comes together in a magic moment of release and re-frame. That can facilitate a lot of change in a single session, making it possible to take a big step forward. The kind of circumstances where this may occur would be for example, a person arriving for therapy with a strong feeling of worthlessness. With analytical hypnotherapy, I would take that person back to the root of that feeling, and have them "review" the moment at which that belief originated. When therapy is at its best, this can be a moment of

Epiphany. The client can experience a complete revelation of the cause of the dysfunctional belief, and with the correct guidance from the therapist, a subsequent re-writing of that belief system at the core level. The result of this can be a profound and definite "knowing" that the feeling of worthlessness rested entirely on a terrible misunderstanding. Once this happens, that worthless feeling simply cannot continue to sustain itself. It has literally been disproven at the deepest level of the unconscious mind, and the feelings fade. This may sound remarkable, but it is part of what really happens in therapist's consulting rooms every day. Here are a couple of genuine recent reviews from my clients to illustrate the point:-

There was one particular session that was my breakthrough moment. While deeply relaxed, John led me through my mind back to my childhood. He allowed me to be able to sit with my 10 year old self, and comfort the hurt child in me. I visualised myself sitting on my bedroom floor of my family home. I saw how sad and hurt I was. Through John's suggestions, in my relaxed state, I was able to identify the very core of my problem. I didn't even know until that very point why I had so much anger and hatred towards myself. I am not going to divulge all of the details, but it was something that my Mother had "joked" about with myself and my siblings, that clearly, as a small child, I did not deem as a joke. I'd had no idea how that had eaten away at my very being, had knocked my confidence right away, and had deeply affected my own parenting skills. I thought my issues were due to my very controlling Father, and his physical punishment towards me while growing up. Guess what though, it was not even to do with him! Outward anger and wrath from my Father was so very less destructive than something said/joked about by my Mother.

Since that crucial breakthrough, I have never been the same person (in a good way,) and I have NEVER looked back! I am a confident Mother. I no longer drive my car like a maniac at 90mph thinking only of smashing into a wall head on with so much anger in my soul. I have not had another episode of severe depression since. My OCD and Anxiety is minimal.

Here's another:- *I was so fortunate to find John when I needed urgent help for my teenage daughter. She had been locked into a frightening cycle of depression and suicidal thoughts that the adolescent mental health services had been unable to release her from. She didn't fit the standard diagnoses or patterns of expected behaviour and was falling through the gaps as a result. In just two sessions, John took my daughter on a safe journey back to the source of her pain, and enabled her to accept what had happened, and move on from it. It was astounding. He released something that has changed her life. A year on, and she is completely transformed. She is able to deal with life and look forward in ways that seemed impossible to her not long ago. John has real integrity and understanding.*

Now the point about this is that even though we make a huge leap forward therapeutically, it is accepted by the unconscious mind as valid, and therefore doesn't fall into the house of cards category. Change that happens in this way really "proves" to the unconscious mind that it has been carrying inaccurate information. Then, the mind and the emotional body can assimilate an enormous amount of revised information all at once.

There are also certain difficulties which are relatively easy to resolve. Minor phobias, such as fear of flying, needles, public speaking, and examination nerves are generally very straightforward matters for hypnotherapists to resolve. There are certain techniques which usually make short work of these types of difficulties, providing they are not supported by generalised anxiety in any significant way. If you struggle with "specific" fears like this you would be wise to find a hypnotherapist to help. Anywhere from two to four sessions should be sufficient to resolve it.

Finally, sometimes big change happens with small things. Sometimes, a person, having suffered with stress and anxiety for years can come back for their second session and tell me that they are feeling better than they have done for years. Here, just the simple process of understanding their difficulty, with a drop of relax-o-therapy using a relaxation recording, has made the world of difference. Why some people move quicker than others is a complicated picture. The really important point though is that we are all moving through our work in this world at our own pace. Don't make the mistake of comparing yourself with everyone else as to how quickly you are healing, or indeed your so-called imperfections because your journey is unique, and there may well be aspects of your work that are deepening your eventual richness, with something which turns out to be a great gift. The alchemists of old believed that the more difficult your journey through the "dark night of the soul", the deeper your transformation, and the greater your joy when you emerge. "The darker the better" they said.

Anxiety has a certain amount of momentum. Think of how a cruise liner has to shut its engines off twenty miles out to sea to slow down in time to reach the port. Old steam locomotives were famed for needing a long stretch of track to slow down even after they stopped the engines. Anxiety is like this too. It has momentum. If you've been unwell for some time, then there is work to do. Don't be disheartened. It's all positive forward movement, and if today is even just a bit better than yesterday then that's something to be happy for. We don't have to be completely well to be content.

Sometimes you'll be doing everything you should be doing and the anxiety may still be running its course, emptying its momentum.

This is important. Remember it. Don't be stressed or frustrated because you're following the plan and it's not working. It is working because everything you are doing is anti-stress, anti-anxiety maintenance. How can that not be doing you any good? It's just that there is still some momentum in the anxiety. Keep doing what you're doing right, and trust that the anxiety locomotive will start to slow down shortly. You can enjoy your life while undertaking this journey. You can be philosophical about your journey too. Perhaps it is helping you to grow in a profound way? Big, quick change can happen, and sometimes does. Mostly though, it's a gradual improvement taking place over a period of time.

EMOTIONAL WEATHER

Sometimes, the World is not on our side. Partly, that's because "stuff happens" all the time. We just feel it and notice it more when we're down. So there's emotional weather due to what's happening in our lives. These are sometimes uncontrollable circumstances.

When stuff happens that makes us anxious we very often overlook the real cause and go back to immediately asking what's wrong with me? This is a mistake. We then start busting our backs trying to identify what's wrong with us. This simply gets us all riled up as we try to "work out" why we're feeling so awful. In fact it was perfectly reasonable to expect that our anxiety levels would rise as a result of finding out that our house has subsidence, our job is threatened, or whatever other crisis we're dealing with. Recognise the cause of the anxiety, and then you can stop making things worse by believing that it's dropped out of nowhere on you, or that you're suddenly rubbish at managing anxiety. To this day I still get caught in this trap if I'm not careful. What am I doing/not doing that's causing me to feel less than great? Sometimes it's nothing you've done. It's what's happening. Stop looking for a profound explanation. Your car broke down. It makes you anxious not having a car when you need it. End of story.

Emotional weather, like the weather outside, can be very changeable. One day it can be sunny, the next day rainy. Some days are overcast and grey. Some days it can be positively stormy. Sometimes you know why the dark clouds are gathering, and I'm sure some days, it's just one of those days where even with the most powerful cloud-busting machine, it would still rain. Tiny imperceptible changes in atmospheric pressure can sometimes create storms. This is called the butterfly effect. It may not be obvious "why" the weather has changed, but let's at least note that it has!

When we look at Eastern philosophy and to some extent the Mayan and Aztec World, we discover that it's always been accepted as a perfectly natural assumption that time itself has different qualities. Yesterday is different from today, and tomorrow will be different again. The ancient and mysterious Chinese I-Ching (Book of Changes) goes even so far as to categorise the different types of time into sixty four unique categories. The Mayan calendar actually names days as having certain qualities, and patterns when such a day with said quality will be repeated. The theory is complicated when you investigate it because there are small and large cycles of time, but the essence is simple. It's basically that there are good times to make investments or advances, and there are bad times. Good times are known as "auspicious" times, and bad times are of course "suspicious", when such investments of energy or effort are unlikely to pay dividends because the quality of the time is simply not right. Then you may be advised to bide your time and wait until the conditions are more favourable.

So, sometimes the "time" is just not on our side. This is unscientific, and some would say superstitious, but is it really so strange an idea? Scientific or not, it is our experience that times feel different for no apparent reason, and there are times when it feels that the weather is against us. Then what do we do? We sit with what is, and stop trying so hard! I know this to be true with weight loss for example. There are times when it's really easy for me to eat less and do more exercise, and there are times when it's really hard and I have to push myself enormously to motivate. Invariably, I exhaust myself if the time is not right. I've learned that it's better to wait for a decent wave when surfing. Success is easier when the conditional weathers are in our favour. When time is on our side, then it's no time to be heel dragging. Then we need to optimise our opportunity with real effort. The real point is this though. We're going to have bad days. Sometimes it's nothing you're doing or not doing. The reason we're not making progress is because there's a storm. Don't make the mistake of being frantic for solution. You'll just whip up confusion and stress. Instead, batten down the hatches and wait it out. It will pass. When it has, hoist the sails and get moving!

FROM PAIN TO JOY

I want to remind you that whatever you're going through right now will change. I've felt truly stuck more times than I care to remember, and even throughout my therapeutic career I've had my moments. Being a therapist doesn't make you immune to overload. We can all be faced with circumstances that would challenge a Buddha. The human condition is flawed by definition. Somehow we must make our peace with the complexity this brings to our lives. Remember that there really is no light without darkness. Some pain is inevitable. You are learning to meet this fact patiently and wisely. The key is to remain gentle with yourself wherever possible. Give yourself permission to feel the pain compassionately, acknowledge the lesson, then forgive and move on.

Life is really long. I was born in 1971 and looking back I feel like I've been here for ages! That's seeing it objectively. Subjectively, it feels like the blink of an eye. What I have personally learned in life is that love, really, is all that's truly important. Our friends, our families, our pets, our communities, our clients, our customers, our World, and what we can bring to each other's lives, both in terms of happiness and reduction of suffering, are the things which make us truly happy. There is much on the periphery too, but if we stay focussed on sharing our caring we won't go too far wrong. When you look for the best in yourself and then find the same in others, you will enjoy more love in life. When you find what's right in life, instead of what's wrong, you'll enjoy more success. When you judge less, and appreciate more, you will enjoy greater peace of mind. If you can cultivate patience with yourself and others, you will learn to see the person beyond the pain. Then you will know kinship rather than division. It's just better this way.

If you're fortunate enough to be able to extend caring and valuing into the wider World without sacrificing yourself in the process, you'll be one of the happiest people alive. Giving is much more rewarding than receiving. It takes maturity and experience to learn this, and it takes real courage to put it into action. We all fear scarcity; it's in our bones. But, that's exactly why it's so important to over-ride the instinct to build a golden cage around ourselves. We can be surrounded by wealth and still be spiritually starving if we're afraid to share. Love is the only currency that truly feeds us. Some rulers of the ancient World apparently lived by the maxim, "To rule is to serve." These are wise words.

In each life, there are many lives. No matter where you are right now, a time will come when you will look back as a different person, in a different time, with a different mind, and understand much that makes little sense right now. Whether it's deep joy, or hell on Earth, always remember that "This too will pass." Feeling cynical and jaded is really not who you are. That's just part of being unwell. When you feel better, you'll enjoy the simplest of things again. Trust that this is true, even if you don't feel it right now.

So, please aim to give yourself permission to live fully. If not now, then set it as your intention for when you are feeling better. Life is challenging at times, but it can have exquisite and moving moments that make it all worthwhile. Make opportunities for this to happen more. Notice the seasons and the landscapes. Remind yourself what you are grateful for from time to time. Spend some of your savings. Accept invitations. Make the effort to stay in touch with loved ones. Tell people what they mean to you. Do something nice for someone without any expectation of favour or reward. Create something. Throw a party. Learn to wind-sail. Fly a kite. Travel somewhere exotic. Volunteer. Stand up to injustice. If you're a billionaire, become a philanthropist.

Your legacy, no matter who you are, or what you do, is the degree to which you make the World a better place. You don't have to open a charity to make that happen. Every kindness you show to yourself and others does that. The World needs healing desperately. That healing begins with each one of us individually. Everything which you heal within yourself will send ripples of kindness out into space and time. It's that which will make the difference in the World. One kindness today, to the right person, at the right time, could literally change the course of the World.

Please don't let fear dictate your life to you. You have a future. Take some risks. Respect your limitations, but be proud of your greatness too. Live courageously, be generous, smile often, love triumphantly, and remember that when you laugh…the light trickles through the chuckles!

I hope that I have lightened your life with this offering. You will have work to do I know, but I hope that you will now have clarity, understanding, a map, and a toolkit to make things better.

Over And Out.

One Last Thing

As an independent author, your Amazon reviews are **hugely important** to me. Customer reviews are considered in the algorithms of online book retailers and positive and numerous reviews help authors to become **visible** among the many millions of books available. Your reviews are literally the lifeblood of our work, so you'll be doing me a highly appreciated favour by leaving a quick review! It could take you just seconds but it will make a massive difference for me! Thank you greatly in advance!

You can leave a review via one of the links below. Other countries will be automatically redirected via these universal links.

Every One Counts!

Thank you.

Here are the links to leave your review or you can simply leave one next time you're in Amazon by searching the title or viewing your recent transactions and clicking "review".

UK Readers - http://goo.gl/2kFqJw

US Readers - http://goo.gl/Y68SG6

You can join me on facebook at:
www.facebook.com/stressanxietydepression

Please come on over and sign up for my newsletter for regular offers and freebies at www.youcanfixyouranxiety.com

There will be more from me soon. Thank you for your support!

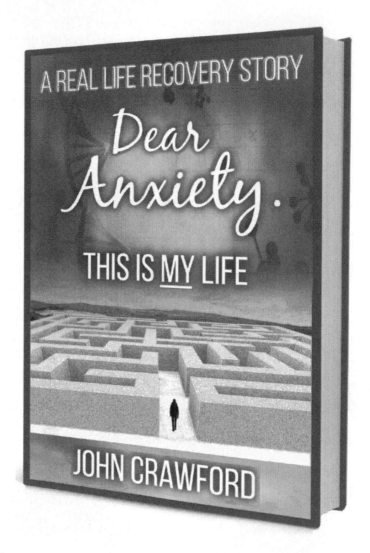

"Dear Anxiety. A Real Life Recovery Story" is my own personal recovery journey told in full detail. That's available here: -

www.books2read.com/u/4N1loN

Don't forget you can get the ebook version of "Dear Anxiety" free of charge (in any format) when you sign up to my Free Reader's Group at www.youcanfixyouranxiety.com or via Amazon directly!

Are you tired of over-reacting? Is anger making your life a miserable place to be? Learn how to identify, heal, and re-program the roots of anger with this professional guide.

Maybe your temper threatens all that you hold dear? Perhaps you just feel easily irritated? Have you ever considered though that your anger might not be a personal failing?

Previously entitled "You Can Fix Your Anger/Cool It" and re-launched in September 2017, Anger Management offers "straight to the point" expertise which can be easily understood and quickly put into practice, so that you can get back to being your awesome self as quickly as possible!

We can find empathy for people suffering with anxiety or depression but often it's only the victims of anger who receive any sympathy. The perpetrators are written-off as a bad lot. This book will explain how chronic anger is just as much a stress-related "condition" as these other difficulties, and why anger sufferers deserve compassion as much as anybody else!

I've been professionally helping people to resolve their stress related difficulties for the last thirteen years, and I've enjoyed working with "angry" people the most. Why? Because they are the least helped among us. I know you didn't ask to be angry. It can be overcome.

Using fictional case studies from real world examples, this book will explain clearly why you may feel so much anger in your being, and explain why your subconscious programming is making it impossible for you to "will" yourself calm. With that understood you'll find practical, workable approaches here to understand and desensitise your triggers, live more peacefully, enjoy better relationship security, be more patient with the world, and get more of what you need without the stress or regret of anger and rage.

Don't wait until it's too late! Get your "yang" back in balance today with Anger Management - A professional guide for everyday folks from an experienced practicing therapist. You will learn:-

- Why the brain creates angry responses when we feel threatened, and what you can do to soothe it.
- How to recognise where your personal anger stems from and how to heal it.
- Why anger can feel good, but become an addiction.
- The brain chemistry! Understand what you're up against!

- Why "controlling" behaviour will drive those you love away, and how to invite them closer instead.
- How to "use" anger appropriately to have people help you instead of resent you!
- Why softness controls hardness, and how to implement that understanding in your life.
- The incredible power of words, asking for what you need, and why "sorry" is the most powerful word in the English language.
- Plus much, much more. Also included in the book is a full professional anger management hypnosis session available for free download.

This clear and insightful book could help you change your life. If you're angry and you don't know why, then don't be without it.

Buy Anger Management today to learn how to rescue your relationships, get more of what you want, feel prouder of who you are, and lead a life free from regrets! You can find this book at these links: -

UK: - www.amazon.co.uk/dp/B01HENG6LW

USA: - www.amazon.com/dp/B01HENG6LW

ABOUT JOHN CRAWFORD

John Crawford is truly qualified to share expertise on how to overcome anger, anxiety, OCD, and depression. Not only has he been a professional therapist for more than thirteen years, he was himself held hostage by severe anxiety and depression for many years in his twenties. His understanding of the field is therefore more than purely intellectual. It's deeply personal and committed.

John ran his own thriving business as a one to one hypnotherapist/psychotherapist specialising in the treatment of anxiety, depression, and OCD from 2003-2016 before taking a year out to focus on writing. He quickly gained a solid professional reputation in the Bristol and Bath area of the UK for anxiety-related difficulties. He has over seven thousand hours of clinical experience in helping people to overcome their emotional and mental health challenges. He returned to work as a therapist in 2017 and is happily continuing to help troubled folks to find their peace again! www.hypnotherapyforlife.co.uk

He is a significant contributor of sections of the training materials used by Clifton Practice Hypnotherapy Training (CPHT), a now international Hypnotherapy Training Centre with twelve branches in the United Kingdom. CPHT is recognised for its outstanding Solution-Focussed Brief Therapy training.

John has spoken professionally for the Association for Professional Hypnosis and Psychotherapy, Clifton Practice Hypnotherapy Training, OCD Action (the largest national OCD charity in the UK), as well as regularly at smaller supervisory events for local practitioners. He has also written for the highly respected online anxiety sufferers' resource, No More Panic. He was a registered and accredited member of three leading therapeutic organisations - Association for Professional Hypnosis & Psychotherapy, National Hypnotherapy Society, and National Council of Psychotherapists, up until 2016 when he closed his one to one practice to focus on writing and teaching. His main qualifications include:-

Diploma in Hypnotherapy and Psychotherapy - Clifton Practice Training (formerly EICH)

Hypnotherapy Practitioner Diploma - National externally (NCFE) accredited to NVQ 4.

Diploma in Cognitive Behavioural Hypnotherapy - Externally (NCFE) accredited to NVQ4.

Anxiety Disorders Specialist Certification - The Minnesota Institute of Advanced Communication Skills.

He lives happily in Bristol (UK) with his wife and cat, and produces music in his spare time.

29598993R00177

Printed in Poland
by Amazon Fulfillment
Poland Sp. z o.o., Wrocław